LIFE GOALS

How to Discover & Achieve Your Own

LIFE GOALS

How to Discover & Achieve Your Own

John Groh

NPI

Northwest Publishing, Inc.
Salt Lake City, Utah

Life Goals: How to Discover & Achieve Your Own

For information address: Northwest Publishing, Inc.
6906 South 300 West, Salt Lake City, Utah 84047
JAC 9.14.94
Edited by: S.J. Davis

PRINTING HISTORY
First Printing 1994

ISBN: 1-56901-420-5

NPI books are published by Northwest Publishing, Incorporated,
6906 South 300 West, Salt Lake City, Utah 84047.
The name "NPI" and the "NPI" logo are trademarks belonging to
Northwest Publishing, Incorporated.

PRINTED IN THE UNITED STATES OF AMERICA.
10 9 8 7 6 5 4 3 2 1

Table of Contents

To the Reader

It may be presumptuous to write a manuscript but it is even more presumptuous to think that someone should read it because it moved to the printed page. The critical question is not why write but why read? You deserve to know why you should read this book.

This book is about the problem of living, specifically, life goals and why so many people ignore the challenge of setting and achieving goals. Have you seen that in yourself? Of not thinking much about life goals? Of not having solid, realistic goals as you page through life's book? Of not doing much with the several you fashioned for yourself? Why do people fail to set achievable goals when they know they should? Why do they not realign goals as life changes? Why do they let good enough alone rather than press on to the excellence they want and deserve? Why do goals fizzle?

We dialogue about these problems in the pages that follow. You—not I—are the resident expert in your life, as I am in mine. What we have in common is a band of human experience that may allow us to find new ways of addressing old problems.

I answer these and other questions at a level that is one step higher than the motivational manuals that hype bigger and better success through sheer optimism. I take seriously our inclination toward—let's call it what it is—evil, our will to fail, and the foibles of 20th century living. Effective goals must grapple with these and other hurdles, though I have not sacrificed humor and good fun, anecdotes, and glimpses into my life.

This book is about more than material success since life is more than that. Life goals that are not empty bottles deal with marriage and family, value structure, faith, and civic responsibility. Many baby boomers are rediscovering the value of thinking deeply about life. Their children ask value-loaded questions about honesty, good, evil, God, and other subjects, and many of them are going once more to the well of values and religion to replenish their store for their own sake, and for their children's. So if you want only a pep talk this book is not for you, though it discusses material success and the value of healthy self-talk.

Like mine, your goals change often in the move from young adulthood to maturity and retirement. Part of life's assignment is discovering how and why our goals change, and if this challenge is for you, so is this book. Every day you live you paint a stroke on life's canvas. I hope this book becomes your assistant, encouraging you to see the whole painting regardless of your stage in life. Seeing life as a whole is part of a process that leads to a balanced life, with balanced goals.

I take the flow of life seriously, from teenage years through retirement. None of us is frozen for long at any stage so a serious discussion of goals covers the full span. More than that, we learn much from how people in other stages and stations face problems and shape healthy goals. Individual chapters highlight problems and challenges of teenagers and their parents, new college graduates, salary and wage earners, sales and business people, marriages and families, and retired people. Each group approaches life goals from a different angle, and we learn from them all.

Why read these pages? Because they help you set and achieve realistic goals and understand the need for purposeful goals throughout life. You will discover the joy of linking thinking and feeling through a regular program of goal visioning. To be is to feel, think and act. Life goals combine feeling and thinking in ways that lead to action so they are an essential part of being human.

Good luck, and good reading!

Acknowledgments

Harry Truman was right when he said about the presidency, "The buck stops here." Authors too must assume sole responsibility for what is written. I do.

But I also recognize the contributions of many others who helped me understand the importance of life goals. More to the point, the following persons read chapters and offered helpful criticism for later drafts: Margaret Asher, Bill Dendinger, Rose Chapman, Sam and Carol McKee, Grace Meinert and Paul Skogebo. Their 370 years of life experience sharpened my sentences and shortened my ramblings. Theirs is a debt not easily paid.

Dr. Ray Martens of Tucson, Arizona illustrated chapter titles with marvelous sketches. I stand in his debt.

Finally, my spouse of twenty-nine years knows more than anyone the foibles and successes of my life goals. Nancy used tact and persistence in encouraging me to finish this book. Our two adult children, Brett and Marguerite, amaze me with their capacity to adjust to rapid change. I thank them for this insight into any set of successful life goals.

For the rest, the buck stops here.

FINISH

I
Getting There From Here

This book is about getting to your life goals—discovering and achieving them in all phases of life. How you get there, what interferes, and how to overcome obstacles on the way are major points of interest. While a straight line is the shortest distance between two points, getting to life goals from the present is not always a straight line. You cannot get "there" unless you know where "here" is. Even if you know, getting there takes hard work.

This chapter shows the need for purposeful goals for people of all ages. We will sharpen our focus with the following question: If teens—of all people!—can profit from resolute life goals, why not the rest of us? Like a merry-go-around, what goes around in life comes around. Life goals are as important for teenagers as anyone. Some of us have passed the vale of teenage travail, but from them we can learn the importance of measuring our abilities and talents, and channeling life energy with clear goals. All of us need life goals, whatever our time in life.

Self-Examination and Goal Action

Is there any question about teenagers' favorite word? It is "Later!" You can probably hang a banner with this word above 90% of their actions and activities. The word fits nearly all situations, whether mom needs help with the dishes or dad is worried about the garbage. Much to their liking, teenagers live in a future that never seems to arrive.

"Yes, I'll go to bed—later."

"Yes, I'll do my homework—later."

"I'll pick up my room—tomorrow."

"Later—see you tomorrow."

What's that, a teenager said something different this time? "Oh Well." For sixteen-year old Tiffany "Oh Well" means matter-of-fact, whatever will be will be. "You went through the intersection when the light turned red," her friend exclaims. "Oh Well," she answers. That is life. That's the track the car was on.

The teenager's "Later" and "Oh Well" are a model for much of life that follows, as adults can testify. These phrases summarize how we delay and avoid self-examination and fail to set clear goals for directing and measuring our lives. The terms show how we fail to charge our energy battery with our self-image, ignore powers of concentration, and shy away from self-inventory.

Self-Appraisal and Life Goals

Like many of us, teens are notorious for avoiding *constructive* self-examination. They defer the rigors of self-examination to another time and place since their instincts tell them that the road of self-examination leads to change and the pain that comes with it. Self-examination raises questions about using abilities, and applying patterns of thinking and feeling in positive ways. Given an option about self-examination, most teens probably would choose "Later" over any alternative. If something concerns their talents, abilities or goals, they find solace and security in that time-worn cure-all, "Oh Well."

When Jesus told us to throw the first stone if we have no sin, he had little reason to fear we would injure teens for their lack of self-examination. We adults have plenty of our own baggage to carry, and few free hands for stones. Old Ed, a man whom I knew, was an exception since he was always interested in self-examination. I have often wondered what would have happened if he had asked the monument dealer to etch this epitaph on his tombstone: "The unexamined life is not worth living." I'm sure for the right amount of money the chisel would have clanged and old Ed would have left his witness in granite for many eyes to read.

What is the right point in life to apply this pithy truth about the unexamined life? On your tombstone? When you are entering retirement? When you are making a job change? When Aunt Mathilda leaves you $200,000? When you lose everything in an economic reversal? Or, horror of horrors, when you are a teenager? We prefer to hang that poster with "The unexamined life is not worth living" in someone else's office. Examining life is something we want to put off until we receive a degree in philosophy, or we let the preacher handle it for us on Sunday morning. Already I hear someone complaining, "We have plenty of homespun philosophers around town without me adding two cents worth! I don't need an examined life."

Think about it. Would you visit a doctor the second time if the sign on his office door read, "Unexamination Room?" Of course not. So why live one unexamined day in your life? Take a big marker and cross out these three sentences right now, and use a heavy black line as you do!

• The unexamined life is worth living.

• Sometime *Later* I'll find the key to my life's examination room.

• *Oh Well*, the unexamined life is the only one I've got.

Like going to the dentist, constructive self-examination hurts at first. For instance, do you prefer eating Sunday-morning sweet rolls or examining your patterns of thinking and feeling? Yes or no: Do you mix thinking and feeling in a positive way so constructive action follows? Adults have nothing on teens in these areas. And what about clear, precise, visible goals? Putting goals on paper is like writing a check to the IRS after sweating over your tax return for a week: the torture of calculation is exceeded only by the torment of check-writing.

Here is the nub of the problem. We cannot have constructive self-examination without compiling a goal agenda that makes sense, but neither can we plan life goals without counting our resources. We hesitate about both since they are closely linked, and procrastination sets in. Procrastination puts things off in hopes that the end never arrives. Once I wrote a poem about hesitating that probably should have been called "Later! Oh Well" rather than "Procrastin." It went like this.

PROCRASTIN
***A** delaying*
    of the fraying
        while men smell
            the odor of death
and prefer
    to refer it
        to another space or
            ***TION**.*

Perhaps it is too philosophical to say that we procrastinate and avoid goal-setting and self-evaluation because they remind us of our Ultimate End. Let's just say that death and taxes plague us as life intruders, and we prefer the well-traveled road rather than walking the rocky path of reality. On that smooth, well-traveled highway travelers carry signs that read "No Death," "No Taxes," "No Constructive Self-examination," and "No Goals." The walking is easy, but the burden gets heavier each day.

That may be why some adults invoke the teenager's "Later" and "Oh Well" without so many words. Day after day we fail to ask where we are going or what we want from life. No wonder there are three kinds of people, including teenagers: those who make things happen, those who watch things happen (Later), and those who say, What happened? (Oh Well).

One time I was traveling in Germany by train when a distinguished looking man started regaling me with his personal philosophy, which sounded very official in German. "Most people look for too much from life," he said. "For me, a little bread, a little wine, and some cheese on a quiet meadow, that is enough." At least he knew what he wanted. He had examined life and discovered that for him too much was too much, so he needed little for fulfillment. He did not say "Later" or "Oh Well."

Energy and Powers of Concentration

Teens have boundless energy for certain activities, and that is why I always felt sorry for the summer camp counselor who had to pack my daughter and fifteen other rowdy girls into bed every night. If this was the night to laugh, laughter filled the bunkhouse for hours with no apparent loss of energy. For his part, a teenage boy can play soccer non-stop with his energy meter above a hundred percent, but the meter hits zero when his mother wants him to vacuum the house.

For teens, energy is wired to self-image. My son did not see himself as a mower of grass, so all energy drained from his heels when I mentioned cutting the lawn. Suddenly this brawny young man lost control of his muscular system and could scarcely lift an arm! However, if Greg called him to play basketball, Presto! In his mind he became an Olympic champion to be pictured on a Wheaties box. Instantaneous battery recharge, I thought.

Teenagers learn what the rest of us practice with varying success in life. Their Energizer battery never runs down if they're beating the right drum, and they keep going and going and going. When a teen's activity and goal are fused, the self-image unleashes energy that is the equivalent of nuclear fission.

Here is the important link to goals. Your self-image energizes your battery by feeding off your life goals. When your rabbit stops in its tracks, it's time to check your self-image and life goals. The teen years show this linkage better than any time in life, and their experience can teach us much. Part of being a teenager is learning how to live in the adult world, and that involves tying a golden thread from life goals to self-image to energy. When the thread unravels, our energy level plummets.

The average teenager learns how the process works and how to modify it through trial and error. For instance, a high school freshman named Jane appreciated the energy that came from her self-image as a child, but she found it more difficult to accept goals that society imposed, such as self-control and responsibility. Her challenge was to maintain a high level of energy while developing the self-image of a young woman with personal independence.

A firm bond linked Jane's self-confidence with feelings about herself, and the reason was simple. Confident people carry their own battery pack and do not need to tap a charger every hour. They know who they are and where they have chosen to go, and they have the energy to get there. Asking confident people if they will get the job done is like asking a Mt. Everest climber which way is up.

We can learn another important lesson from teens since they are masters at applying the power of concentration. This carries over from childhood when they learn to sock body, soul, mind, and spirit into an activity that pays rich rewards,

so it gets undivided attention. Parents of teenagers stand in awe of their concentration. A mother asks, Why can't these kids hear me shouting although they pick up every word of the MTV video? Sheer concentration! You could probably shout "Fire!" at McDonald's without moving a single teenager. Riveting conversation makes them ignore such non-essential information. Sheer concentration!

We use our power of concentration with varying success, and sometimes we need to ask for help. Victor Hugo of *Les Misérables* fame did not always feel like writing so he forced himself to concentrate by having his servant remove all his clothes from the room and disappear for several hours. Then, clutching paper and pen, the naked Hugo had little choice except to write.

Learning to concentrate is an important building block for life goals. You need to know how and when you concentrate best, and how to elevate your powers of concentration. If you concentrate on constructive self-examination, your pay-off will beat the odds in Las Vegas. Using concentration for this purpose is like buying IBM stock in 1946, or Microsoft's forty years later. You've got a sure winner.

Self-Inventory

The exercise in the accompanying table opens the door to your self-inventory. These questions can reveal your abilities, talents, and skills and show patterns in how you think, feel, and act.

Choose the right time for this constructive self-evaluation. When do you concentrate best, early in the morning or late at night? Before lunch? Take time to do the job right. You are painting a word-picture of the self-image that will nurture your life goals, and these goals will smooth some of the rough edges of your self-image and identify other important facets. Work through the chart and questions in any order. There are no wrong answers; yours are the right ones, and you alone know them. You can finish the exercise in a few minutes, and

what can be more important right now? Please don't say "Later" or "Oh Well."

After finishing the table labeled "Thinking, Feeling, Doing," read the full text aloud. Start at the top and go across, or start at the top and go down, or read across from the bottom up, or use any order you choose. Do these statements summarize your normal pattern of thinking, feeling, and acting? Do you recognize yourself? If not, add more data until you are satisfied. Then take a blank sheet of paper, title it "My Thinking, Feeling, Acting," copy the sentences one after another in full paragraphs, and read each paragraph aloud.

Now in any order read aloud the open-ended sentences that you completed. Add any statements that are necessary to sum up your major talents, abilities, and skills. Then take a blank sheet of paper, title it "Self-Examination: My Talents, Abilities, Skills," and copy the statements in any order in a single paragraph. Read the paragraph aloud.

Congratulations! You have taken a critical step in discovering important parts of your self-image together with your significant skills, abilities, talents, thinking, and feeling processes.

THINKING, FEELING, DOING

THINKING	I enjoy thinking about	My favorite subjects for thinking are	I don't get far when I try to think about	A person I'm most like when I think is	These words best describe my way of thinking:
FEELING	The feelings I show most often are	The kind of feeling I enjoy most is	I have a hard time expressing these feelings:	A person I'm most like in expressing my feelings is	These words best describe my way of feeling:
DOING	I base many of my actions on (thinking or feeling, choose one) because	What I find easy to do is	What I find hard to do is	A person I resemble in the way I act is	These words best describe the way I act:

QUESTIONS FOR SELF-EXAMINATION

In a group of people, my best social skills are ______________ and ______________.

One-on-one, my best social skills are ______________ and ______________.

My friends tell me I do these things especially well: ______________.

On these things about me my friends are right: ______________.

On these things about me my friends are wrong: ______________.

QUESTIONS FOR SELF-EXAMINATION

In a group of people, my best social skills are ___________, ___________________________, ___________________________, and ____.

One-on-one, my best social skills are ___________________, ___________________________, ___________________________, and ____.

My friends tell me I do these things especially well: ______________, ____________________, ___________________________, ______________________, ____________________________.

On these things about me my friends are right: _________________, _______________________, ______________.

On these things about me my friends are wrong: _________________, _______________________, ______________.

My favorite subject for reading/study is ____.

In life I'm most interested in___________________________, ____

Right now the best thing my tombstone could say about me is: This person…

____

____.

I show my abilities best when I:

____.

One good side of me that a lot of people miss is:

____.

My physical appearance is:

____.

If I could wave a magic wand, today I would:

____.

The best points of my personality are:

______________________, ______________________,
______________________, ______________________.

I feel a lot of confidence when:

____.

I think about the future because:

____.

People keep telling me:

____.

Religious faith is:

____.

My mother (is/was) good at:

____.

My father (is/was) good at:

____.

I want to:

____.

Several important things about me that I haven't mentioned are:

____________________, ____________________, ________
______________________, ______________________.

What really matters to me is:

____,
and ____________________________________,
and ____________________________________.

Responsible Choice

One of George Moore's novels tells how the Irish government put peasants to work building roads during the Great Depression. For a while the peasants worked well, singing songs since they were glad to be working again, but little by little they discovered the roads they were building led nowhere. They stopped at dreary bogs. The men grew listless and quit singing as they realized that the government had put them to work only to provide employment and food. Moore made a striking comment about what happened: "The roads to nowhere are difficult to make. For a man to work well and sing, there must be an end in view."[1]

This truth is second nature for teenagers since the future counts for them. Their phrase "What's Up?" inquires about the present for the sake of the future. It is like asking who's going where and for what reason?

Instinct and Reflection Time

An inquisitive spirit gets toddlers into trouble when they find Draino under the sink, but it also distinguishes us from Darth Vader or a pet parrot. Our interest in finding what is enjoyable, our pursuit of social interaction for its own sake and for purpose, and our urge to create a satisfying future turn us into inquisitive kittens.

Last spring I watched two house finches having their springtime fling on my patio. With a nest carefully built, they instinctively planned the future. Egg-cracking time would arrive before Easter, and then they would care for the baby finches. The life story of mom, dad, and the brood was the instinct to live and propagate, and year after year these birds answer the teenager's perennial question, "What's Up?", with the same activity. Theirs is the beauty of instinctual goal-setting, not an inquisitive spirit. They waste no energy setting goals, but neither do they have the luxury of modifying behavior toward non-instinctual aims. Unlike the peasants building roads to nowhere, these birds cannot stop singing.

Some days we may feel like exchanging places with finches, but our skin is the only skin we're in, so the teenager's "What's Up?" is one of the most valuable questions we can ask. Our society has enough wealth to give teenagers the luxury of reflection time to think and grow. We consider it unwise to thrust our daughters into matriarchal duties at puberty, and we want sons and daughters to expand their boundaries before joining the work force. Theoretically, we've given all teens the luxury of asking, "What's Up?"

Of course, what teenagers learn and how they learn it varies widely. Teens stretching their life-bonds from childhood to maturity sop up what parents, friends, and mentors have to offer. Their success and failure in stretching life-bonds becomes part of their pattern for living, and changing that pattern later in life is usually not easy. Teens learn much, and how they use what they learn is even more interesting to watch. One day a teenager brought home a report card riddled with poor grades. When his parents asked what he had to say about this, he replied, "One thing for sure, you know I haven't been cheating!"

Asking where we want to go without reflectively examining talents and abilities needed to get there is as foolish as would-be mountain climbers who prepare only by drinking several quarts of beer every night. But with the results of our constructive self-examination now in hand and using time for reflection, we're off to find the Wizard.

Setting Personal Goals

An important lesson in the teen years is how to formulate a personal future, how to set personal goals. Our capitalist society intensifies the worth of this lesson with its individual rights and democratic freedoms. Teens have the opportunity to achieve personal excellence, but sometimes the wide variety of choices teaches teens—and adults—the wrong lesson. They think that all of life's material niceties and freedoms are there for the taking, or they mistakenly believe that some giant dispenser has put them on the list for automatic distribution.

Life goals cut through this jungle for teens and the rest of us since well-formulated goals tie a firm knot between freedom and personal responsibility. Goals teach us the foolishness of aspiring to some freedom or material success for which we take no responsibility. They help us ask concretely what is probably the most important question for daily living: What am I going to do with the rest of my life?

Many graduation speakers harp on this question. A "Shoe" cartoon showed a young bird graduating from school, and he offered his father this advice about the commencement speech he was supposed to give for the graduation: "Draw on your years of experience, regale us with a few stories from a full and vibrant life. Speak to us of the challenges ahead, the lessons you have learned, the advice you have for our generation." Then the young bird added, "And keep it to four minutes."

We keep thinking, if only I did not have to ask myself each day, What am I going to do with the rest of my life? If only I could take care of that question once and for all, or once every ten years. Life goals matter because they force us to address this question, and the question matters since it forces us to life goals. When teens ask "What's Up?" they raise a similar question, or at least open themselves to its possibilities. You answer this question personally through life goals because they are mind-sketches of your future. They show which choices you make for growth and gain out of all the alternatives available to you. So go to it if you find it easier to ask "What's Up?" rather than "What am I going to do with the rest of my life?" Just do something so you stop sitting on eggs—like those finches—and think that is all there is to the exciting story called life!

When we ask "What's Up?" in relation to life goals, we circle once more to our inventory of skills, talents, and abilities. Wouldn't it be a cruel joke for someone born without legs to aspire to professional hockey? Being realistic about our gifts and skills is the first step toward genuine, successful life goals.

Life goals are especially important when concentration lags. Not knowing what you are trying to do is bad anytime; when for some reason you have trouble concentrating, not having specific goals is a greater calamity. Keeping your goals handy is a sure way to help your mind concentrate on the task at hand.

You use a turbo-injection system when you tap your conscious *and* subconscious mind to establish and attain goals. You find pure joy in writing black on white paper what you want from your future, beginning with tomorrow. Once you establish goals, you will never again ask that familiar teenage question, "What's Up?", without knowing exactly what you want to uncover.

Affirmation

Some things don't change much, and one of them is the teenage attraction for the word "Cool!" My memories may be dim but I think we used the term in the 1950s. Even then "Cool!" expressed feelings of enjoyment, affirmed someone's talents or actions, and covered situations when we wanted to express a positive sentiment.

Calling yourself "Cool!" or being positive about yourself is sometimes a more difficult task than saying good things about others. From childhood we learn the virtue of humility, and most kids dislike braggarts as much as bullies, but, paraphrasing Barry Goldwater, extremism in the pursuit of expressing positivism is no vice. Being positive is not bullying others or bragging about self; it is identifying and celebrating yourself as a unique and singular part of the human race.

Being Positive

Saying that you are "Cool!" may be an unusual use of teen jargon, but the psycho-dynamics have a firm basis. Drinking water from a poisoned well is stupid, so why should we expect positive behavior from a person who says only the worst about herself or herself? The less positive we are about ourselves, the less positive are our relationships.

Let's not sell ourselves short by emphasizing negative characteristics at the expense of our good points. Shortcomings do not prevent people from achieving monumental ends. In a recent book Jane Goodsell tells us that Aristotle bit his fingernails. Did that stop him from thinking? Wealthy J. Paul Getty installed a pay phone in his English country house so that he would not be charged for calls by his guests. A character flaw or shrewd business? Pablo Picasso reportedly could not learn the letters of the alphabet. Did that affect how he mixed colors in beauty? Sigmund Freud would not travel alone since he did not know how to read a railroad timetable. Did that keep him from thinking new thoughts? Woody Allen once lamented, "My one regret in life is that I am not someone else." With all his laurels, obviously the joke did not apply to him. King Alfonso of Spain was so tone deaf he could not recognize his country's national anthem. Was this a throne-toppling flaw? Cezanne thought so little of his paintings that he gave some to his small son to cut into puzzles.[2]

Rephrasing an old saying, there is more between your ears than dead wood. Chances are that you are scarcely tapping your brain's capacity since there are millions of cells to use after you exhaust the drawer in which you are working. You have mental powers that none of IBM's most powerful computers can emulate.

The first electronic computer was a monster. Located at the University of Pennsylvania, it weighed thirty tons and filled the space of a box car. Large fans cooled 18,000 vacuum tubes, and on average a tube failed every seven minutes. The computer's first assignment back in 1946 was two hours of work on a million top secret cards; it performed calculations in nuclear physics for the untested hydrogen bomb.[3] Today we pack this computing power into silicon chips that rest on a tabletop, yet the miniaturization of computer power has not begun to equal the creativity, genius, warmth, affection, perception, integration, and other powers of the your mind.

It is fool's wisdom to underestimate the human mind. Talk about power, hear this. An illiterate farm laborer from Derbyshire, England instantaneously calculated how to double a farthing 139 times. Others checked Jedidiah Buton's answer and proved that his thirty-nine digit answer was right. When he saw Shakespeare's *Richard III* the first time, he memorized the number of words spoken by each actor, and every entry and exit. An American named Zerah Calhoun determined in an instant how many seconds there were in 1,183 years, seven months and twenty-seven days. Check his answer: 57,234,384,000 seconds. Without paper and pencil, George Bidder figured the number of light waves striking the human eye to produce the effect of the color red. His computation took a second or two since it ran to fifteen digits.

Constant negative self-feedback shrinks the size of the canvas that we use to paint subconscious pictures and compose our future. People who consistently refuse to affirm their gifts and talents end up with fewer of them to use because their skills and abilities wither without the positive reinforcement. The destructive process of feeding on self rather than feeding self can lead to flame-out, over-activity without purpose, fatigue, psychological and spiritual sickness, interpersonal friction, and a host of other maladies.

We have no ironclad assurance that self-affirmation inoculates us against all of these plagues or gives us a promised land without life problems. But not affirming your way of thinking, feeling, and acting and your gifts and abilities gives you a better chance of coming down with something more than the flu. A little affirmation goes a long way with the subconscious, like with my old hound. When I scold him for tracking mud he acts like Rodney Dangerfield: no respect from nobody! A pat on the head turns the world bright again.

We have heard the statement a hundred times, but it is just as true as the first time: "Start each day with a positive success." This is an important tool in being positive. Successfully complete a task that shows one or more of your gifts or skills in action, and then relish your achievement. Some people start the day with prayer and meditation to celebrate their ability to concentrate on the Wholly Other as life's focus. God bless them! Some people begin the workday answering yesterday's mail since they enjoy writing good letters. May their fingers fly! Whatever the day's first task, do it with gusto and reward yourself. You deserve the reward since you are "Cool!"

A second way to ensure positive reinforcement is by setting realistic deadlines for all tasks. A project with no due date is not a project but a hobby. If you are serious about attaining a goal you will stack up interim dates until you meet your deadline. This turns a venture into a finished product. A date stamp bearing only future dates confirms the discipline of self-affirmation, and you unleash mega-kilowatts of internal energy when you require yourself to finish the task on time. Goals without deadlines are like sitting on a three-legged chair: you are guaranteed to tip and fall.

Meeting a deadline means it's celebration time, so celebrate your deadlines. Deadlines are not self-electrocutions. They build expectation, like a bride and groom waiting for their wedding, and they show that you successfully meet your expectations. We celebrate too little in life since celebration takes time, like self-examination and self-affirmation. We're too busy, have too many responsibilities, or cannot think of ways to cheer minor accomplishments. Celebration is positive reinforcement, or another form of self-talk that says, "Well done! You're cool!"

Visioning

One more thing about being "Cool!" is that you are

heading for the stars when you apply positive self-affirmation to your goals. This is a final step; it links your skills, abilities, and capacity for self-affirmation with the aims you set for life. We call this "visioning."

Visioning does not always sound exciting. The city where I live created a "visioning" program last year because the city council wanted to integrate peoples' dreams about Scottsdale into a comprehensive vision of the city's future. While this program had people stifling yawns, visioning personal goals is always exciting. It is intensely personal since every visioned goal begins with the word "I," and it uses as many senses as possible and paints mental pictures in Technicolor. Visioning lets you emotionally experience in the here-and-now your feelings of joy and satisfaction at reaching your goal.

I use visioning to paint on my conscious and subconscious mind an unforgettable image of my goal. I see, feel, hear, smell, and touch what happens at the time of goal achievement, when I meet my deadline (that is why you construct goal statements in the present tense, not future).

If we do not provide our subconscious with food for the future it cannot lead us there. The subconscious mind has thousands of images to draw on as we move through life. For example, psychologists tell us that we associate the sense of smell with our earliest recollections and strongest memories. If I smell a dank, dark place, one of the first things I remember is the basement where my mother stored homemade root beer. But let's consider how we can use this subconscious power in visioning. Say that one of your written goals is a retirement home on the Carolina shore ten years from now. Shouldn't you use the powerful sense of smell to reinforce your goal-vision? Can you smell the new paint and wallpaper as you walk through the living room? Fresh flowers on the kitchen table? Salty air outside?

Visioning uses a small part of the mind's expansive power. We will discuss more about visioning in later chapters, but start now to see, feel, hear, smell, and touch your written goals while visioning them as pictures in your mind. Work through your list of goals one by one. Place yourself smack in the middle of the mental picture at the precise moment that you are accomplishing your goal. Focus on details, see yourself as the main actor, and use all the senses as you feel the joy of success. You are on the way! You are "Cool!"

Cover your rear-view mirror and steer your subconscious to the future! Enough already with a past that you cannot change! The past is important but not so important that it alone should control your future. Full throttle, seat back, let's fly toward a future that we have a better chance of changing than our past.

Now is no time to regress to "Later" or "Oh Well." Your constructive self-examination is in hand, your self-outlook is positive, your energy light flashes green, you know the value of deadlines, your self-image pivots on goals, your life goals point to the future, and you visualize your goals several times a day. That is how you get to "there" from "here." Best of all, you aren't using a rear-view mirror!

How much time is left to answer the question, "What I am going to do with the rest of my life?" Let's imagine that your life-span is three-score years and ten, seventy years. If we compress seventy years into a single day from 7:00 A.M. to 11:00 P.M., what time is it for you?

10:25 A.M. if you are fifteen years old,
12:40 P.M. if you are twenty-five,
1:50 P.M. if you are thirty,
Just past 4:00 P.M. if you are forty,
Quarter past 5:00 P.M. if you are forty-five,
6:25 P.M. if you are fifty,
7:40 P.M. if you are fifty-five,
8:40 P.M. if you are sixty,
Ten minutes before the 10:00 P.M. news
if you are sixty-five,
11:00 P.M., you run out of time.

II
Beating Your Path to the World's Doorway

Dear Brett,

Your graduation from Stanford University is another good time for a father-son chat. Until you call me on the phone I will do the talking, and my end of the conversation will be on paper.

My letter heading recasts the old saying, "Build a better mousetrap and the world will beat a path to your doorstep." I changed it since life goals involve beating your own path, not someone beating theirs to you. Usually the world does not come running to you even if you are a new mousetrap-builder. You must do the path-beating, and to beat a path you have to find it, in fact, make it.

That is as shocking for a college graduate as for the rest of us, I am sure. Our skills and abilities, including those honed by higher education, do not magically transform us into the earth's axis. Unless we know what we are doing the world will tell us what to do, and the difference between the two is great. You will wait a long time for the world to fall over itself finding you; you, not the world are the path-beater.

Since babyhood you have continued to push out the boundaries of your life. It took about a year for you to distinguish yourself from your mother and the world around you. Before that the whole world was hungry when you were hungry, and what a cry the world made when you cried! In the terrible two's you still wielded an imagined omnipotence over everything, including our German shepherd Bismarck. Then you started extending your boundaries, this time from a core personality that recognized the difference between you and the world. You have kept at it since then, down through your most challenging college experiences.

It will not stop, as those of us farther along life's path know. Extending boundaries through life goals beats your path to new areas of experience in the world. That is life's excitement, and it does not end until you stop at death.

Life goals are your plans for beating new paths. You will change your goals often in life, but their purpose remains the same: they are your best tools for expanding horizons, spreading boundaries, and finding fulfillment in as many areas of human experience as possible. Without them you might as well curl up in a corner, dream dreams for new mousetraps, and wait for the world to come to you.

Do you remember our tripping each other with tongue-twisters? "The skunk sat on the stump; the skunk thunk the stump stunk, but the stump thunk the skunk stunk." You always liked "How much wood would a woodchuck chuck if a woodchuck could chuck wood?" Finally I have the answer! 700 pounds! While a woodchuck usually does not throw things through the air, it clears out thirty-five cubic feet of dirt underground for a shelter to live in. At twenty pounds a cubic foot that is 700 pounds of dirt. Now if a woodchuck can chuck that much dirt backwards, couldn't it chuck that much wood?[4]

Furthermore, if a woodchuck can chuck that much wood, why would it want to invent a woodchucking machine that works slower? For me that is the more important question, and that is why I want you to consider beating paths to the world's doorway instead of tinkering on a better mousetrap the rest of your life.

Settle back and enjoy yourself with this letter. I want to describe why your goals should include other people, how much life goals cost, and how they poke beyond the end of your nose. Check what you want to discuss later. While I am writing at your graduation, I hope that what I say will be useful throughout life.

People Goals

Does your room still look like a hermit's, like when you lived at home? You did not design it for receiving visitors unless they were comfortable with clothes on the bed, stacked books and papers, and other signs of college life.

Now I know you are no hermit, despite some appearances. You use language, like other human beings, and sociologists call us "social animals," a human pack. Not many people find a solitary existence gratifying since being with others is good for mental and physical health. People help you discover who you are and challenge you to become something more. The less interaction you have with other people, the more satisfied you will be doing the same things the same way, and boredom and disinterest often follow.

That is why your life goals encompass other people. If you want to beat a path to the world's doorstep your life goals must be large enough to celebrate interdependence with others, for that is part of what it means to be human.

Support Groups

Several years ago I met in ten sessions with a dozen men

who discussed at length the joys and sorrows of being men today. It was an interesting experience for us as we cried and laughed over common experiences, heard others telling our own story, and formed a kind of community unknown to us.

Men are good at avoiding this kind of encounter. We think it is not "macho" to show pain, let alone share it with others, but your mother and her friends are smarter. They are more relational, whether by nature or force of male pressure I do not know; they weave a web of support for each other through breakfast gatherings, club meetings, and bridge nights.

The me-alone emphasis has not run its course for men and women, and many people continue going it alone. They think that the individual is life's end-all, but loneliness is often a consequence when individualism is overburdened. In an interview in 1977, Shirley MacLaine suggested that

> *the most pleasurable journey you take is through yourself, the only sustaining love involvement is with yourself. When you look back on your life and try to figure out where you've been and where you're going, when you look at your work, your love affairs, your marriages, your children, your pain, your happiness—when you examine all that closely, what you really find out is that the only person you really go to bed with is yourself. The only thing you have is working to the consummation of your own identity. And that's what I've been trying to do all my life.*[5]

Brett, with this attitude Ms. MacLaine probably will keep on trying to satisfy her individualism with little success. She seems to have forgotten that we are people, and people need one another.

I urge you to include support groups in your life goals, all kinds of them. Your friends, relatives, co-workers, adults at church, and other organized and ad hoc groups fill this bill. You will probably form and join many support groups during life, some by necessity and others by choice. Look for the best from them and you will find it. Contribute what you can to support someone who is suffering temporary pain, and do not be afraid to ask for their support when you need it. Your problems are yours to solve, true, but that does not mean you have to suffer problems and pain alone. Other people can be sounding-boards, can discuss alternatives, offer counsel and emotional support, and brace you with their help.

One of my life's biggest mistakes has been trying to do too much alone. Too often I ignored resources that could have tempered anger, soothed grief, and given emotional support. Part of that was a male hang-up, learned behavior that I am still trying to modify. Consider using your list of life goals to find support when and where you need it. Vision yourself participating in group conversation where participants level with each other, support one another, and practice human solidarity.

A lot of so-called little people became unsung or recognized heroes because others supported them. Borden Burr hatched the football huddle and Italo Marchiony invented the first ice cream sandwich. Maurice Turner devised the folding telephone booth while Hayword Law thought of painting white stripes down highway centerlines. Andrew C. Lawson became a father at age eighty-seven.[6] I wager that at some point each of them received pivotal support from one or more persons.

Life goals that make room for other people are worth their weight in gold since they pay off. Cooperating with others is a sure way of multiplying your gifts and theirs, growing more together than you can apart.

Rejection

As you learned while growing up, rejection is part of life. Any person who grew up without scars from rejection probably never left his room, and locked the door in his sister's face besides! Life goals can help with rejection, especially when your mistake is the cause.

Surely Stanford had no perennial bitchers, did it? I mean, people who gnaw daily at the guts of life? They will probably ask St. Peter for directions to heaven after one glance inside the pearly gates. I know you are no complainer, but like the rest of us you have your days and weeks. When you feel like complaining, read the following sentence aloud and listen carefully to the underlined words. Does the sound of these words ever sound like you? "The *plump, phlegmatic plutocrat* smelled of *flatulent* excess, *griped, crunched* peanuts, sought *treachery,* liked the *cacophony* of *jazz,* and drained the *sap* from everyone." According to one poll, these are the ten worst-sounding words in the English language, and for impact I put them together in a sentence.[7]

Being down-in-the-mouth turns people off, and for good reason. It lowers spirits, spreads gloom and doom, and encourages mutual rejection. So if you tend in this direction occasionally, think about including a short-term life goal that portrays you as a perennial encourager, not a bitcher. See yourself smiling broadly on Monday morning and expressing appreciation to others for who they are. Imagine yourself as a person you want to be around because he keeps life moving to where the air is clean and the sky is blue.

Some people feel rejected after making a mistake. This reminds me of why your mother kept repeating Big Bird's words from "Sesame Street," "Everybody makes mistakes!" You and I share the trait of perfectionism, and it is a big pill for us to keep swallowing. To think that we could ever be imperfect! No wonder you got so mad when you could not craft your English paper exactly the way you planned. No wonder I get angry with myself over mistakes that just should not have happened but did.

I recently heard a good story about a mail order house that received an irate customer's letter. "*I purchased a do-it-yourself birdhouse from you,*" the man complained. "*First, it is too big, and second, it keeps blowing out of the tree. Please send my money back immediately!*" The company quickly replied. "*Dear Sir: The enclosed check covers the amount of your purchase. We made a mistake and sent you a do-it-yourself sailboat. But be happy. Somebody somewhere just finished dead last in a boat race in a leaky birdhouse.*"

Nobody is perfect, not even computerized mail order companies—or brokerages. In 1992, a clerk at Salomon Brothers hit the wrong button by mistake and triggered a sell order for an estimated $500 million worth of stock. And it happened five minutes before the stock exchange closed!

Hopefully we can laugh at our imperfections. Ethel Barrymore once said that you grow up the day you have your first real laugh—at yourself. That belly-laugh is one of the best in the business.

One way to battle perfectionism is with a short-term life goal that targets this tomfoolery. See yourself making an inconsequential boo-boo and then laughing along with others, and practice visioning this goal with color and emotion. Soon you will find it easier to say peccator (I have sinned) about little things that you fail to accomplish absolutely, positively perfectly. Let's take the pledge now to leave absolute perfection to God.

I know that generally you are not a good loser, but neither am I. People make fun of us with good reason when we cannot enjoy a game as a game. Remember how you had to win at Monopoly or pout? You did not have to administer that dose of rejection to yourself. Why? Because not everything in life is about winning or losing. In 1964, an American father and his young son were enjoying a beautiful Saturday in Hyde Park, London, playing catch with a Frisbee. Few English people had seen a Frisbee by that time, so a small group wandered up to watch the strange sport. Finally a Brit in a Homburg asked the father, "Sorry to bother you. Been watching you a quarter of an hour. Who's winning?"[8] Nobody was. It was not a contest but a game.

Life is about people goals, and interaction with people concerns more than winning or losing. You may even want to consider a short-term goal that shows you losing graciously at your favorite game, perhaps even Monopoly!

Mating

For you to beat a path to the world's doorstep, life goals

must include other people. Mating is part of that assignment for most of us.

Mom and I are happy that at least until now you have found no lifelong mate. We have enough trouble supporting you single! Our generation grew up with the motto "Eat, drink, and get married," but who knows, you may choose life as a bachelor. Then again, you may have little choice and end up as one. Chances are good that you will tie the knot with someone along the way.

Maybe "mating" is not a wise choice of words since it reminds us of animals, zoos, and the peacocks' courtship dance. After all, the lifelong commitment we call marriage has more to it than pure mating, which is life's reproductive force. The word should give pause to male chauvinists like us. Much as we would like to think that we choose a mate and the other obliges, the process is more complex than that. Women rightfully think for themselves, and this adds a new ingredient to the mating game. Despite all these caveats, I will use the term.

I want to sum up a few thoughts about mating without offering a long treatise on staying married after you leave the altar. How have your mother and I enjoyed twenty-nine years of marriage? There is a simple answer: by the grace of God and through hard work. Robert Frost once asked how his two eyes "make one in sight," and that is a helpful way to think about marriage. Two people keep separate lives and interests, but they see as one when it comes to understanding their relationship and what it should mean. That takes some learning.

Romantic love, the original flush of falling in love, usually does not last a lifetime. It is ephemeral since its primary goal is reproduction of the species, which is important. The real question comes when that honeymoon is over, the kids are screaming, and the mates want to know what is next. This shock can be overwhelming. Part of the problem may be due to over-reliance on sex as the marital cure-all. "Sex is the flame which uncontrolled may scorch; properly guided, it will light the torch of eternity," Joseph Fetterman warned.

In my book no married person's set of goals is complete if it ignores the pivotal relationship with a spouse. One life goal can be a master plan for your spousal relations, although it will change often as your relationship matures. Half of the battle is being conscious of the need for maturation in marital love since nothing in life stays the same for long, including that relationship.

Your mother and I had our share of troubles, but we constantly pursued greater intimacy in our thoughts and feelings. We corralled personal preferences that conflicted with our common good, and in value clarification sessions we weighed personal and marital values. In maturity we discovered that the romantic passion of love does not compare with hearts and souls that intertwine.

It would take several pages to regale you with some of the problems we faced, including early-poverty style furniture, but despite occasional bitterness and frustration we always tried to make it possible to talk. Through it all we maintained strong lines of communication so we did not throw out our relationship with the problem.

That reminds me of one of O. Henry's stories about a very poor couple. As a sign of love the woman decided to sell her long hair to buy a good-looking chain for her husband's watch. Meantime, the husband sold his watch to buy some beautiful combs for his wife's hair. As you can see, being generous without communicating is not the answer.

Use life goals to envision what kind of mate you want, how you will relate with her early in marriage, and how you will mature with her as days pass. To me it is incredible for a married person to ignore a spousal relationship in a set of life goals.

Life Goal Costs

Underline this in red: Life goals cost something if they are going to accomplish anything in your life and vocation.

Despite what this says, people tell us not to look a gift horse in the mouth. Well, life goals are not horses, and neither do they give free gifts. They are going to cost time, money, and commitment, and you should not take them on if you will not pay the price. The old hymn had it right: no cross, no crown.

Some life goals are nearly universal in character while others are very specific and limited. Some are short-term and some long-term. Not all are of equal importance, although all are important or you would not include them in your goal list.

Being selective about goals includes selecting-out some for the time being. Reportedly Queen Victoria underlined all of her diary because supposedly every word was so very important, but maybe the real problem was her undeveloped skill of selection. Life teaches us that not everything is equally important. If it is, we stand in need of criteria to arrange our priorities. Non-selectivity may be a sign of jumbled values (more on that below).

My advice is that your life goal list should never include more than twenty goals at once. Some may be broad. For instance, you see yourself overcoming a general tendency toward negativism. Another may be specific, like celebrating the purchase of a new car by feeling the seats and smelling the interior. Consciously or unconsciously you will establish a priority in your list. You will work toward attaining all your goals but recognize that deadlines vary from one to the next, giving each goal a temporal priority.

Ranking goals according to priority means ignoring what does not matter. That usually is easier when you have fewer responsibilities and challenges, but take a lesson from Joe (Satchel) Page, one of baseball's best relief pitchers. Many people thought the 1949 Yankees had a pitcher named Reynolds-Page because Reynolds started the game and Page came in and finished off the opponents. Someone once asked Satchel how he remained calm in pressure-packed situations. He said that he ignored the men on base while he kept them from stealing; they could not hurt him as long as he struck out the batter. He ignored what did not matter.

Some people mistakenly believe that they are better off ignoring big problems than confronting them. Why? Because big problems, like big life goals, will cost more time, money, and commitment. Their reasoning is correct but their conclusion is wrong.

Fear of tackling big problems can spread like a disease through the rest of life. Leo Rostow tells a story about Fate coming to an island long ago and calling three of the island's inhabitants before him. He asked what they would do if he said that the next day a giant tidal wave would immerse the island. The first answered, "I would eat, drink, carouse and make love all night long!" The second said, "I would go to the sacred places and make sacrifices to the gods and pray without ceasing." Then the third man said, "Why, I would assemble the wisest men and begin at once to study how to live under water."[9] I hope you will always make the effort to tackle it no matter how large the problem, knowing well that any life goal will cost you.

Time Costs

Life goals resemble religious faith in one way. Faith as a gift costs nothing, but it exacts a heavy cost once you have it since it compels you to believe, live, and act as a person of faith. Someone described the paradox this way: "Trust as though it all depends on God; work as though it all depends on you." Life goals freely bring what they promise and pour down gifts as your subconscious works day and night to attain what you set before it. Like faith, life goals cost time and money, and without paying both you will not receive their gifts.

Since you expend large amounts of time pursuing life goals, organizing your time efficiently is a top priority. In life there are no "gentleman's C's." When you arrive at the end the grade is Pass or Fail, so organizing for action is not a mere option. Since time is money, organizing life and work reduces the money you waste.

Recently a time management expert advised that the best place to start organizing is with a clean desk. Remove everything from your desk, all the big and little piles. Put every item into a labeled file folder dealing with that subject, or into a new folder (cheap compared with the cost of your time). As you do this, list items from your desktop on a Master List as things to be done. Now your desk contains only this Master List, kept on computer if possible.[10] You add new items to the Master List daily as they come in, and remove those that you complete. This process helps you correctly answer an important question: Which do you value more, pleasing habits (such as a piled-high desk) or pleasing results? You are a "pilamaniac" if all you can find on your desk are glimpses of wood between piles.

Then comes the actual work of making time to do it right the first time. How much is your time worth per hour if you average your annual income? How will you get the most bang for the buck? Mark all items on your Master List with A, B, or C; A for urgent and very important, B for necessary but comparatively less important, and C for things that you want to do if and when you have time. Then pick the A items you want to concentrate on the next day and put them on top of the day's agenda. After completing them go on to other A items you select for that day, or B items. If you still have time, finish some C items.

This system helps budget your time by making a priority list of what you do first. Rather than following a daily calendar slavishly you control what you will do and for how long, starting at the top. If emergencies interrupt your work, return to where you stopped. Use your life goals as criteria for designating A items at work and home. You have a real problem if the criteria do not mesh with your goals.[11]

Just as important as organizing work is organizing your time for reading, writing, speaking, and thinking. Have you ever met someone who brags that his last real thought struck him in the hallowed halls of "X" college? By avoiding time to think they are missing one of life's real joys, and besides, a straight line connects thinking with reading, writing, and speaking. To beat your path to the world's doorway you need excellence in all four.

In 1854 a school in New England dismissed a young child after he attended classes for only three months, supposedly because he suffered from mental retardation. His father accused him of being a misfit and often beat him unmercifully. At age twelve, the boy got outside employment to support himself, and few imagined that the young man would ever amount to anything. During his lifetime, Thomas Edison registered over a thousand patents and became one of the century's foremost inventors. To top all, he was deaf but considered the disability an asset because it taught him to listen within. That was thinking time.

Brett, do you remember as a child when we asked you why you were going to school? You said, if you recalled our answer, "To learn to think." Thinking is important since life is a series of tests—and you thought you were done with exams! Academic suicide is defined as taking an exam without thinking, and life's tests also demand a thinking hat.

Writing and written communication? Who am I to advise? Nonetheless, here are some brief recommendations. Work at sentences under twenty words, avoid the passive voice when possible (even if Jimmy was hit by the ball), and write and polish until clarity shines through like a diamond. Make sure your thinking is clear, then test how well your words carry your thoughts.

I have compiled the following phrases that you can string together as needed so that you will never be at a loss for words while writing company reports. The instructions are simple. Take any line from the A items, add a line from B and one from C, and close with a line from D. Try one now, adding a comma here or there as necessary, and you will be amazed how much this expands your verbal repertoire. Any combination can serve as a summary statement for your report. Now that you have the idea, note how easy it is to use these convoluted phrases. Congratulations! You can now concoct the kind of gobbledygook that often passes for good writing in reports.

A ITEM:
The lugubrious nature of this characteristic,
Systematically examining all the quotients involved,
Components of the systems analysis within
behavioral objectives,

B ITEM:
appropriately modified by variables in use,
technically speaking,
in this regard,

C ITEM:
does not hold temporal qualities of a desirable nature
fails to consider dimensional attributes attributable
without cause
should be based on a voluminous study of the data

D ITEM:
all the extraneous circumstances notwithstanding.
although impetus for qualification of the data is
assumed.
although assimilation through qualitative
analysis may prove otherwise.

I am poking fun, of course, to make a point. Good writing flows from good thinking, and both are hard work and take time. While convoluted thinking has its place, usually in the philosopher's chamber, putting thoughts on paper clears up a great deal of muddled thinking. Many people can profit from a life goal that celebrates improved writing, so envision yourself celebrating a one-page masterpiece you just finished. Expect to pay a price for this goal.

Another area that will cost you time is the life goal of growing up "from" others throughout life. Probably our parents are the most important people we need to grow up "from," and we can use writing skills to advance the process. Here is how, Brett.

I hope that in the future you will have the gumption to write dead letters to mother and me. While we dearly love to hear from you we also want you to keep growing up from us. You will face situations when all that you can think about is what dear old dad would say, and how his customary advice has no real bearing on this situation. Precisely then you should sit down, write a long letter explaining my shortcomings and veritable foolishness on this point, letting it all hang out. Then, save your stamp and destroy the letter. The process will do wonders for your writing skills (combining emotion and intellect) and even more for your goal of continued growth throughout life. The last letter I wrote to my father was after he died, and I said uncomplimentary things that do not deserve the light of day. Thank God the letter is nowhere to be found, although it helped me grow in my late forties.

Do not forget dear old mom. She will keep throwing apron strings around your neck—intentionally and unintentionally—until you die, and you must keep cutting them. Did you hear what Whistler said on seeing his mother walking in the garden? "Mother, you're off your rocker!" Enough said.

You have your own gifts, and you will celebrate them as your lifeblood throughout life. Your need for independence from me and other adults is real. You are no John Stuart Mill and I am no James Mill, who supposedly was John Mill's "author." You did not read Greek at three, master Robertson, Hume, and Gibbon at seven, and return to re-read Roman history at eight, like John did. But thank God, neither do you think that you came into the world by immaculate conception, like John Stuart did. He said it well in the first sentence of his autobiography: "I was born in London on the 20th of May, 1806, and was the eldest son of James Mill, the author of the History of British India."[12] Poor John, no mama was necessary. What was called for were dead letters to his father and mother!

Let me add that your life goals are empty shells without

time for thinking. It takes time to think, evaluate, sort, choose, and prioritize goals and count their cost, as Bertrand Russell complained: "The real trouble with the world is that the stupid are cocksure and the intelligent full of doubt." Overcoming doubt through applied intelligence is part of what makes life goals exciting. In the Old West cowboys said that "every jackass thinks he's got horse sense," so let's let jackasses be jackasses and concentrate on getting our horse sense in line.

People without time to think run short of vision-fuel and remind me of trying to fish in shallow water. One time two pious Lutherans went ice fishing up north (I'll stick with them since I am like them). While chopping a hole in the ice they heard a voice boom out, "There are no fish in there!" After hearing the voice several times one of them gazed toward heaven and asked, "Lord, is it you?" The booming voice returned over the PA system, "No, I own this damn ice rink!" They were a little short of vision-fuel.

Some people may want to formulate a goal to control one of the greatest thought-killers of all times—television. Let's admit it, TV is a mind-killer. Figures show that by the time you and your classmates hit kindergarten you had seen about 5,000 hours of television. We tried to limit exposure, but not enough.

Television kills thinking, including the reading, writing, and speaking tied to it, by producing a "now" mentality that seeks immediate fixes for all problems. When heroes repair a large-scale environmental disaster in thirty minutes, it lowers personal and societal interest in long-range planning and solving problems realistically. TV desensitizes us to violence and stimulates instant gratification. In both family and society it heightens individualism while diminishing the sense of community. Sometimes the only community spirit in the family den is when somebody says, "Get out of my way, I can't see the TV." Television stresses materialism with a constant stream of commercialism, and stunts intellectual growth. When people discuss a television show they usually limit their information to what they saw since the medium is their primary source of information. As images flow over and control us they seem to make us passive observers of life. It is little wonder that we lose a sense of control over our lives.[13]

Talk about the cost of life goals! Take a person who sets as a goal to cut in half the hours spent in front of the tube. That will gain him a lot of time while depriving TV advertisers of viewing credits. Like breaking any bad habit, this one will cost time and energy, and perhaps money for a new book.

Your vocation is another area where life goals cost time and money. I prefer the term vocation over job since it connotes satisfaction from the human activity of work. Being objective about one's vocational potential is a bottom-line consideration. At least short-term your vocational goal should rest firmly on a realistic appraisal of gifts, skills, and training.

Long-term vocational goals are another matter. I think everyone should have at least one "stretch" vocational goal. If the person is young like you it looks ahead twenty or thirty years, or ten or fifteen years if they are older. Sit down sometime and write out a resume for the vocation you want to fill twenty years from now. The full description may not come easily, but keep pounding until you formulate it. Beware if you decide to make this a life goal for it will take time and energy for the incremental steps. The alternative is to keep on keeping on as you are, resting on your laurels.

In 1622 a Spanish galleon named *Atocha* sank after a raging hurricane hit Havana and dragged her onto Florida's treacherous reefs. The ship carried a secret cargo of over forty tons of gold, silver, and emeralds, and for 350 years people tried to piece the legend together. Finally, in 1971, an historian named Eugene Lyon discovered a remarkable document in the Spanish archives in Seville. Wormholes made the document hard to read, but the last page convinced him of the ship's location. Here was the missing link.

He called his friend Mel Fisher, who already had spent two years searching for the ship east of the Marquesas Keys. Fisher raised more money and set out again with divers. No one expected him to spend fourteen more years searching 120,000 linear miles before he found the *Atocha*. Along the way, the team located black chunks of metal (1973), and finally, in 1975, Fisher's son discovered an ancient bronze cannon stamped with *Atocha*. A week later disaster struck when Fisher's son and wife died in a freak accident in an overturned boat, and three years later Fisher still had nothing in hand after spending twelve years and over $6 million from investors.

Finally on July 20, 1985, ten years to the day after his son's death, Fisher found the *Atocha*. Emeralds in gold settings had a value of $60 million. Then came treasure chests loaded with gold and over a thousand silver bars, with serial numbers matching the original cargo manifest. The total find was worth $400 million.[14] Mel Fisher's long-range vocational goal of sixteen years came true. It cost time, money, and much more, but he knew with certainty what it was. It was his stretch goal.

Money Costs

Now on to another area. I know that you and others your age do not want to think about retirement since it is so far off. On the other hand, planning for retirement is a life goal that costs time and money, and you must judge whether it is worth the cost of starting early.

If I were your age I would consider the following information very carefully. News reports say that your favorite federal fund will be broke by the year 2040 unless Social Security taxes increase from their present level. That is just after you retire, but listen, there is more. Each of your retired aunts and uncles has four workers in the economy to support their retirement benefits. In about thirty-five years only 2.5 workers will be supporting you if American demographics remain unchanged. Isn't that sobering?

Herbert Hoover once said, "Blessed are the young, for they shall inherit the national debt." With congressional cooperation the national debt tripled during the Reagan and Bush administrations in the 1980s and 1990s. This year alone twenty-five percent of the federal budget is borrowed money, and next year will be worse. All federal income taxes from people west of the Mississippi go toward paying interest on the debt.

This tells me that you should formulate a financial goal on retirement as soon as possible, and it should be comprehensive. Anyone who thinks that money grows on trees is bound sooner or later to get caught out on a limb. One way to keep from losing your shirt is to roll up your sleeves on retirement planning.

The Rolling Stones sing it right for young folks like you: "Time is on my side, yes it is." Aristotle the philosopher said it another way when he called habit the secret of success in anything. A great builder builds monuments by laying one brick at a time, and a great artist works day after day and over time produces powerful works of art. To build the wealth you need for retirement you must use the power of compounding, the financial habit of daily growth as one penny earns another.

I do not want to sound like a huckster for compounding, but look at this. Putting away only $100 a month for thirty years in a tax-deferred investment gives you a retirement fund of nearly a quarter million dollars ($223,108). This assumes an annual return of 9.9%, which is the average return of the S&P composite index of common stocks from 1926 to 1987. Many months you will have more disposable income, and sometimes the return will exceed the mark. The point is that you should set your retirement life goal and then pay the cost of attaining it, and compounding will do the rest. Never allow your only retirement account be a Social Security number like 402-21-9231.

You may want to remember the handy rule of 72 when you consider investing. How many years does it take to double your money? That depends on the rate of return you receive. Whatever the percentage, divide it into 72 and you will know many years it will take to double your money. For example, if you receive a 5% return it takes 14.4 years (72 divided by five); for 12% it is six years. This rule shows that the best choice is investing for the long term at the highest safe return.

There will be times when for a hundred reasons you do not

want to stick with a regimented savings plan. When that happens remember this story from Grady Nutt of "Hee Haw" fame. At age six, he sang gospel songs in Texas churches while his mother played piano. She roped Grady's younger brother Don into the act at age three; mostly he just stood there looking cute while Grady carried the singing load. The parents gave their kids strict instructions: "Stand still, hands at your sides; don't look around; sing loud and clear; don't let anything distract you." One night at a church supper in Amarillo, Don got the sillies while the two boys performed on a table. Their mother had dressed them in identical sailor suits with pants buttoned onto the shirtails. Then, Grady continues, his brother Don

> *started clowning. He began unbuttoning my pants from my shirt! I was terrified. Straight ahead...one button...hands at side...two buttons...loud...three buttons...clear...four buttons...don't let anything distract you...five buttons...my dad was standing against the back wall in hysterics...six buttons...I had tears running down my cheeks...seven buttons...he wouldn't rescue me...DOWN THEY CAME!! The audience was delirious! Mom was playing by touch, because she couldn't see the keys for the tears! I finally broke a rule and reached down and pulled up my pants. I sang every note. I didn't let anything distract me!*[15]

Do not be distracted from your retirement goal when it is tough sledding! Like all life goals, it will cost you but deliver more than promised.

Faith and Value Costs

Another life goal worth considering is your value structure and the power of religious faith. It is foolish to jump for them without counting the cost and your readiness to pay.

You heard plenty about religious faith while growing up, but here I want to emphasize that faith affects the great triad of how we think, feel, and act. It is no accident that religion has endured through the centuries of human civilization. It still attracts billions of people today, and for good reason: by nature the human being is *homo religiosus*, a religious person. While each of us may hold the gift of religious faith in differing degrees, we sense that there is more to the universe than we see. How we deal with that insight is the tip of our religious iceberg.

Telling stories is a vital part of religious faith. Since faith concerns our ancestral past and points ahead to the future, learning how to tell stories is helpful for faith and life. I hope you will hone this skill so your children and grandchildren hear stories from you.

You know from experience that Sunday School teachers make a big hit with kindergartners if they are good storytellers. These kids like all kinds of stories, from Superman to the Good Samaritan. One teacher told the Good Samaritan story in vivid terms so the kids would understand what happened, and when she got to the end she asked the class, "Now what would you do if you saw somebody lying at the side of the road all wounded and bleeding?" After a brief pause a thoughtful little girl in a red dress piped up, "I think I would throw up!" That story made an impact.

Do you want something exciting to do on Saturday night? Here is a dare: write your own obituary, omitting the death date, of course. Include who you were, what you did, for whom you did it, your religious convictions—anything you want. The next step is the important one. Now construct a life goal to get you there, specifically to the religious faith and action your obituary portrayed as important. Remember the cost in time and money if you are serious about the journey.

What should I say about a value structure? The most important thing is to make a set of values your own. That means you know which values count, why they count, and where they stack up in your hierarchy of values. Is love more or less important than suffering? Where does honesty fit? Which values reach beyond the personal to the social realm, and why?

An eminent theologian named Robert J. Marshall tells

about a graduation speech that the seminary's most renowned professor gave to his class. He advised the graduates to "never give up [their] disgust."[16] If you lack a sense of disgust you probably also lack a sense of integrity, so maintaining a sense of disgust keeps your value structure intact through integrity. The focal point of my value structure is integrity, and value spokes fan out from its hub. Henry Fielding rightly described conscience as "the only incorruptible thing about us," and conscience hangs on a thin thread of integrity.

Life goals that intentionally ignore the cultivation of values are not only valueless, they also lack an anchor to moor them and a magnetic pole to pull them. I hope through the years your life goals show specific values that you are cultivating because they are good, true, and beautiful values. Doing this will cost you, as Jahwaharlal Nehm warns: "To be in good moral condition requires at least as much training as to be in good physical condition." The resulting value-fitness is worth the cost.

Deserting values you hold dear is as deplorable as not cultivating values. We can gain instruction and strength from people who valiantly defended their values, who prevailed when circumstances tested their values.

Remember Stalin's gulag prisons? In most cases resistors or suspected resistors spent the rest of their lives there. In the early 1950s a Jewish Russian doctor named Boris Kornfeld was sent to the Ekibastuz prison for political subversives. In the camp he became a Christian and for a time wrestled with a demand that he sign waiver papers "legalizing" punishment for the "insane." One day he visited a patient who was suffering from pellagra brought on by malnutrition. He had prescribed chalk, good white bread, and herring to stop the diarrhea, but the man was dying. As Kornfeld walked away, he saw an orderly (another prisoner) finishing a loaf of white bread meant for the pellagra victims. Kornfeld reported the orderly to the commandant, who confined him for three days. But since the commandant was tired of the doctor's refusal to sign waivers, he recognized that Kornfeld had arranged his own execution.

Kornfeld knew what was coming, and one day he emptied his soul to a little man who had been operated on for intestinal cancer. He related the full story of his faith to the patient, rambling on all afternoon and into the night. Early the next morning that patient heard a commotion in the operating area, and soon the whispers of fellow patients told of the doctor's fate. Eight blows from a plasterer's mallet had split Kornfeld's head while he slept, and his fellow doctors could not save him. It remained for the little man alone to carry this story out of the camp. His name was Alexander Solzhenitsyn.[17]

Brett, I know some of the cost of defending values since an institution once fired me for that, changing my life's direction. It was worth it. I sleep well.

Commitment Costs

Your life goals cost time and money, and commitment too. That is not something new. How much commitment did it cost American inventors in 1899 when the Director of the U.S. Patent Office asked that his office be closed, announcing that "everything that can be invented has been invented?" What about Alexander Graham Bell when a banker pointed to his new telephone and said, "Take that toy off my desk?" A production manager reportedly told the inventor of the Xerox machine, "That's what we have carbon paper for." Horse sense dwells in a stable mind, and a stable mind pays the cost of commitment when others question what you are doing. It will cost you.

I saw a "Hopes and fears ladder" that makes good sense. The ladder symbolizes life with the top rung representing your whole complex of hopes, what you want to happen in the future. The bottom rung represents your fears, what you do not want to happen. Now choose a rung number that shows where you think things are at the present time: ______. Then choose a number showing where you think things were five years ago: ______. Finally, choose a number where you think things will be five years from now: ______. Some suggest that the shift in numbers from past to present roughly measures your sense of accomplishment. Conversely, the shift in numbers from present to future may be a rough measure of your sense of optimism.[18]

Hopes and Fears Ladder

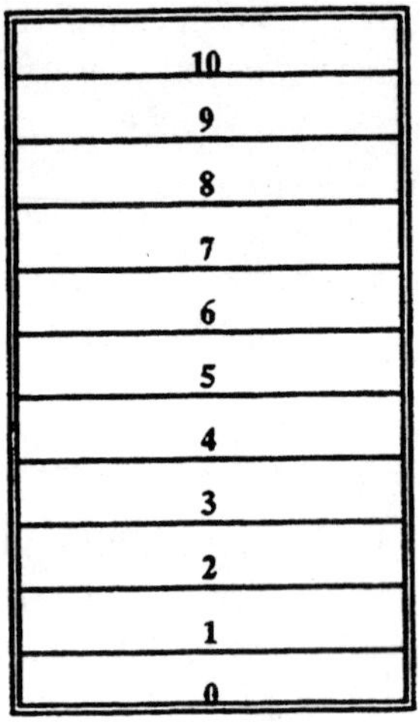

You could call this the Hope and Mope Ladder. One letter separates the two words although their meanings are light-years apart. One looks to the future and counts the commitment cost to get there while the other grovels in yesterday's despair and broods over wrecked plans. Using life goals to instill and maintain hope is a good way to build your sense of optimism, but it will cost you since you are your own midwife for hope.

Another thing that takes commitment are those characters and events that are pivotal in your life. Here is why I say this. Truly pivotal people and pivotal moments will mold you, and it takes commitment for your life goals to incorporate them.

Remember the story about three baseball umpires discussing their work behind home plate? One said, "Some's balls and some's strikes, and I calls 'em as I sees 'em." The second chimed in, "Some's balls and some's strikes, and I calls 'em as they is." After they finished the third piped up, "I sees 'em comin' across the plate and some's balls and some's strikes, but they ain't nothin' till I calls 'em." You have the power to name the persons and events that are pivotal in your life. You may not always pick them, but you name them. By calling it pivotal you empower "who" or "what" happened to be of great importance in your life. You call it a strike, and your life goals reflect it.

Let me tell you about two pivotal events in my early career. One happened in the mid-sixties while I was a ministerial intern in Schenectady, New York, and officiated at a funeral. At first there wasn't much out of the ordinary except that it was my first funeral, but the event soon became pivotal by giving me a clear sense of death's finality. I had been to funerals, seen death, and thought I knew all about it. This was different. The man died in bed in the heat of July, and his body was not discovered for five days. The resulting body bag was reason enough for a closed casket during the funeral. At the cemetery I led the way, downwind, as pallbearers bore their heavy load to the grave. Since they shook the casket a great deal, no mortician could have concealed the atrocious stench of death that soon reached my nose. In an instant I knew more about death's finality than all my reading and experience had taught me. This was a pivotal event and I named it.

Another one came the weekend of Dr. Martin Luther King, Jr.'s assassination. You will recall that he was killed on a Friday. Two days later was Palm Sunday so I entitled my sermon "Behold the King Comes!" to fit the day's lessons. Besides reviewing Jesus' palm-strewn entry into Jerusalem, I discussed King's entry into the promised land the Friday before. My sermon may have been acceptable elsewhere but not in the Chicago suburb that housed our congregation. After services the church treasurer told me that the treasury was suddenly bare and he could not pay my salary until the church elders discussed the sermon. I reasonably suspected that he was exerting overt pressure so I laughed heartily and said, "Harold, that's all right. My wife has a good job and we can hold out as long as necessary." For me this was a pivotal event, one I named. It showed that you must be ready to pay the price when you stand up for what is right.

Generally you do not control if or when pivotal people or events impinge on your life, though you may contribute to chance timing. But you can name them as decisive and use them to enrich your commitment to life goals that need support from past experience.

The last item about commitment is this. You have to spend commitment chips to do a good job with life goals. It takes committed work to compose and write down well-stated goals, and more work to visualize them several times daily.

Follow these steps to imprint goals on your subconscious. First, create a precise visual image of your goal, filling the scene with as many vivid details as possible and including objects and color. Use every available sense. You are the scene's central star. For example, if you plan on vacationing in the Virgin Islands with a deadline of January 1996, compose a goal sentence like this. "I sense soft breezes on my cheek as I sit on a beach in the Virgin Islands." Second, add emotion and feeling to that image: "I feel happy and relaxed and soft breezes caress my cheek while I sit on a beach in the Virgin Islands." Third, be sure to envision the moment of goal achievement in the present tense, the here-and-now, not the future. Use only present tense verbs (I am, I feel, I run) in your written goal list, not future tense. At all costs avoid a passive verb ("I am being served by waiters") since you are the star of this movie.

Visioning your goals in this way releases immense untapped energy. It puts into play a large portion of your brain (including your subconscious) that normally loafs without your guidance and control. Estimates are that your mind contains ten to fourteen billion neuron cells, each capable of storing one to two million bits of data. For computer nuts that is equivalent to 210 billion bits of data. Let's put it to use by committing the time and energy required for visioning.

Beyond the End of Your Nose

That is enough about the cost of life goals. Now let's talk about something closer to home, namely, your nose and seeing beyond it. You will beat a path to the world's doorway with life goals that extend beyond your nose tip. Having life goals with pea-shooter range is like running 200 meters and calling it a mile—you're short.

One way to ensure that you are on the right track is by not turning the world into basketball-size, reducing its vastness. Some people are whizzes at that. Ask them about anything in the world and they respond, "What does that have to do with me? Why should I be concerned? Who cares?" Reducing the world to a basketball is comforting but very foolish. These persons not only miss 99% of what happens in the world, they also neglect the chance to stretch their boundaries, drink from humanity's deep well, and become more interesting persons.

Since you like rugby more than basketball, substitute a rugby ball if you like. The problem is the same. Fitting the world inside a size seven head is ultra-individualism and a fool's folly. One result is that you become a bore for anyone whose world is slightly larger than a rugby ball, and remember, bores can be divided into two classes: those who have their own particular subject to harp on, and those who need no subject.

People with shrunken worlds are often shocked by fast moving developments. Two days before his election Pope John Paul II said, "It's too early for a Polish pope." An American businessman named Chauncey Depew opposed investing in Henry Ford's new company with the comment, "Nothing has come along that can beat the horse and buggy." Radio pioneer Mary Sommerville never caught up with TV after she said, "Television won't last. It's a flash in the pan." Your friends the Beatles? John Lennon mistakenly stated in 1966, "Christianity will go. It will vanish and shrink. I needn't argue about that. I'm right and will be proved right. We're more popular than Jesus now."[19] If your world's circumference is about 25,000 miles, like the earth's, the rapidity of change usually will not surprise you.

Making the world a basketball leads people to think that fads will last forever. That is dangerous, especially when they invest money in such misguided beliefs. No less dangerous is the onslaught of mental myopia. This nearsightedness brings unforseen results, like stumbling into a pit without seeing the edge. You can hide the biggest star in the universe by holding a penny to your eye. You will catch a bad case of myopia if all your life goals have pea-shooter range, so beware. Those pits are deep.

Remember your grandfather's house in Missouri and the skeleton key we used on the doors? Remember those keyholes? All you saw when you looked through was what the keyhole showed you, and usually that was not much. People with keyhole vision have no breadth and their life goals show it, if they have any. Maybe bumper stickers that say "Visualize World Peace" are on the right track. At least those people look and think beyond the end of their nose, and that is a start for goals that cover more than limited personal interests.

There is a way to let the world be the world and to tie your life goals into the world as it exists. That is to celebrate the fraternity and sorority of the world's peoples. Making room in your goals for different kinds of people is admirable; more than that, in our international age it is realistic.

To talk about "one world" and a "global village" linked through television is not empty conversation. Surely the world is now more of a single perceptual unit since we have seen the blue ball floating in space. We still have the Germans, Japanese, Russians, and other nations that were state enemies when I grew up, but "them and us" are "we," engaging in a common, human battle against pollution, world hunger, and economic and political instability.

Through the years you have become a much better soup-eater as you amplified your tastes and sampled more of the earth's soups. If you are like me you will have to continue fighting the soup-battle that Grady Nutt describes this way:

"Most of us make the mistake of judging all soup by the only soup we've ever known."[20] Keep tasting and you will see how good the whole world is.

When you are visualizing life goals with all five senses, consider putting in a goal that celebrates all the world's peoples, perhaps even their soups. To the extent that goals point beyond your nose you will fill life with an exciting world that runs from the Amazon to the Nile, from black Africans to yellow Chinese. This is your world, not the inside of a rugby ball, so enjoy it. Since you will be working in an international business environment this is an especially important consideration.

One more thing about getting beyond the end of your nose is this: civic duty starts where your face ends. Please remember that.

Millions of Americans are quick to take their portion and more from the common pot we call civil government (federal, state and local levels), stepping smartly into line for Social Security benefits, Medicaid, all available tax breaks, and other "entitlements." What do they offer in return except compulsory taxes? Little or nothing, and the water level of the civic pot falls as a result. There is much more to democratic government than paying taxes, and our nation can run only so long as people put more in than they take out. That is the essence of democracy, although many people have not learned the lesson.

Civic duty can include voting, giving your opinion to editors and elected officials, and serving on juries. These are minimums, and I hope you will consider life goals that make larger contributions to the pool of civic assets. That may include public office (remember, the cheapest way to have your family tree traced is to run for public office), voluntary service on boards and commissions, political contributions, encouraging and helping others in political campaigns, and other options. Just do something above and beyond the minimum.

Indeed, little people can make a big difference. Until

August 10, 1976, Betty Williams was just another housewife in Belfast, Ireland. She was driving home after visiting her mother that day when the car ahead spun out of control after a British solder shot its IRA driver in the heart. The car pinned a woman and her three children against a school railing, killing the children and critically injuring the mother. "When I saw on television the children were dead, I just couldn't take any more of it," said Mrs. Williams. She decided to knock on doors in Anderson town to see how many people felt like her. Within hours, she, her sister, and a friend had hundreds of signatures on a peace petition. Soon two youth rallies involved 30,000 Catholic and Protestant women; they were evidence of a desperate longing for peace on both sides. Women from the factions met to plan joint actions, but soon Betty Williams and her co-leaders faced denouncement, obscene letters, and death threats. "I was scared out of my wits," she admitted, "but we will not be intimidated any longer."[21] This one person who saw beyond the end of her nose made an impact.

Oh yes, I forgot to mention something. You may get dirty hands while playing in the political mud bath. Have you heard about the fictitious speech one politician gave about his opponent? Read it aloud for the biggest impact. Among other things he said that his foe "was a flagrant heterosexual. His sister, who has always been obsessed by sects, once worked as a proselyte outside a church. His father was secretly chagrined at least a dozen times by matters of a pecuniary nature. His youngest brother wrote an essay extolling the virtues of being a homo sapiens. His great-aunt expired from a degenerative disease. His nephew subscribes to a phonographic magazine. His wife was a thespian before their marriage and even performed the act in front of paying customers." The opponent himself? "He perambulated his infant son on the street. He practiced nepotism with his uncle and first cousin...He has urged our Protestant and Jewish citizens to develop more Catholic tastes. Last summer he committed a piscatorial act on a boat that was flying the American flag."[22] So be ready for gainsayers and hecklers.

Your life goals should demonstrate a commitment to civic and community well-being. You may not always have a goal dealing with this element of responsible living, but certainly at points in life your set of goals will show that you see beyond your nose. Life will be fuller when you do.

The rewards will not always be immediately clear, and some things will go unnoticed by others. Like so much of life, it takes time for bread to return on the waters. For instance, during World War II a woman in Ohio was deeply fearful about her son fighting overseas so, besides praying, she wrapped Red Cross bandages and did volunteer work to help save lives. One day her son's ship went down and water swept him over the side, but he survived thanks to a life belt. Later examination showed that a woman named Mary Staples had inspected, packed, and stamped the belt in Akron, Ohio. She was his mother.

Congratulations for plowing all the way to the end of my letter. Now you know the truth about building a better mouse-trap. The way to do it is by constructing life goals that beat your path to the world's doorstep.

You are on the way if your goals cost you time, money, and commitment, take in people, and reach beyond the tip of your nose. I hope that you find these guideposts helpful throughout your life. Even more, I hope you discover joy and happiness in goals that stretch you to reach the uncharted seas that bring excitement, peace, and fulfillment. I have!

Love always,

Dad

III
No Time For Knots

I have never been much good at tying knots since our small Missouri town had no Scout troop. The kids respected anyone who could tie even a slip-knot, but most of the knots we tied were the self-inflicted kind, those that grew like carbuncles when we unrolled a pile of rope. Untying knots was an even more mysterious art than tying them. Meanwhile, those living near lakes and oceans gained much broader experience with lines (do not call them ropes, says my spouse, an old salt). A person is not much of a deck hand if he cannot tie and untie knots, and sailors even use the term “knots” for speed.

Most inventors of knots are anonymous, and that is probably good, considering such knot-names as the granny knot, thief’s, figure eight, sheepshank, cat’s paw, weaver’s and midshipman’s hitch. Matthew Walker is an exception since he gave his name to the Single and Double MW knots. If you cut an artery you hope that the emergency room doctor can tie a surgeon's knot to close it.

This chapter is not about knots but about having no time for self-made knots. These cripplers bind our mind, body, and spirit; they fatigue us, slow our motion, cut endurance, and distract us from life goals. Just what should we do with knots in the lines? We want to learn how to avoid the common complaint, "I'm all tied up in knots."

As we press toward life goals we need to learn the daily art of cutting knots. They fill our lives above and below water, and to make things worse a knot-tying machine runs at full throttle inside us. The only way to stay ahead is to cut knots daily. That is what we mean by "no time for knots."

My mother was a nineteenth century baby, and when she died in 1987 at age eighty-eight and a half she ended a life of about 32,303 days, 775,260 hours, or 46,515,600 minutes. While her heart beat almost 3.5 billion times, she had her share of physical, mental, and spiritual knots. Her subconscious mind added insult to injury as it cruised on automatic, rehearsed earlier knot-tying episodes, and created a future that imitated the past. She never spent a day on a boat but was one of the best sailors I have met. An expert knot-cutter when she wanted to be, she used a long knife to dismember knots that dragged her backwards. While she did not fully exploit this capability, she taught me the wisdom of cutting knots.

Knots Above and Below

Knots cling to our lives like parasites. They cause bodies to ache as ligaments and muscles clench in tension, and minds to lose the power of concentration as "small stuff" overwhelms and fatigues us. Our spirits visit the dumps too often and we feel like giving up. Sometimes we resemble an old windjammer with hundreds of unwanted knots in the rigging and piles of knotted rope below deck. No waterproof seal separates the physical, mental, and spiritual layers of our lives, and seepage spreads ailments from one level to the next. Our fast-paced lives show the close connection of body and mind, and stress damages cells, organs, emotions, and how we think and feel.

Clinical Illness

Any physician who wants to remove his own appendix is the town's laughingstock, so the medical profession takes preventive measures and urges doctors not to treat themselves or their families. These rules make the well-being of the sick the highest priority, not the physician's pride.

If you have been ill to the point of needing a doctor (clinical illness), you know the foolishness of trying to cut your own knots of physical illness. This is sage advice: Consult a physician when you have physical symptoms of illness, or think or feel you are sick. If you get a clean bill of health, go back to knot-cutting.

A mark of wisdom is knowing when to see the doctor. During World War II Medal of Honor winner Joe J. Foss shot down twenty-six enemy aircraft in the Pacific theater. He survived battle without injury, but years later a lowly blade of grass nearly leveled him. He tells the story about this phone call from death in these words:

I remember the time and the place when it happened. I was in Alaska in 1966 filming a segment of my show on seals. I bent down and picked up a blade of grass to chew on it. Within the next few days, I started to feel weak and I couldn't eat. My doctors didn't know what was wrong. My film crew remembered me chewing on the grass and went back to Alaska and brought a sample to the doctors. They found out the grass was tainted with an arsenic-based crop spray. I almost died and that's when I decided I should keep my promise and live a better life with God.[23]

With a fighter's wisdom, Joe Foss knew when to see a physician.

Trying to treat clinical mental illness without professional help is also dangerous. While the primary responsibility for change rests with the patient, psychologists and psychiatrists provide the guidance and assurance that give strength for change. Sometimes therapy includes medication.

We cannot ignore the spiritual dimension of physical and mental illness. The interleaving of body language often shifts symptoms from one realm to another, and pastors, priests, and rabbis stand ready to help when affliction rains down. These spiritual guides are among the first to hear the problems of people, and they make medical or psychiatric referrals when required.

Non-Clinical Maladies

I use the term "non-clinical maladies" for the run-of-the-mill knots that tie us. These knots are places where life's flow gets so narrow that we lose energy, where the day is a muddled mess since we do not know where we are going, and where fatigue comes from a motor that is racing while we are in neutral.

It is quite normal to be pleasantly tired at bedtime, and when we are we look for John Milton's "timely dew of sleep" to fall on us and wash tiredness away. The other type of fatigue lingers after the morning light, and we lack energy, zeal for life, and the capacity to stick to tasks. After receiving a doctor's clean bill we should confirm our diagnosis of fatigue with a close friend. We can ask, Have I changed lately? Can you notice my listlessness? Real fatigue cuts the spirit from under us; it sucks the sap and leaves only wood in the tree of life. An old Spanish proverb says it well: "He that loses wealth, loses much; he that loses friends, loses more; but he that loses spirit, loses all."

Comedians sometimes make exhaustion the butt of a joke. One comic told about a man who suffered grief from his business, the stock market, and his wife. Fatigued to the bone, Sam decided that it was all over so he took an elevator to the top of the Empire State building and did a swan dive. Standing at an open window on the 37th floor (guess why?) was Joe, who saw him flying by. Joe yelled, "How is it going, Sam?" "So far, so good," came Sam's reply.

People suffering fatigue find little humor in their condition. Fatigue is total depletion of energy and loss of vitality. It may bring effort that leads nowhere, draining all desire to "go on." It often results in a loss of perspective, and sufferers see people and things in distorted relationships, not as they are. Well-known counselor Wayne E. Oats writes that "the most telltale evidence of the loss of perspective is when you begin to belabor the point in discussion, 'sweat the small stuff' in decision-making, procrastinate about big decisions, and/or become inappropriately irritable with your fellow workers, your family, etc." Other signs of fatigue are poor judgment and "confusion of the heart," when "the double bind of a double mind" traps you.[24]

Muddled life goals contribute to fatigue since running in reverse and drawing life patterns from the past can tie our lives in knots. To know the wisdom of goals you do not have to accept Thomas Aquinas' view of a teleological cosmos, a universe going somewhere. Fatigue from muddled or absent goals is enough proof for many people.

Others suffer fatigue from an unbalanced array of life goals. They aim high in several important areas such as vocation and financial gain, but their personal life lacks direction. They fail to establish clear goals for personal growth in areas such as emotional and intellectual development, social interaction, private time, and spiritual maturity. If people fail to cultivate all these areas their life mechanisms begin shutting down, and they relapse into inactivity. Fatigue is a symptom of life out of balance.

Another kind of non-clinical malady takes root in fear of the unknown. This can develop into generalized fear, so that a creaking roof startles you and every siren sounds like an ambulance coming for you. Hans Christian Andersen, the famous fairy tale writer, had a lifelong fear of being buried alive and left a note by his bed every night that said, "I only seem dead." Imagine how many fantasy dreams he missed worrying that someone might overlook that scrap of paper! Fear of the unknown paralyzes some people; they slow to a crawl and their lives take on a funeral director's personality. They might as well hang Hans' strange sign around their necks every morning.

Those who fear the unknown fail to count the real cost of the supposed disaster they face. The only way you can force an unknown fear to reveal itself is by confronting it head-on. An old man once gave me some sound advice about this when he said, "Whatever problem or difficulty you face, count the true cost to you if everything goes wrong. Then you'll know how really bad it is." Years ago in the Old West cowboys used to say, "A brave man doesn't admit courage. Cowards don't admit fear." Those words carry a big clump of wisdom. To admit fear is to look squarely at what we fear. Cowards will not do this since they deny that any fear is stalking them. It takes the real courage of a brave person, not the bravado of a coward to count the cost of what is feared. Then a person can do something about the non-clinical ills that come from a fear gone wild.

I feel sorry for people who are afraid of everything, from mice to microbes. There is danger everywhere, especially if you are looking for it. The U.S. Consumer Product Safety Commission keeps track of injuries that require medical attention, or result in limiting normal activity. Take the report from 1980, for instance. Baseball caused more "recreational accidents" (478,000) than football (470,000), and more people hurt themselves dancing (26,000) than practicing martial arts (19,000). Hapless fear-mongers face numerous dangers in their homes. More accidents involved lawn mowers (68,000) than guns (60,000); fireworks maimed 10,000, but pencils, pens, and desk supplies injured 45,000. Six thousand Americans said musical instruments wounded them. Is it safe to brush your teeth? Probably, unless you live in Durham, North Carolina. Researchers poring over medical literature found thirty-one reported cases of people swallowing tooth brushes, and strangely enough, four were in Durham! Believe it or not, being blown up by an air mattress is also a real fear. A Florida man using a hair dryer to inflate an air mattress was injured when it blew up and caused $6,000 in damages.[25]

Finally, there is the malady called "problems in general." Sometimes an overwhelming array of problems freezes us into immobility. Problems become a splint for life, like your body reduces movement in a back that has a broken rib. The difficulty is that the stiffer we get the less we move. Problems restrict our range of motion and limit activity; they drain our energy and turn us in on ourselves when we should focus on the future and its goals.

We add insult to injury by turning challenges into problems, a transformation that is all too natural. As the eminent psychiatrist M. Scott Peck observes,

> *the tendency to avoid challenges is so omnipresent in human beings that it can properly be considered a characteristic of human nature. But calling it natural does not mean it is essential or beneficial or unchangeable behavior. It is also natural to defecate in our pants and never brush our teeth.*[26]

A true problem-lover wallows in the naturalness of turning challenges into problems, thinking that is the last word. Now he has reason to do nothing since he faces problems to endure, not challenges to overcome. The long-term result shows a great difference between the two. Nagging problems increase wear and tear, rewards are few, and feelings of inadequacy wrap the problem-lover like a wet blanket. Life as a daily array of problems fits Henry Ford's definition of history, "One damn thing after another!" Welcome to life as seen through the welder's black glasses!

Whether struck by fatigue, fear of the unknown, or problems by the thousands, our compliant bodies add their two cents worth. Old basketball injuries ache more than they used to, and neurological stress stiffens our muscles. We feel punk in the flesh because we are punk in the mind. Body-knots take on their own life, and chiropractors make a living on "tight spots" in shoulders and backs. Good medicine for body-knots is a regimen of healthy exercise, together with balanced life goals that meet our needs. Flexible goals in all spheres of life reinforce the body's flexibility. Have you watched a yoga master contort his body to unimaginable shapes, stretching supple limbs into strange designs? This flexibility pokes fun at a rigid body composed of knots, with tentacles reaching into mind and spirit.

We all suffer periods of minor depression, but when our body, mind, and spirit show the effects of non-direction it is a different kind of animal. We are trying to sail a ship to no destination with muddled navigational charts. The whole thing groans and moans, shudders and shakes while we haplessly try to get underway by untying a single knot here, another there. We have too many knots above and below deck for smooth sailing, and all the signs show it.

Religious faith can play an all-important role in confronting and conquering life problems, fatigue, and fear. The long history of humanity teaches an unforgettable lesson about the value of linking life goals with religious conviction. All world religions include ideas of beginning, renewal, rebirth, and starting over, and even people without religious convictions feel the newness of spring as nature casts off winter's cloak. We ignore this powerful lesson at our peril.

Faith faces the odds head-on. One old woman, a master storyteller, liked to embellish the story of the Titanic with flourishes that showed the power of religious conviction in the face of insurmountable odds. As she told the story, the ocean liner's band played "Nearer My God to Thee" to keep the passengers calm. When the horns could no longer toot because they were filling with water, everyone knew the giant ship was going down.[27]

Some people dismiss the solace and strength of positive faith and turn to a conspiracy theory that helps them perpetuate their self-imposed suffering. I call this the Black Death of personhood. To grasp how completely these people seek to avoid responsibility you must understand a little about the Black Death. This pandemic killed millions as it swept from Asia to Europe in the fourteenth century, and no one knew exactly how it spread. People blamed everything from Jews to poisoned wells, laying responsibility everywhere except with the real carriers and causes of the bubonic plague. One viral strain moved through respiratory contact and brought sudden death. The bloodstream of infected rats and fleas traveling with them carried the second strain; its gait toward death was slower.[28]

The Black Death of personhood blames anyone and anything except the one responsible. The consummate form of using a scapegoat, it allows people to complain about life-knots without looking internally for roots, causes, and solutions. Since it lets a person off the hook for his problems, the Black Death of personhood spreads big clumps of knots that need cutting.

Your Automatic Knot-Maker

Do you know that inside yourself you have one of the best-oiled, most efficient machines known to humankind? That it works night and day without rewinding? That it follows regular rhythms and has great power? That you are dead without it? No, not your heart; it is your subconscious mind.

To make it easier to identify your subconscious we are going to call it Old Sub. After all, why not be friendly with something that accompanies you everywhere you go twelve months a year? Old Sub deserves a nickname as much as the twelve months:

Snowy, Flowy, Blowy,
Showery, Flowery, Bowery,
Hoppy, Croppy, Droppy,
Breezy, Sneezy, Freezy.[29]

Surely these nicknames outshine the mundane months, just

like Old Sub sounds better than "your subconscious."

Old Sub is always busy with something since that is its nature, the jungle law it follows. Old Sub contributes to the dynamic that makes learning possible, helping us apply what we know from the past as circumstances change. By forming a collage of experience and emotion from a broad spectrum, it preserves a sense of self and of who we are. The subconscious is the closest faculty we have to inbred animal instinct; it provides responses to all circumstance, even if they are not the best ones.

For better or worse, Old Sub is a perpetual motion machine always processing something—and sometimes playing tricks on you. For example, when you least expect it Old Sub can cause a memory lapse. For fifteen years Charles Schulz had been drawing sketches of Snoopy typing on his little portable typewriter. All of a sudden one day, he said, "I started a [comic] strip and completely forgot how to draw the typewriter."[30] Now why would Old Sub do something like that?

Subconscious at Work

Let's get this straight from the start. Inside of you is one of the most powerful historians in the world. Old Sub comes computer-equipped (remember the brain's power?) and relies heavily on blocks of memory, especially those associated with emotions. It knows every historical sleight of hand: how to skew data, use selected sources and ignore others, argue points that common sense dismisses as groundless, and array unrelated events into a grand schema covering all your life. Remember the old TV show called "This Is Your Life?" Old Sub produces that show for you daily.

Think of it this way. Old Sub is your private, personal historian, constantly collecting and processing information and feeding it back in packages that apply to the situation at hand. See how much you rely on Old Sub? Who else could do such a magnificent job for you? Who else knows as much about you, where your comfort zones lie, and where you feel uncomfortable? Who else could exercise such a guiding role over your future?

Old Sub is such a good historian that it seldom forgets anything it considers important, but on the other hand, Old Sub lays no claim to comparative objectivity, a quality coveted by historians. Old Sub is subjective by nature since it uses selective data from your life. Is there any wonder that it prefers rehashing old times rather than offering objective views of what is best for tomorrow?

Remember when I called Old Sub a powerful knot-tying machine? One way it ties knots is by heightening your sense of fear, based on past experience. Another is making you uncomfortable with where you have not been before. A third is reminding you that you will break your rubber band if you stretch it too far (like you almost did in 1983; remember?).

Let's take the first. Rabbi Abraham Twerski tells a story in his book *Like Yourself* that explains how Old Sub sets us up for a fall. A man returned to his apartment late one night after work, utterly exhausted. He fell into bed without undressing but kicked off a shoe that landed on the floor with a loud thud. Though tired he recognized his thoughtlessness, how the shoe probably disturbed the downstairs neighbor, so he carefully removed the other shoe and set it quietly on the floor. In twenty minutes a ferocious knock awoke him. He staggered to the door and found his downstairs neighbor glaring at him and shouting, "Damn you! Will you hurry up and drop that other shoe? I'm going crazy waiting!"[31]

Old Sub tells us to wait for the other shoe to fall. Like the neighbor, we look for the bad to come in a one-two punch. Haven't you experienced that sequence many times, Old Sub asks? I ask, don't you feel the knot pulling tighter?

Old Sub knows Shakespeare's line well, "The past is prologue." That is why it excels as personal historian, using the past to program your future. I am not going to knock history or your past accomplishments since we learn much from history, including personal history, and we draw inspiration and find challenges in trying to understand history. But too many people live under the control of their rear-view mirror. Every other sentence begins with "I always…," or "I never…," or "It's no use…." Old Sub buffaloes them into seeing the past as prologue to a duplicate future.

These rear-view mirrors mesmerize us as Old Sub makes us concentrate on the past and generates negative self-talk that constricts our environment. As a result, we have fewer comfort zones and more knots outside these zones. We are comfortable in fewer areas and situations. We see what we expect to see as we study the images Old Sub shows us in rear-view mirrors. We hear what we expect to hear and think what we expect to think. We become self-fulfilling prophecies. And why not? Old Sub's job is to replay past experiences to keep us comfortable.

Simply put, we act the way we see ourselves since we must live up to the self-image Old Sub projects. Using a rear-view mirror produces rear-view mirror self-talk. Computer hacks tell us why this is true in their description of poor computer programs: "Garbage in, garbage out!" In Old Sub's hands, all too sadly, the past is prologue to a foreclosed future. And take it from a historian, a lot of history is not fit to be repeated!

For our self-image we draw on images in the mind since they are "reality" for Old Sub. Trouble mounts when Old Sub confronts new challenges and problems and applies the same old images and pictures as solutions, though they may not fit. The results are more knots in body, mind, and soul.

This is why problems do not evaporate but multiply if we do not tackle them. They are like cul-de-sac streets that end in circles, and we go around and around with no way out as long as Old Sub keeps using old solutions for new challenges. Ben Franklin gave sage advice when he wrote, "Things that hurt, instruct." We render that advice useless if we add "sometimes" and stick with Old Sub's solutions to problems. Our version usually reads, "Things that hurt tie us in knots."

It need not end that way if we discover how to make Old Sub an accomplice in change. As he prepared for retirement, a renowned New York psychiatrist said that working with four little words was the most useful idea in helping people turn around their lives. The first two words were, "If only." He said that many patients spent their lives living in the past, anguishing about what they should have done in various circumstances. Their "if only" caused serious emotional drain (we call that a lot of knots). The antidote was simple. The psychiatrist urged patients to replace them with two other words, "Next time."[32]

Using "Next time" instead of "If only" trains Old Sub to look to the future for guidance. If Old Sub is as powerful as we have seen, it will gladly incorporate the visioning data you feed it. Granted, you will never fully rehabilitate Old Sub to work from your visioning agenda alone; it will always retain the residual task of "house historian." However, you can tip the scales in favor of your life goals. Dr. Jean Houston says that "we live largely in the attic of ourselves with the first, second, third, fourth, fifth floors unoccupied and the basement locked."[33] Why not let Old Sub use your life's basement for rear-view gazing and rehashing the past? Why not open the first to fifth floors for getting rid of knots and pushing toward future life goals?

To understand the power of the subconscious and how we can steer it, consider how several people responded to the threat of death and severe physical impairment. Actress Patricia Neal faced tremendous personal tragedy in her life. In 1960 a taxi smashed into her baby's carriage, and the child lived only after months of surgery and hospitalization. Then her oldest daughter died suddenly. In 1965 Ms. Neal herself suffered three massive brain hemorrhages and five heart attacks that impaired speech, vision, and mind. After an agonizing battle she miraculously passed through the valley of death and later won an Oscar. One day a reporter asked for her secret of survival and recovery. She waved a hand toward a large copper plaque nailed to an overhead beam that read, "Fear knocked at the door. Faith answered. No one was there."[34] Patricia Neal force-fed Old Sub with faith that sustained her and survived when others might have quit.

Second, Dr. David Rabin reports that when he was in

medical school no disease frightened him more than amyotrophic lateral sclerosis (ALS). Was it the way the medical class examined an old man stricken with this killing disease, his voice almost gone? Was it the neurologist's booming voice as he pronounced the prognosis: "Hopeless! This is creeping paralysis!"

Dr. Rabin reflected on these questions after he developed the illness. In two years he lost the use of his hands. Then came a tracheotomy and the fear of losing all interpersonal communication; he would retain his powers of perception, but communication would be one-way. Refusing to give up, he searched for a means to combat impending isolation and found it in a computer operated through one switch. Any muscle group provided a way to communicate. "For me, my eyebrow muscle is strong enough to depress a light switch and thereby gives me access to the full power of the computer. Other patients have a functioning finger or toe. The first person to use a similar computer program had a switch fitted to her mouth and bit down."

Retraining Old Sub with this newly important life goal, Dr. Rabin conversed with family and friends, told jokes, and worked independently. "Coping with ALS is a grim ordeal—but it is not hopeless," he wrote through a single eyebrow.[35] This prince of a man occupied every story of his life-mind!

Let Good Enough Alone

Not everyone has Dr. Rabin's gumption to face the future and redirect Old Sub's preoccupation with the past. That reminds me of when I tried to untie knots as a child. After several unsuccessful attempts I got fed up and thought, "Let good enough alone. If I keep this up I will have more knots than when I started."

Have you ever looked at a beam of light as it came through a hole in a dusty barn? What did you see? Flecks of dust floating right before your eyes? If so, that was a "let good enough alone" experience. If your eye followed the shaft of light to its origin, you had the glorious experience of seeing more than dust. You saw light pointing beyond itself to brilliance.

Old Sub wants us to let good enough alone because that makes less work for the subconscious. Don't disturb the rhythm, it says: stay the same course, endure if necessary, and let good enough alone. This talk from an automatic knot-tying machine can tie your life into one knot after another, and with enough knots you are fatigued, problem-laden, and overloaded.

If possible, Old Sub wants to immobilize you and lash you down with knots in three areas. They are boredom, inactivity (inaction), and indecision. The reason is simple. The more bored, inactive, and indecisive you are, the easier Old Sub's job is. Your knot-tier turns itself on automatic and scarcely has to lift a finger. If you let good enough alone, all Old Sub does is replay old biographical videos of your life.

We know that unused muscles lose their tone and eventually degenerate, but applying that lesson to life goals is harder. Let's take boredom as an example. Boredom is a perfectly healthy response to Old Sub's insistence that we should let good enough alone. Don't read anything new. Don't change your schedule in any way. Don't say anything different to anyone. Don't take the dog out except at 10:00 P.M. Don't have intercourse on Sunday. Don't eat anywhere but Denny's. Put together enough don'ts and you have a menu for boredom. You may be doubling up with knots in body language but Old Sub is spending time on easy street!

Or, your subconscious tells you not to make a decision because grave consequences may follow. If you talk with your boss you may get fired, it says. You are imagining the problem in the first place so there is no reason for a decision here, it says. You have gotten along nicely for ten years without regular exercise so why decide differently, it says. You may be doubling up with knots but Old Sub is spending time on easy street!

This is automatic knot-tying at its finest. Your subconscious gets its way by replaying the past to forge your future. You prefer another way but feel stifled and indecisive about changing so the result is fatigue, boredom, an ever-expanding array of problems, and a host of non-clinical maladies.

Old Sub also gets help from Subs working on other people. Cultures and societies impose all kinds of good and bad constraints, and even as children we learn that "this is life," and these are the alternatives.

Simon Schama describes an interesting example of how Old Subs in a culture interact and cross-fertilize in his book *The Embarrassment of Riches: An Interpretation of Dutch Culture in the Golden Age.* Schama concludes that the "primal Dutch experience" was the "struggle to survive rising waters." People saw this firsthand when dikes broke and rising waters swallowed whole towns. Because of its "diluvian personality," Dutch society understood itself as a precarious community that could be maintained only by constant physical and moral vigilance.[36] These experiences formed a common Dutch pool from which all Subs could draw, raining down hesitancy and extreme caution on a whole group of people, just as each national culture forms its own pool.

Battling with Old Sub is not easy, but letting good enough alone is no solution when you end up worse than before. Have you ever felt washed out or washed up? Did your soul ring hollow like a tin cup? Was your mind so tied in knots that you could not think straight about what was wrong? Did you feel badly about your depressed circumstances? What was your response when Old Sub said, "Live with it and let good enough alone?" Did you take a knife to your knots?

When you consider using talents and skills in new ways, what is your usual response? What is your self-talk when you ask, "Why don't I use my gifts?" Do you say you don't know why—that you cannot translate skills into new arenas? That you cannot focus well enough to ask the right questions? Do you enjoin false humility and assume that these questions are out of bounds? Do you search out the payoff you get from not fully using your talents (since apparently something inside you profits from self-restriction)? What do you respond when Old Sub said, "Live with it and let good enough alone?" Do you say, "I have no time for knots!"

The trouble with most knots is that they get tighter as more strain is exerted, much like the non-clinical maladies we face. Some of us are prone to slink into self-imposed solitary confinement as boredom builds, inaction increases, problems proliferate, and fatigue flowers. Old Sub gets us eating out of its hand and then confines us to quarters to make its job easier. The result is a continuing diet not of hash but of rehash; our senses dull, life looks greyer, and we see only dust in a bright beam of light.

One nineteenth century Vermont farmer was a true enigma. He lived alone with two sisters in a farmhouse, painted art on the sides of his barn, and carved large pieces of wood and stone into images of people and things. People called him "kind of queer." He enjoyed isolation and did not care much for visitors, especially curious ones, so for some time the gate leading to his house carried a sign warning in big red letters, SMALLPOX.[37] Russell Risley wanted people to let good enough alone so far as he was concerned. Do you? Or are you ready to cut knots?

Daily Knot-Cutting

We are talking here not about self-surgery but knot-cutting, and though there are similarities the differences are major. First, you use no anesthesia in knot-cutting while there may be some pain. Second, you use finely honed skills to cut the knots Old Sub strings through your body language, not a scalpel. Third, you conduct preventive maintenance to keep Old Sub from tripping you up. Fourth, you throw straight lines (not ropes—remember, we are old salts!) toward your life goals and future through visioning. You are practicing "well-medicine," making and keeping yourself well on all fronts.

To practice daily knot-cutting you need to recognize the

close relationship between self-integration and self-health, or self-healing. It only seems natural that when all your parts cooperate without strain, each part works easier and wastes less energy. When you integrate abilities, skills, wants, needs, and life goals, you establish a camaraderie of function and purpose among all parts of your person. Living the examined life means that you cut knots each day, and the returns on your invested time and effort are well-medicine, self-health, self-healing, and an integrated life with balanced goals.

There is also a close relationship between self-transformation and re-imaging yourself. If Old Sub pays attention to your life goals, your subconscious receives a transformed "YOU" to work on. Injecting new data into Old Sub's computer bank enlists your most powerful ally in transforming how you feel, think, and act. This directly affects your relations with others since you change others most effectively by changing yourself.

Re-imaging includes cutting negative knots, checking lines with preventive maintenance, and throwing lines to the future through life goals. This is no one-time job but a joy we experience daily.

Cutting Negative Knots

It is too bad that ropes no longer play the important role they did in the old westerns. One highlight of the show was when the bad guys wrapped the Lone Ranger and Tonto in what looked like a hundred feet of rope and cinched the knots. The music's tempo increased as the good guys twisted to free themselves, then suddenly one discovered that he could saw the rope with a boot spur. In an instant they jumped free and rode off to find the villains. This drama portrayed the simple truth that it is usually easier to cut a tight knot than untie it. In sum, we find a form of liberation if we locate and cut the nodule knots Old Sub ties.

One major knot to cut is the habit of thinking negatively. That may be easier said than done, but it can be done if you change several other habits. One is lopping off the words "I always" and "I never" from your vocabulary and substituting the phrase "Next time." Another is taking your "temperament temperature" every hour for several days. What are you feeling like, and what words immediately come to mind about yourself? Try expressing how you feel in positive terms instead of comparing yourself to someone. You can do it!

Cutting the knot of negative self-talk will not vanquish all the evils of the world, or overcome social ills in major cities, or change the nation's economy. But talking positively at every opportunity sends a message to Old Sub that you are exerting control. Affirmative self-talk and positive talk to others is a small step but still a step.

At least you are doing something, which is better than nothing, and you are a little bit like a certain old woman. She heard that a cousin she had not seen in years moved to the small town where she lived. Reportedly the cousin was in ill health, so the old woman picked some roses and went out to see her. The story continues:

> *Mrs. Scott reached what she thought was the right house, rang the bell, and a woman's voice answered and told her to come on in, which she did. And there she found an old woman in the bed, looking poorly, too. So Mrs. Scott went over to her bedside and kissed her on the cheek and gave her the roses and told her she was sorry to find her unwell and hoped she'd soon be better. Then she took a seat and prepared to visit and was just launched into an account of Dad and his big toe, which he had told her was sore every morning of the world during their forty years of marriage, when the old woman rose up in bed and asked, "Just who do you think you're talking to?" And Mrs. Scott said, "Why, aren't you my cousin, So-and-so?" And the woman said, "Why no, she lives two houses down the street. I'm Mrs. Vasser Scoggins!"*

With that the old woman told her she was sorry but to keep the roses anyhow. "And after a suitable interval she got up and left; I never did know if she found her cousin. It really didn't seem to matter; what was important was that she had *done something,* she had *acted.* She didn't just sit home and think about it—or worse, talk about it."[38] This old woman's positive words and actions rolled right over negative thoughts. She knew how to cut knots on the run!

Another negative knot for cutting is letting George, Mary, your spouse, or anyone else do it, especially if "it" is your problem. This cop-out mentality burrows into many levels of life, but sometimes consequences are more grave than others. Please note that copping-out is not the same as stepping aside for a professional. For instance, I will help at an accident scene but gladly make way for paramedics when they arrive. But you suffer from cop-out-itis if you want George or someone else to do what you alone can do in your life. Before long you engage in charades to defend your inaction, and knots multiply in body language. Taking responsibility for life should be as natural as eating and breathing, but Old Sub has genuine interest in helping you avoid self-accountability if that means more work for your subconscious.

Knife in hand (isn't this gruesome?), let's go to work on that large knot called not assuming personal responsibility. Take a piece of paper and write this short poem by Robert Frost, entitled "Assertive":

Let me be the one
To do what is done.[39]

Post it prominently where you see it several times a day and put copies in your calendar and address book. During a quiet hour consider its meaning in several areas of your life including finances, personal relations, and intellectual and spiritual growth. What should you do differently to take responsibility since your actions do make a difference? As Walter S. Robertson said, "The only way to get rid of responsibilities is to discharge them." Or, "It's up to me if it is to be."

One result of taking responsibility is that you will say no to the requests of others more often. Management advisors recommend that corporations should have a vice president in charge of eliminating outdated policies and procedures, and in your life you are the vice president for this function. You will discover that some activities are not essential since they no longer fit into your schema of life. You must be willing to cut these knots as you assume daily responsibility for how you live.

Another negative knot for cutting is the lack of vigorous physical exercise. Many books and manuals describe in detail the physiological benefits of regular exercise. There is no need to repeat their exhortations here, but see your doctor before you begin a program, and start slowly. The psychological benefits of an exercise program are equally important. Will Rogers once cracked, "Even if you're on the right track you will get run over if you just sit there." These words find a target in anyone who thinks he can shape up his psychological mechanism while ignoring the physical side. "Just sitting there" is bad physiological and psychological medicine.

To cut this negative knot you may want to establish a life goal for regular physical exercise. Doing the real thing is easier if you envision yourself walking, running, playing racquetball, or engaging in other forms of physical recreation.[40] Varying your tempo and gait offers relief in a self-discipline such as this, and focusing on a real, physical goal as you walk or run makes the goal attainable. Walking promotes thinking, maybe because of increased blood flow to the brain. In any case, walking and other regular exercise provide Old Sub a different image for its data bank. Walking also exercises the senses as feet go clip-clop, birds sing, dogs bark, and other sounds, sights, and smells strike your senses.

One last negative knot for cutting is the dour, grim face of a person who lacks humor. Whether you are fatigued, de-energized, problem-laden, or just plain "normal," being dispirited about life is a sure way to compound all that can go wrong. Some people complain that I like humor too much since I tell jokes while teaching a regular adult forum at church, but, like C. S. Lewis, my response is that the devil fears humor.

Humor is one way we can take responsibility and control for who we are and what our life is. When the doctor told a patient whose check bounced, "By the way, your check came back," the patient responded, "That's funny, so did my lumbago." What makes this funny is that the patient admitted his mistake while reminding the doctor of his own imperfection. He knew enough about his illness to insist responsibly on better treatment.

The Book of Proverbs says a merry heart is good medicine. Norman Cousins, *Saturday Review* editor, discovered the wisdom of this proverb in 1964. He suffered from a life-threatening spinal disease and could not move in his hospital bed without excruciating pain. He took the bet when specialists wagered 500-1 odds against recovery, checked into a hotel room, and with his doctor's help planned a healthy regimen of laughter. Cousins watched Marx Brothers movies and "Candid Camera" episodes and enjoyed other belly-shaking humor. While he needed painkillers to sleep in the hospital, he now found that ten minutes of laughter brought two hours of painless sleep. His best-selling *Anatomy of an Illness* describes his experience in detail.[41]

Remember President Reagan's crack to the emergency room doctor after the attempted assassination? "I hope you're a Republican!" was his valiant effort to assert control and maintain a sense of responsibility in unnerving circumstances. He could have said nothing in that bloody room but used humor to summon as much self-control as possible, appealing for the physician's best treatment.

Charles Schulz' *Peanuts* strip often shows people seeking and avoiding personal responsibility. Most of all, Schulz lightens life with humor and provides a liberating perspective on daily situations, such as when Lucy is constantly tempted to jerk the football from Charlie's foot.

An episode in Schulz' life shows his philosophy written in large letters. In 1981, he had bypass heart surgery for blocked arteries. When he entered the hospital, a nurse put a large felt-tip pen on a cabinet and asked him to "draw something on the wall" before he left. Four days after surgery he was lying in the hospital bed, with his wife sitting beside him. It was 10:30 P.M., and Schulz felt that he had to honor that earlier request. Suddenly a cartoon idea popped into his mind.

> *I climbed carefully out of bed, picked up the pen and began to draw a series of five Snoopys, showing him struggling with an inhalator to make the three balls rise to the top and remain there for a moment. All patients could identify with this frustrating exercise, devised to keep the lungs clear and get them back to good working order. The last panel showed him collapsing with exhaustion and triumph...here I was standing at the wall, drawing again, exhilarated with the feeling that I had gone through something I had not been sure I was brave enough to attempt, and that maybe, somehow, drawing cartoons really was what I was meant to do.*[42]

In this dramatic episode Schulz used humor to exert control over a seemingly insignificant thing like raising inhalator balls, and important things like reclaiming his vocation.

Humor is good for you since a good laugh gives your whole body a kick. You stimulate heart and lungs, temporarily raise your heart rate and blood pressure, and breath more oxygenated blood. Your body releases natural painkillers called endorphins and produces immune cells, and your caloric burning increases seventy-eight times over resting. In what Norman Cousins calls "internal jogging," your organs bounce all over in a massage that also affects your diaphragm and facial muscles.

Laughter cannot cure everything, but it certainly helps with self-inflicted maladies, especially in bringing a new perspective. A recent health bulletin tells how to build your self-practice of humor. Look for humor in daily life and the newspapers ("Vandals make off with toilet seats from police station—police have nothing to go on"). Laugh at yourself (one man looked at his passport photo and decided he wasn't well enough to travel). Take mental breaks, and like "Candid

Camera," look for humor in people's behavior. Use contagious humor and enjoy good laughs with others. Create a first-aid kit of humorous cartoons, jokes, funny quotes, and video collections for when you need a lift.[43]

Guidelines for Knot-Cutting

Life goals are guidelines for the daily knot-cutting that overcomes problems, fatigue, and lack of energy and direction. If we are serious in these tasks we will discover that although life goals change often during life, they are the best guidelines for discovering what holds you back. What you set out to accomplish in your twenties changes in your fifties. What a college graduate formulates as life goals becomes a different set at retirement. Especially in the thirty-five to forty-five age bracket, tension builds in the area of personal creativity. People ask themselves whether they want to stagnate or proceed to a new generative phase. The outcome depends partly on how well they worked through earlier challenges. So setting and attaining life goals is a never-ending process that is pivotal for cutting knots, conducting preventive maintenance, and throwing lines to the future.

The ancient Greeks used two words for time that help us think clearly about life goals. *Chronos* was their word for hours, days, seasons, day-to-day time, and regular time. It covered everything under the sun, like time to laugh and time to cry, time to sow and time to reap. *Kyros* was their word for the right time, the opportune time, the critical time. It is the time of the mountaintop moment, of insight, of special grace and blessing. New Testament writers used this distinction to emphasize the importance of God's salvation time.

One way of checking your time-pulse is to ask, "What do I—can I—could I get excited about?" If your mind and spirit tingle with excitement about something, chances are this is *kyros*-time for you. Your framework for life goals should be *kyros*-time since goals are for the right, critical, opportune time. That is why you are working to accomplish them. With this perspective on the rest of life, your *chronos*-life, you can easily give new material to Old Sub, cut knots daily, and conduct preventive maintenance. Your life-goal vision puts daily life into proper perspective since life goals are guidelines for daily living.

An inquirer once asked an eighty-five-year-old woman from the Kentucky hills, "What would you do if you had your life to live over?" The person who answered reviewed life from a fresh perspective. She said:

> *If I had my life to live over I'd try to make more mistakes next time. I would relax...I would be sillier than I have been this trip. I know of very few things I would take seriously.... I would climb more mountains, swim more rivers and watch more sunsets. I would eat more ice cream and fewer beans. I would have more actual problems and fewer imaginary ones.*
>
> *You see, I am one of those people who live seriously and sanely, hour after hour, day after day. Oh, I have had my moments, and if I had it to do over again, I would travel lighter...I would start barefoot earlier in the spring and stay that way later into the fall. I would ride more merry-go-'rounds. I'd pick more daisies.*

Your challenge is to look forward with a perspective that is equally strong and vibrant. That power enables your clear voice to say, "I have no time for knots."

Preventive Line Maintenance

Preventive maintenance checks your life-lines for knots and also ensures a short life for problems. The amount of knot-cutting is reduced if you avoid situations that cause knots.

Some people keep a written list of their traits, skills, abilities, and gifts, updating the list often and adding new items that come to mind. They use the list to measure how well they apply personal resources, and in this way it becomes a checklist for preventive maintenance. Facing a new life challenge, what specific gifts or skills should I use, they ask? How can I employ a dormant ability? What training and intellectual advancement would round me out as an individual? Some people arrange the list in priority order around subjects such as family relations, job, or financial planning, and then they check how well they are using personal resources in each area. This extends positive thinking into as many life areas as possible. Important building blocks in a positive life are a realistic appraisal of strengths and a determination to shore up weaker points. You keep the lines untangled in body language by maintaining a realistic self-inventory and strengthening weaker traits.

Another part of preventive maintenance is a regular checkup of life goals. We assume that you have started compiling a list of life goals that are important to you. As Pogo said, "If you don't know where you are going you're apt to end up someplace else," so there is no better time than now to make your list. At all costs you should phrase goal statements in a positive manner. Research analyst William Koppe gives a succinct reason: "If your goal is to avoid error you are not interested in your main goal."[44] For example, a life goal should not say, "I am less grouchy than usual." Better to write and envision this goal: "I feel my whole body pulsing with joy and happiness at the new day." The accompanying table lists characteristics of life goal statements that you should monitor in regular checkups. Perform a maintenance check on your life goal list at least

Characteristics of Good Life Goal Statements		
Yes	No	
X		Does each life goal sentence begin with the word "I"?
X		Does this life goal contain a present-tense verb, not future tense?
X		Does it have one or more verbs or adverbs describing an emotion ("joyfully," "smilingly," "tingle with happiness")?
X		Do you include the senses of hearing, touch, smell, and taste in goal statements whenever possible (sight is in your visioning)?
X		Do you cluster life goals into related groups (for example, financial, interpersonal relations, personal growth)?
X		Have you assigned each goal a deadline date for achievement so Old Sub knows the time period that is available?

monthly, make required changes, and compile a list of your revised goals.

A final maintenance item is to ensure that you are living the examined life day by day. One good way of doing this is to include this aim as a life goal: "I feel good about my life goals and enjoy an examined life that smells like newly baked bread." This statement contains visioning material that can help keep your lines straight.

Throwing Lines to the Future

Several years ago I toured a giant aircraft carrier. As we inspected the area housing the anchor chain the guide told us this giant chain was supposed to jingle down a large channel, following the anchor to the ocean bottom. I thought about what a problem the sailors would have if the chain got tangled or the heavy links jammed.

As you work toward life goals you are not handling one-foot chain links, or even tossing a rope from skiff to shore. You are throwing to the future lines that connect with your heart, mind, body, and spirit. If you cut negative knots regularly and conduct periodic maintenance, visioning your life goals is the most important way of saying every day, "I have no time for knots."

Have you considered the fact that you will spend the rest of your life in the future? We recognize mentally that yesterday is past and tomorrow is the first day of the rest of our lives, but it is much harder to grasp this truth psychologically, spiritually, and with our whole being. Mastering it clarifies the Greek distinction between *kyros*-time and *chronos*-time. The future, tomorrow, is always *kyros*-time since it is decision time, critical time, gift time, mountain-top time.

Poets tell us that time flows like a great river under a bridge. Since human beings can look upriver to a future that is becoming the present, we can throw visioning lines that directly affect our present life goals. Visioning is the end of the novel that you are writing in your life goals; it celebrates the success of achievement before it happens so Old Sub can steer you there. One authority tells us that visioning helps restore the "ecological balance" between inner and outer worlds.[45] It is a way to create a harmonious whole that integrates you, your talents and abilities, and the real world around you.

Visioning is not easy, effortless, or uncomplicated. Merely hoping that someday you will use visioning is not the same as visioning life goals with persistence. Like the old cowboy said, "A wishbone ain't no substitute for a backbone." Neither is visioning a one-day quick fix for a lifetime of misdirection, since Old Sub must learn to accommodate you in the saddle. But it is a helpful way to turn energy-drain and fatigue into excitement, and that is why visioning is the consummate daily knot-cutter.

Visioning shows that you consider problems serious enough

to do something about them. In *The Road Less Traveled,* Dr. Peck has a revealing paragraph about the need for discipline in handling problems. He writes:

> *Yet it is in this whole process of meeting and solving problems that life has its meaning. Problems are the cutting edge that distinguish between success and failure. Problems call forth our courage and our wisdom; indeed, they create our courage and our wisdom. It is only because of problems that we grow mentally and spiritually.*[46]

Dr. Peck hints that discipline is not the opposite of pleasure but the gate to pleasurable courage and wisdom. Similarly, the discipline of visioning opens your whole person to growth as you face problems wisely and courageously, and forge a future that grows from courage and wisdom.

You should engage in visioning two or three times a day to firmly fix life goals in the subconscious. You may want to combine visioning with a concentration or relaxation technique by assuming a meditative position on a chair, lying flat on the floor, or taking another position, including yoga. I type my life goals on a single sheet of paper and work through them one by one. Dedicate as much time as you need to visualize each goal as clearly as possible in your mind's eye at the precise moment of goal achievement. I usually spend no more than ten minutes on the set. Some people record the dates of their visioning on the reverse side of the goal sheet to maintain the discipline.

Inevitably we envision some goals more easily than others. The images flow more freely, we smell the fresh forest air, and everything clicks. If that is the case, use several easy goals first in your visioning, then move to those more difficult for your mind's eye to "see" in imagery. Some people say they find it hard to "see" goals because they seldom "see" anything with their eyes closed. They should consider visioning with their eyes partially open and a narrow slit between the eyelids. Others put open hands in front of the eyes to peer into the future through their palms.

At bedtime you may want to give Old Sub a special challenge to wrestle with all night. Visioning a goal as you go to sleep presents it to your subconscious for all-night processing, and do not be surprised if the way seems clearer the next morning.

The last point about visioning is to use all your senses. Many people loaf through life with their senses running at half power—unless they see lightning strike or smell barbecued steak. Use as many senses as possible in visioning. Your life goal images should include things you can taste, odors you smell, sounds you hear, and things you touch. Most important is to use your mind's "seeing" capacity to experience the joy of a goal achieved. Your goal scenes will be more memorable and make a bigger impression on Old Sub if you dress the scene with flashy colors (your sweater or necktie), action (your dog walking beside you), and familiar items like a lamp from home or office.

It is no accident that Mozart was a musical thinker who thought auditorily. We might say he visioned that way since he reported, "When I compose I sit down at the piano. All I'm doing is I'm playing what I'm hearing. And whence it cometh from I know not, but I thank the good Lord it is at least Mozartisch." Einstein used imagery as a visual way of thinking. An important advantage of the visual image is that it condenses large amounts of material and dynamic flow into one unit. Dr. Jean Houston explains that visual thinking works with conglomerate units like one through five, or five through ten. These units are constellations of information, conglomerates that integrate intellectual and emotional data. Visual thinking works with a unit like one through five without splitting it into sub-parts, while linear (non-visual) thinking considers this material by dividing it into the sub-unit numbers of 1-2-3-4-5.[47] Visioning or imaging works holistically, and that is how we use it to rehabilitate Old Sub in the pursuit of life goals.

Some things are unchangeable. For example, it is impossible to sneeze with both eyes open. An ostrich will never bend its knees backward like a person. Horses will always breathe through their nostrils. The number of kernel rows on an ear of corn is always an even number. The tomato remains a vegetable and not a fruit—unless the Supreme Court alters its 1893 decision.

But knots are changeable. If we cannot untie them we can cut them. That is why it is important to declare with a loud voice, "I have no time for knots." The discipline of daily knot-cutting keeps lines free to throw to your future. Reading this chapter and this book will not make your life goals a reality, but cutting negative knots, preventive line maintenance, and visioning your goals will give you control over the automatic knot-tier inside you. If you truly have no time for knots, Old Sub will not let good enough alone.

IV
We Want All of You

For millions of Americans, daily life is not super-salespeople in action or business entrepreneurs making important decisions. It is getting out of bed, hauling themselves to work, and battling the day until quitting time. These wage and salary earners are carpenters, assembly line workers, bank tellers, pizza deliverers, and accountants. They also are middle-level managers, nurses, teachers, and people working in 13,000 jobs described in the Labor Department's Dictionary of Job Titles. They are the backbone of the nation's economy.

Life goals are for all people, whatever their vocation. They are not restricted to a few elite people; the supersalesperson's $150,000 income is not a prerequisite and neither is a college degree. For life goals you need a beating heart, a working brain, and an interest in integrating your life.

This chapter's focus is the daily struggle of all workers to adopt life goals and put them into practice. Why is it a struggle? Because employers claim the right to peak hours, peak production, peak mental work, and full allegiance. They tend to say, "We want all of you!" If you yield, your job can consume nearly all your physical and psychological energy, and work can become life's end-all. "We want all of you" is often the result, whether employers suggest it or not.

Charles Lindbergh discovered what a culture means when it declares, "We want all of you!" His nonstop solo flight in 1927 made him an authentic hero, but soon after he landed the biggest news about him was that he was such big news. He flew the ocean alone, but even more remarkable, he dominated the news unlike any person to that time. At age twenty-five he became a celebrity, a person known for being well-known, and the culture owned him. Lindbergh stayed on public display until 1940, marrying an ambassador's daughter and enduring a son's kidnapping and death in 1932. Mobsters volunteered their help to find the kidnapper while disclaiming their own involvement, and Al Capone offered a $10,000 reward for information leading to the child. Despite his early accomplishment, Lindbergh died a celebrity's sudden death after imagining that he had become a public spokesperson. His pronouncements were dull and vicious, he was a reputed racist and pro-Nazi, and Hitler gave him a decoration. Soon skyscraper beacons were renamed to remove all reference to him, and Lindbergh Peak in the Rockies became Lone Eagle Peak.[48]

Whatever your line of work, you face Lindbergh's struggle although yours may not be as public or as intense. Struggling for goals in all areas of life is a basic right. You alone can put life and work into proper perspective, taking responsibility for your work and job changes along the way. Giving your employer his due makes work an art while preserving the integrity of your life goals. But you become a work celebrity if you subsume life goals to your work.

Your Struggle for Life Goals

Doctors, lawyers, merchants, chiefs, salaried workers, and wage earners must fight to assert the priority of life goals. While Uncle Sam's finger points at young people and says, "I want you" for military service, our culture, society, economy, and jobs constantly demand, "We want all of you!" We have to invoke the full strength of our humanity to lay prior claim on our lives with life goals, and if this is a serious pursuit the resulting struggle continues throughout life. The outcome of the encounter shows how well we arrange life and work and our willingness to establish goals for all areas of life.

Right to Life Goals

Human beings have the intrinsic right to establish goals for life since that is one thing that distinguishes us from the animal kingdom. We humans use language, think, and think ahead, and we have the right to life goals, although many forces seek to deny that right.

For the first time in the West, the excesses of the French Revolution showed what was the nature of totalitarianism. Its basic thrust is to own citizens wholly in all respects. A totalitarian regime uses social, economic, and political tools to suppress the human spirit and erase all feelings of personal responsibility. The 20th century has seen the most devastating attack on the right to life goals in modern history with totalitarianism as the perpetrator. It came in many forms, in Italy under Mussolini, in Germany under Hitler, in the Soviet Union under Lenin and Stalin, and in Japan under Tojo. These dictatorial regimes owed their origins to the totalitarian need for total control, and after World War II other tyrants arose in post-colonial environments.

A totalitarian tendency was also evident in some societies that escaped the scourge of these rulers in the twentieth century. Democracies had to create massive concentrations of power to defeat totalitarianism, and governmental bureaucracies sprouted to manage arms and equipment for total war. Top-secret plans for the atom bomb planted new towns in the southwestern United States. Political power flowed to an increasingly imperial presidency while congressional tenure lengthened. After World War II the North Atlantic Treaty Organization (NATO) defended western Europe as a standing army. Radio and television plied new wares manufactured in the postwar boom, and a more centralized economy, culture, and society emerged in the United States.

American life in the 1990s is by no means life in a fascist state, but many organizations and structures have a natural tendency to overwhelm us as individuals. The sense of "being owned" or controlled is heightened by employing companies, capitalism, and a political system that seems out of touch with many Americans. Also, mass media and advertising make us one of the crowd whether we like it or not.

This drift toward centralization flies in the face of American history. As a nation we bloomed in what the eminent historian Daniel Boorstin calls the "Fertile Verge." America was a "verge," a place of encounter between something and something else, and individualism flourished in that context.

Americans met geographic verges as they traveled westward, enticed by mountains, rivers, deserts, and oceans that did not confine them to the original colonies. Our political verges led us to a clear self-awareness that we were different from the "old" countries, and in nation, state, and community we created thousands of new laws to deal with this insight. Beacons along the way were the *Mayflower* compact, the Declaration of Independence, and the Constitution. Our technological verges led to a new world as we reshaped the old, clumsy German musket into a Kentucky rifle that was longer and more slender, and that used a ball half the weight. Americans used it as backwoods sharpshooters and Revolutionaries. Our technological specialty were the factories that sprang from nothing, like the railroads that ran from nowhere to nowhere to entice population.[49]

These verges helped create three ways of thinking and

feeling that are characteristically American. Hear Boorstin:

> *First, there is our exaggerated self-awareness. On the verge we notice more poignantly who we are, how we are thinking, what we are doing. Second, there is a special openness to novelty and change. When we encounter something different, we become aware that things can be different, and our appetite is whetted for novelty and its charms. Third, there is strong community-consciousness. In the face of the different and the unfamiliar, we [who are similar] lean on each other.*[50]

As a result, our American tradition of individualism rebels at the suggestion that everything must be the same. We will not accept that we have no right to life goals, or that an employer or organization can "own" us lock, stock, and barrel.

Because of the century's totalitarian pressures and America's history of individualism, we must return to the theme of the "unexamined life." Unless we evaluate life we may not notice the tentacles that may squeeze it to death. That is why your struggle for life goals is linked directly to your right to have life goals. Making that claim is the first step in untying the noose of organizations (including employers) that seek to own you.

It takes little effort to live a life of quiet desperation in an organization. Making no waves, following the boss's nuances, amassing "perks," and gaining access to the center of power are equivalent to slipping into semi-consciousness. Goethe called it selling one's soul to the devil, but did he know something that we do not?

A fictitious story about a Harvard Law School graduate describes our predicament. This young lawyer worked for a prestigious Washington law firm, putting in twenty hours a day seven days a week with the hope of becoming a senior partner. After six months of intense labor one of the senior partners privately told him that if he continued at this pace, "we'll consider naming you as a partner."

At midnight one Sunday night he decided to leave the office early and surprise his long-suffering wife. When he arrived home he noticed a Cadillac in the driveway so he parked his car and crept in the back door. He found no one downstairs but saw a light shining under the bedroom door upstairs. He crept up the stairs with his shoes off, opened the door quietly, and looked in. There the senior partner and his wife were engaging in amorous activities of the first magnitude.

He quietly closed the door and crawled downstairs, went out the back door, pushed the car into the street, started it, and drove slowly to the corner. Then he pushed the pedal to the metal, racing through deserted streets to the law office at sixty miles an hour. Forgetting even to turn off his car lights, he ran into the building, dashed past the locked elevator, and sprinted eight flights to his office. There the young lawyer rushed to his desk, felt the security of his leather chair against his back, put his head in his hands, and gasped to himself, "My God! I nearly got caught!"[51]

This humorous story has the ring of truth. Sometimes we sell our right to life goals for a pot of vocational porridge. For a time we may resist while under the influence of youthful idealism, but all too soon we capitulate to forces seeking to control us. If we give up the right to life goals, we give in to the unexamined life.

One reason this happens is that life has many unsolvable problems, unlike much of the work we do. Work teaches us how to solve problems well, and television, advertising, the market economy, and the advice of friends and relatives reinforce this message. How can someone solve a murder on TV in thirty minutes while I battle this one marital problem for years, we ask? Let's concentrate on solvable problems, mainly on the job where we get paid for it, we think. Soon that becomes the source of life's satisfaction instead of life itself. So we capitulate.

Our technological society's stock in trade are specific problems with specific solutions. Do you need to split the atom and create a chain reaction? You have it, and that solves that problem. What others are there?

Do you want an adhesive that will not require moistening

to hold the flaps of envelopes? Do you want a highway surface that will not crack under given variations in temperature? Do you want a pen that will write under water? Do you want a camera that will produce an image in twenty seconds? Do you want that image in full color?[52]

We can solve these problems and more. Do you need to learn Windows on your computer at work? We'll fix that. Do you need an exact calculation of how many miles of telephone cable the job requires? You can do that. Solvable problems make the larger problem of living life seem more distant, more difficult, and perhaps not worth the effort.

It is no wonder that we give up the right to life goals in favor of meeting the easier challenges of daily accomplishments. Totalitarian influences come close to bowling us over, threatening the human spirit, and we have a daily struggle on our hands if we want to pursue life goals, whatever our occupation.

Personal and Work Compartments

Separating life into "work" and "personal" compartments does not work for most people. Some try this approach as a way to fight the life-goal battle without clearly asserting the right to life goals. "Work is work, and my personal life is my concern," they say, but the divorce takes its toll, slowly or more rapidly, earlier or later in life. Schizophrenia works no better in approaching life and work than it does in operating a personality. Andr Maurois says, "Business is a combination of war and sport." War and sport do not mix easily unless one knows what he is doing, and compartmentalizing life and work is not the way. The U.S. Department of Health, Education and Welfare reports that fifty-seven percent of white-collar workers and sixty-four percent of blue-collar workers are unhappy with their jobs. They would choose differently if starting again was an option.[53] There must be a better way than merely allying life with work.

Burnout shows the fallacy of this approach, and it is a

major problem. "Jobs are physically easier, but the worker now takes home worries instead of an aching back," says Homer Bigart. Dividing personal and work spheres presents problems, including inadvertent transfer between the two.

Burnout, the opposite of wholeness, can come in any job. Its slogan is "Try harder" and its formula is living beyond your limits. Any sustained energy deficit can lead to burnout. Dr. G. Lloyd Rediger describes several aspects of the syndrome and its telltale physical and emotional signs. His list includes the following:

Physically: Low energy. Weight changes. Exhausted appearance. Significant change in sleep patterns. Motor difficulties such as lack of coordination, tremors, twitches. Frequent headaches and gastric upset. Loss of sexual vigor. Hypochondriacal complaints.

Emotionally: Apathy, one-track mind and loss of creativity. Paranoid obsessions. Constant irritability. Constant worrying. Loss of humor or development of "gallows humor." Sporadic efforts to act as if everything is back to normal. Complaints of loneliness. Inability to be playful or become interested in diversionary activities. Excessive crying. Random thought patterns and inability to concentrate. Hopelessness.

Some of these characteristics may also appear in a person who is tired, bored, or discouraged, but it is the depth, pervasiveness, and combination of factors that suggest burnout, which is full exhaustion of resources.[54] Burnout often needs professional care as a form of depression.

The fallacy of trying to separate life and work also becomes clear if a job is more dreadful every day. Some loathe work because they misinterpret the intentions of others; soon they consider themselves victims, mistakenly drawing this conclusion from their own fears. In 1980 the *New York Times* printed the following short story. "They met in a bar, where he offered her a ride home. He took her down unfamiliar streets. He said it was a shortcut. He got her home so fast she caught the ten o'clock news."[55] Did the ending surprise you? Did you make an assumption based on fear?

Some employing organizations may try to portray our job-tasks as herculean in nature to pull us into the company's time warp and make it difficult to preserve separate life-work compartments. In a slip of the tongue Mayor Richard Daley of Chicago said in 1967, "Together we must rise to ever higher and higher *platitudes*." He did not get the English quite right, but in many organizations, including companies and governmental agencies, the idea of rising to higher plateaus is a staple. Such talk can sweep you off your feet and propel you into a company culture that controls personal life, or make it so unlivable as to possess it.

In most organizations people meet a strange puzzle that management consultant Jerry B. Harvey calls the "Abilene paradox." The puzzle is that "organizations frequently take actions in contradiction to the data they have for dealing with problems and, as a result, compound their problems rather than solving them."[56] This affects how employees feel about the company, and it too can throw a monkey wrench into compartmentalizing life and work.

Company travelers know what the "Abilene paradox" looks like since they see its tracks often. One of its signs is action anxiety. People can get very anxious when they think about doing the right thing, and as a result they stay on a straight course without wavering. Imagine, for instance, that you are a manager who is heading up a research project that makes no sense. You will probably choose to suffer action anxiety rather than tell the company president that the project is worthless. Because of your inaction the company compounds its problems. Telling the emperor he is without clothes causes anxiety, and that is why most people leave it unsaid.

There is another sign of the Abilene paradox. Organizational members have negative fantasies about what will happen if they act the way they know they should. The manager imagines that if he told the truth he could lose his job or suffer loss of face and prestige. These negative fantasies give him a psychological reason for continuing to saw wood when the company heats with gas.

Real risk is another sign of the Abilene paradox. If the manager tells his supervisor that the project is worthless, he risks being fired. This consequence may be possible, but is it likely? Some people who are unable to accept the reality of risk in personal life are also unlikely to accept personal risk in a work situation, even when it cries out for truth and change. If the person does nothing the organization continues digging its grave, wasting valuable resources on a worthless project.

Part of the Abilene paradox is fear of separation. The manager referred to above fears ostracism, no longer being connected. Separation may mean being called "disloyal" or a "non-team player," or being separated from other workers temporarily or permanently. Fearing separation, the manager contributes to collective deception by taking no action. This happens, for example, when no member of a research committee supports a project individually but all members adopt it collectively.

When eventually the worthless project fails, as it almost certainly will, the company's compounded problems are over. Wasted time and money disappear for good down the black hole, and the "Abilene paradox" prevails.[57] Meantime, the manager who failed to take action may realize that compartmentalizing life and work does not work. If he follows a similar course in his personal affairs, he will waste time, money, and even his life, like the company wasted resources.

Professor Harvey pokes fun at organizational structures that regularly pursue the "Abilene paradox." He calls them "phrog farms" (after a frog) because the companies turn many people into "phrogs" that croak in the company swamp. He explains, "All organizations have two essential purposes. One is to produce widgets, glops, and fillips. The other is to turn people into phrogs." Bullphrogs generally get to be "phresident" in phrog farms, and phrogs usually are not rewarded for how well they sing in the chorus. To counteract the phrog mentality Harvey recommends paying people as pairs, teams, or organizations, and he urges people to take responsibility for their activities in the organization.[58]

Among all workers, bureaucrats are probably most inclined to try to separate life and work. Surprisingly, in contemporary life just about all of us are bureaucrats in one capacity or another—or at least many of us. Modern enterprise has created bureaucracies in many non-governmental areas, besides a vast governmental bureaucracy. Think of the many branches, departments, and divisions created with roads, steamships, railroads, airlines, electricity, postal service, telephone, radio and television. Schools, colleges, museums, libraries, and even churches have bureaucracies.

The bureaucratic frame of mind is caution, avoiding the need for any decision, and following regular procedures. One French civil servant had a sign on his desk epitomizing the bureaucrat: "Never Do Anything for the First Time." Uppermost in the bureaucrat's mind is keeping things on track, keeping himself moving toward retirement, and clearing the road for a full pension.[59]

Whatever the industry, a bureaucrat-worker may claim that personal affairs and work exist in separate compartments. The truth of the matter is that if life were lived like the bureaucrat works, few if any personal matters would remain. Life and life goals are much more than caution, avoiding the need for decision, and following regular procedures. A bureaucratic mind that functions alike in personal and work affairs has not yet begun to struggle for the right to life goals. Bureaucratic workers in all industries have a deep need for life goals.

Work Problems

One reason that life goals are worth struggling for is that work problems do not disappear on their own. If people want to change problems at work, chances are good that they must put a full-court press on life itself, and that involves life goals. While some trust their luck and wait for problems to disappear, they should heed R. E. Shay's advice: "Depend on the rabbit's foot if you will, but remember it didn't work for the rabbit." Luck alone will not do the trick for work problems. Charlie Brown gave an added warning about that: "When my ship comes in, I'll probably be at the airport."

Take, for instance, sexual harassment of women on the job, a problem that will not disappear if left alone. The solution of this social and economic issue depends on women and men struggling for life goals that leave no room for sexual harassment.

During the American Revolution one young woman had the courage to apply life goals to all of life, including work, where she faced major problems. Disguised as a boy, Deborah Sampson Gannett of Boston ran away from home and entered the Continental army at age twenty. She was exceptionally tall for her time (five feet, seven and a half inches) and "fleet as a gazelle, bounding through swamps many rods ahead of her companions." Her unshaven face aroused little suspicion since many soldiers were too young to shave, and she was so modest that she pried a bullet from her own wound to avoid a physician's examination. When her sex was finally discovered, she received an honorable discharge, and Paul Revere tried to secure a congressional pension for her.[60] Deborah Gannett knew that, for a woman, work problems in the army would not disappear on their own, so she assumed a masculine disguise for all of life to pursue her goal of serving in the Continental army.

Some people rely on procrastination to avoid work problems. Don Marquis defines procrastination as the "art of keeping up with yesterday," but seldom will problems be overcome by ignoring them and hoping for the best. Dr. M. Scott Peck, a psychiatrist, notes that "problems do not go away. They must be worked through or else they remain, forever a barrier to the growth and development of the spirit." Confronting problems is painful, but people who ignore problems are not willing to delay gratification. That is why their problems persist. They will not put aside something pleasant, such as the status quo, for something potentially more painful, such as working through a problem.[61]

One manifestation of procrastinating is staying on a job too long. Some workers find that their work no longer holds their interest, but their response is to procrastinate and make little effort to solve the problem by finding a different job or career. They remind me of a statement by Jerome J. Jerome: "I like work; it fascinates me. I can sit and look at it for hours." Those who procrastinate in a lackluster job need a sign for their desks containing a fictitious tombstone epitaph written by George Bernard Shaw. It said, "I knew if I stayed around long enough, something like this would happen." If this worker waits long enough he will die at his desk, no matter if life passes him by.

Area Goals

Like the rest of us, salaried workers and wage earners must engage in a struggle for life goals. We need to assert the right to life goals unequivocally, in and out of the work place. Compartmentalizing life into "work" and "personal affairs" fails us since the bleed-off from work is constant and work problems do not disappear on their own. We must face the challenge squarely with feet firmly planted in goals that cover all areas of life.

The Greek philosopher Aristotle praised the "Golden Mean," balancing extremes. That is good advice in the formation of life goals. For example, limiting goals exclusively to finances or physical fitness can lead to an unbalanced life while a balanced set of goals sets reasonable aims in all areas of life. For me that includes the physical, mental (intellectual), economic (work, investment), social, emotional, and spiritual aspects of life. In addition, a well-balanced list of life goals should provide for the civic portion of life, our citizenship in nation, state, and community.

A good way of reviewing life goals for balance is to ask, "How well do these goals assemble my life's puzzle?" If our goals cover all areas of life we get a composite view of life's future, perhaps for the first time. Life goals change as time and our vision of the future change, and as gaps appear we address them with new goals. One part of life enlivens another, and as we achieve a life goal we see ways of bringing others to fulfillment. Through it all Aristotle's advice on the Golden Mean is worth heeding since a well-balanced life avoids burnout.

Now is a good time to see whether your goal list portrays a well-balanced life. What targets are important as you review your physical existence in a body? How do you want to move into a different future, psychologically, mentally, and intellectually? Do you need to move some of your emotions out of the adolescent stage? What financial and investment objectives are most important as you consider the future? How sound are your social relationships with others, and what needs fixing? Where do you leave room for seeing beyond yourself to the transcendent, to forces that motivate you and bring a sense of unbounded joy? How do your goals portray your civic responsibility to community, state, and nation? Questions like these ensure that your life goals cover all areas.

Haste makes waste when a person fails to formulate a set of well-balanced goals. Sometimes we get in such a rush that we do not use goal formulation to provide structure and motivation for a full life. It is like catching a record-sized fish without capitalizing on your catch.

One rainy day in 1932 a young Georgia farmer went fishing in a home-made boat, and while plying the lake he hooked a largemouth bass bigger than any he had ever seen. George Perry, nineteen years old, took the bass to the local general store. There he learned that *Field and Stream* magazine had an annual "big fish of the year" contest, so he sent in a notarized certificate showing the fish's weight of 22 pounds 4 ounces. Then Perry and his family had a very expensive feast as they ate the fish for dinner. Perry received all of $75 in fishing gear from *Field and Stream*, but the bass's size has never been equaled. If he had taken the fish to a taxidermist for mounting, it would still be earning thousands of dollars in exhibit fees each year. Someone catching a larger largemouth today can expect fame, endorsements from manufacturers, and a million dollars or more in cash.[62] For George Perry, haste made waste.

Hammering out a set of balanced goals puts your life into the perspective you design. In the process you arrange your life's priorities and examine all areas of life to evaluate why you may be minimizing certain parts that others find enriching. Your arrangement of goals puts work in its proper place since you work to live, not live to work.

Perhaps there is no better summary of the struggle for life goals than the story of the famous Rhode Island Sweet family since its members struggled for life goals that let them work to live, not live to work. A newspaper in Providence, Rhode Island carried this advertisement in 1830:

> Waterman Sweet, bonesetter, hopes to meet the applause of all who may be under the necessity of employing him. He may be found at the Market Cellar, where he has a lot of good butter for sale, fit for table use.

Colonial America had few medical schools, and people with a natural flair for healing did much to relieve the suffering of the sick. The Rhode Island Sweets were such people. By vocation they were artisans who worked as blacksmiths, carpenters, stonemasons, and wheelwrights, but their avocation was Bonesetting. Beginning in the mid-1600s family members handled sprains, bone dislocations, and fractures with skill that an orthopedic surgeon could envy. They had an uncanny knack for setting bones and often succeeded where others failed. One early son said he could not fully explain how he set a boy's thigh bone; he simply saw every skeletal bone in his mind's eye and knew where to put it.

Remarkably, the family never exploited this natural ability, and none of them sought fame or fortune through Bonesetting. Generally a father chose one or two sons for instruction in the art. Bonesetting was the Sweets' avocation, an important part of life but not their work. All they asked for their services was remuneration for the time it took from their regular jobs.[63] As a sideline Bonesetting gave meaning to their lives. It was part of a well-balanced life that did not allow work to overshadow the rest of existence.

The Sweets teach us that the right to life goals is a right worth asserting. Trying to separate "life" and "work" into niches seldom succeeds, partly because work problems do not go away on their own. Making a commitment to life-goal rights, with goals in all areas of life, is the key to a well-balanced life.

Life-Work Perspective

Putting life and work into perspective is easier said than done, but only you can do it. Your task is to mark the boundaries over which your work will not pass. You establish a symbiotic relationship between life and work, even as you take responsibility for work, job changes, and landing a job.

Symbiosis

Symbiosis is two dissimilar organisms living together and enjoying a mutually beneficial, symbiotic relationship. Your life and work have such a symbiotic relationship when you integrate them effectively. Work enlivens life, and life enlivens work. You feel good about going to work because you feel good about life; your life is rewarding partly because your work is rewarding. That is symbiosis.

There is a simple way to learn whether you hold life and work in proper perspective, and whether they complement each other. You can tell by your answer to this question:

Which do you choose, A or B?

A. What you want from life depends on what you want from a job.

B. What you want from a job depends on what you want from life.

You are on the right track if you chose B. Chances are good that in a job you will not fully find what you are looking for in life. Your work may contribute to life's joys and satisfactions but can never provide them all.

This statement seems so self-evident that we may dismiss it as irrelevant, but it takes effort to explain what you want from life besides work's satisfactions. If you paint your life-goal canvas large enough to include all areas of life, you can enjoy work's pleasure along with life's other bounties. A balanced measure of life goals fills a satisfying life to the brim because life is more gratifying when you understand that what you want from a job depends on what you want from life.

People who expect too much from a job can suffer boredom on the job, or become bores themselves. Loading all of life's questions into an 8-to-5 regime is a formula for disaster, and it is no wonder that jobs become "boring" when they do not meet all these expectations. If a job becomes a bore, all that can be said about boring people applies as well. Christian Nestell Bovee complains, "There are few wild beasts more to be dreaded than a communicative man [read "job"] having nothing to communicate." Walter Winchell defined a bore as "a guy [read "job"] who wraps up a two-minute idea in a two-hour vocabulary." A bore is "a person [read "job"] who talks when you wish him to listen," said Ambrose Bierce.

If you insist on staying with a boring job, perhaps you should consider occupying your spare time with writing. Try composing replies for these problems, which Ann Landers once listed among the most unusual raised by her readers.

> *1. The man who hid his wife's dentures so she could not leave the house to vote for a Democrat.*
>
> *2. The bride who called home to tell her mother that she was returning from her honeymoon. Her husband, a mortician, said he could enjoy sex only*

with women who were dead or played dead. He told her to lie in the bathtub twenty minutes before coming to bed, and pretend to be dead.

3. The man who wanted his 1939 Dodge to be his casket.

4. The young woman with a leg crippled by polio who wanted it amputated so that, with an artificial limb, she would not limp at her wedding.

5. The man who lived in an apartment with a pig for a watchdog—and the neighbors complaining.

6. The woman who enjoyed housework in the nude but was surprised one day when she met the meter reader while going to the basement to do her laundry.[64]

Another way to pass time on your job—if you loaded too much of life into it—is studying these unnatural laws for application to your job-tasks. Murphy's Law, of course, claims that "If anything can go wrong, it will." Zymurgy's First Law of Evolving Systems Dynamics warns, "Once you open a can of worms, the only way to re-can them is to use a larger can." The Law of Selective Gravity is brief: "An object will fall so as to do the most damage." Hoare's Law of Large Problems suggests that "Inside every large problem is a small problem struggling to get out." Finally, the Ninety-Ninety Rule of Project Schedules is always applicable. It says, "The first ninety percent of the task takes ninety percent of the time, and the last ten percent takes the other ninety percent."[65]

Your body may give strong hints that your life-work arrangement is out of joint and lacks symbiosis. It is an excellent reflector of stress since it has millions of nerve receptacles and untold ways of sensing tension. You may be tired upon awakening because each night you dream, on average, three or four dreams of ten minutes or more. Although you stay awake all day at the job, you will close your eyes thirty minutes while blinking. You hope that stress on the job does not thicken your blood's makeup since the chemical content of its serum resembles sea water. Keeping your blood flowing freely through 60,000 to 100,000 miles of your circulatory system is important. Little wonder that the company's barbershop keeps busy; in a lifetime most people grow twenty-five feet of hair on the head.[66]

Some companies recognize the symbiosis of life and work by allowing employees to take off "mental health" days when necessary. While it may count against sick or vacation days, a day off can do wonders in the struggle to integrate life and work and maintain proper perspective on both.

Taking Responsibility for Work

There is no contradiction in saying that you should take firm responsibility for your work while maintaining proper distance between your job and the important values of your life. The connector here is responsibility, but, as usual, it is a two-edged sword.

People who are hesitant about taking responsibility for life will usually be just as hesitant about taking responsibility for their job, and vice versa. Pope John XXIII once gave an interesting insight into job responsibility when he said, "It often happens that I wake at night and begin to think about a serious problem and decide I must tell the Pope about it. Then I wake up completely and remember that I am the Pope."[67]

The remark is instructive, apocryphal or not. There is no absolute freedom in any job, nor can a person work well without taking responsibility for his work. Henry Brooks Adams wrote complex sentences, but what he said about liberty and responsibility is pertinent. He wrote, "Absolute liberty is absence of restraint; responsibility is restraint; therefore, the ideally free individual is responsible to himself." Self-responsibility in life and work makes you as free as possible. Being irresponsible in work is not freedom; it is slavery to the job.

A clear sign that you are self-responsible is that you do not rely on the doctrine of "fairness" in your job. Some people repeat this cliché to avoid work responsibility. Fairness compares you with others, and you and I can always ensure that we come out aggrieved. Why should you dedicate so much energy to your job when Mary has a better position and does less? Isn't that reason to slack off? We follow mental routines like this to avoid taking charge of our jobs and lives.

One wise old sage said, "After all is said and done, more is said than done." He is right. People complain a lot about fairness on the job but do little to assert responsibility and change what needs changing. For example, one positive step is to organize a support group with others who are in the same boat. Or ask your manager to set up a think-tank to propose solutions to problems. These efforts are the human equivalent of the mass maneuvering that animals follow for survival. Herds of reindeer run in V-formation but circle defensively if attacked by wolves. For about eighty percent of all fish, swimming in school formation is a protective devices against predators. Fish at the edge of schools are "eyes" for those in the center, who merely have to follow, and this sharpens the school's awareness.[68] We can learn something from them about acting together when necessary.

Job Change

Life and work are symbiotic if you put them in proper perspective and take responsibility for both. The proof of the pudding appears in a forced or involuntary job change that tests the backbone of your life-work perspective. Such a forced change is being "fired," "let go," or receiving a "pink slip." The origins of the term "firing" provide little comfort. Apparently the idiom first appeared in 1871 and meant "to eject or throw (a person) bodily from a place, to put out by forcible means." There are unsubstantiated reports that the Navy used the term earlier to describe how sailors who were discipline problems were strung over the end of a cannon "spread-eagle" and "fired."[69] To be "fired" also means being subjected to extreme heat and flame, as in a kiln.

Whatever the term's origin, a firing is seldom a thing of beauty, but voluntarily severing a work relationship is little easier for most people. They recall the agony of a six-year-old as he pulls his first tooth. Gene Fowler could just as well have been describing the pain of job-switching when he wrote, "Perhaps no mightier conflict of mind occurs ever again in a lifetime than the first decision to unseat one's own tooth."

Some are not impressed by the fact that the average worker changes jobs eight times in a lifetime. Each year at least forty million Americans are making transitions by changing jobs or careers. The average job hunt takes about four and a half months, with an extra month for each $10,000 sought in salary or wage above $40,000. For someone facing a job change, the only one that counts is the one coming next month.

The majority respond to imminent departure by compiling and sending hundreds of resumes to prospective employers, but, on average, a hundred resumes produce one to four invitations for an interview. The reason for this low ratio is that most companies use resumes to screen applicants out, and many companies offer only one invitation to interview for 245 resumes received. This is the "average." Some companies go as high as one in thirty-six, and others as low as one interview invitation for 1,200 resumes. A job search must take advantage of other avenues that include making personal contacts, going to employment agencies, using college placement firms, contacting executive search firms, and placing and answering newspaper ads.[70]

Viewed in the larger perspective, job changes are part of life's ebb and flow, the river of change that runs from cradle to grave. To resist change or deny its existence is like tilting windmills, as British Prime Minister Harold Wilson said so well: "He who rejects change is the architect of decay. The only human institution which rejects progress is the cemetery." Translated, that may mean that the gravedigger's job is forever while the rest of us face occupational change.

The study of change and transition is an important area because it can illuminate some of life's dark times, including job changes. In a book entitled *Seasons of Man's Life* (1978), Daniel Levinson reached an interesting conclusion about time periods in the lives of men. He found that relatively stable periods of six to eight years alternate with periods of transition. During a transitional stage the fundamental tasks are to "question and reappraise the existing structure, to search for new possibilities in self and world, and to modify the present structure enough so that a new one can be formed." A comparable study of women has not appeared, but it could show different stages and periods of time.[71]

Whether male or female, you can use this lifeline graph to plot your job shifts and other important life events. The graph may deliver insight into life stages and how well you weather change. Here is how you do it. Draw a heavy line from left to right as your lifeline, beginning at birth and ending with your present age. Put vertical marks on the horizontal line for age and your lifeline will look like this.

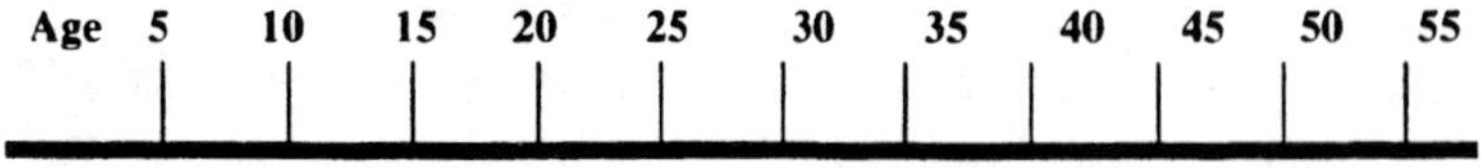

Now comes the fun. Draw vertical arrows (up and down) to show your life's turning points and formative experiences. If the turning point was *positive*, extend a vertical arrow up from the base line. If the experience was *negative*, draw an arrow that extends down from the time-line. Label each arrow with a word or phrase so you know what it represents. You can show the intensity of each experience or turning point by increasing the arrow's length, with longer arrows showing more intensity. Then, connect arrows of approximately the same length above the time-line, and those below. These connections may show patterns of change or transition in your life.

Here is the third step. What was the nature of each major transition? Ask these questions about each transition and you may find out. Was it controlled or uncontrolled? Gradual or sudden? Desirable or undesirable? Personal or communal? Temporary or permanent? Predictable or unpredictable? You will also gain insight by asking what was at stake in each major transition.[72]

You can use this lifeline for many purposes, including a general life review as you create goals. It can also help you interpret a forced or voluntary job shift. Job changes can be harder or easier, depending on whether they coincide with major life transitions, and knowing when the two converge can be helpful.

Job changes have many similarities with other major changes in life. In any transition the first stage is the ending of the earlier phase. Since we may not control the ending we may deny that one is happening; a new stage may overlap the old, but the old must end. We should pay close attention to feelings of grief that accompany endings, share these feelings with family and friends, take time for self, listen to our bodies and spirits, and use rituals to signify the passing.

The second stage of a major transition is the wilderness. Like Dorothy in the *Wizard of Oz* we may say, "Toto, I don't think we're in Kansas anymore." While we know where we are not, we don't know where we are. The wilderness is a difficult place in which to live, and since we lack control it can be scary. We may try to escape this "between time" by retreating to the past or moving too rapidly to a future, and our bodies and spirits often reflect the stress reaction that is common in this kind of wilderness. It is the time to remember that "This too will pass."

Remember that creativity and growth can occur during a wilderness transition. You make the wilderness bearable by listening to yourself, allowing unstructured time and space, and maintaining certain routines and open communication lines. Being gentle to yourself, keeping a journal, and drawing on faith resources can help in days of transition. You affirm yourself and draw on faith, family, and friends to support you.

The final stage is a new beginning, which sometimes seems too long in coming. Beginnings happen in their own good time; unlike some endings and wildernesses, they seldom can be rushed. Sometimes we move to an external beginning, like a job, while the "internal" has not commenced, and it may take six months to "settle in" and make the beginning real from the inside out. An internal beginning gets going only after we pass the first transitional stages. Some parts of endings may persist for a while, frustrating the start of a new career or phase of life. Among the obstacles that can hinder a new beginning's appearance are hesitation, dependence, fear of success or failure, a false start, and unfinished business from the past. Also, a beginning may appear more slowly if trauma caused the prior ending.

To help external and especially internal beginnings to emerge, we listen to our feelings, mind, and spirit, and an attitude of playfulness helps remove tension. Consulting a trained person (pastor, priest, or professional counselor) for conversation and counseling can be helpful. You will have little difficulty recognizing when a real internal beginning is underway. One writer says it feels like "experiencing the beginning of spring" as your body, spirit, and emotions give clear signals that you have passed the transition and moved to a new stage.[73]

Taking time for silence and personal reflection is a key ingredient for negotiating life transitions, including job changes. We can learn much by conversing with ourselves—if we take the time and enforce the necessary silence. Edward H. Richards, a poet, offers sound counsel for times of transition:

A wise old owl sat on an oak;
The more he saw the less he spoke;
The less he spoke the more he heard;
Why aren't we like that wise old bird?

Counselor Wayne E. Oates says, "Silence is not native to my world. Silence, more than likely, is a stranger to your world, too. So, if you and I are ever to have silence in our noisy hearts, we are going to have to *grow* it."[74] Silence is a healer that is worth its weight in gold during major transitions, including job changes.

People who are changing jobs should review all career options for which they are qualified, including new fields.

Some jobs that famous people held earlier in life may surprise you. Poet Robert Burns was a farmer and Johnny Carson a magician. Perry Como cut hair, Howard Cosell was a lawyer, and Albert Einstein spent time as a patent clerk. William Faulkner painted houses, Clark Gable cut lumber, and artist Paul Gauguin was a stockbroker. Evangelist Billy Sunday was a ballplayer and Babe Ruth a bartender. Haberdasher (Harry Truman), truck driver (Elvis Presley), boxer (Bob Hope)—the list goes on.[75]

Careful planning can help you to land a job or change careers. Success in either one hangs on your taking responsibility for the search; no one will do it for you.

Richard Nelson Bolles lists three steps for successful job-hunting and career-changing in his book *What Color is Your Parachute?* They are what, where, and how. He tells the reader to define precisely and in detail "WHAT it is you want to do? WHERE do you want to do it? HOW do you identify the person who has the power to hire you, and show them how your skills can help them with their problems?"[76] The "where" is the kind of company or business in which you want to work, and the geographical location.

This simple-sounding approach demands a heavy investment of time and labor. To know what you want to do requires a careful review of your skills and abilities and how you have used them. Precise analysis of prospective employers will narrow the field and improve your chance for success. Finally, you need to show a prospective employer how you can address a major problem for the firm.

Many people fall into the first job offered, or take a position because friends and relatives pressure them. Later they may initiate a career change. Vocational classes, seminars, and degree programs sometimes open doors to new careers, and packaging oneself attractively aids in the search. A person making a self-initiated change should plan the switch carefully and ensure sufficient financial resources for the interim; some career changes result in unexpectedly lower standards of living. Courage is necessary for voluntary job changes, but with the help of life goals it can be learned.

We leave the nuts and bolts to job-hunting and career-changing manuals. Here we note that part of the job hunt is keeping life and work in proper perspective. A requirement for good hunting is knowing what you want from a job, since you already know what you want from life. Readiness to take responsibility for your job is a quality sought by employers. Weathering job endings and wildernesses smooths the way for external and internal beginnings in a new job. This is part of the struggle for life goals that strengthens your loud "No!" when an employer claims, "We want all of you!"

Giving What Is Due

Telling a company that it cannot have all of you is right, but telling a company that it cannot have part of you is a recipe for failure. Employment is a *quid pro quo* arrangement in which the employee offers services for the employer's remuneration. Giving back what is due is common sense, just as Jesus advised his disciples to "render unto Caesar the things that are Caesar's, and unto God the things that are God's." Paying debts is good business, especially if it is rendering service for a salary or wage.

What Is Due?

American history records many instances where employees owed almost everything to their employer. In some mill and mining towns, companies owned lock, stock, and barrel, and that included buildings, services, grocery stores, and amenities. Mine workers received constant reminders that they were in debt to the company for everything, including grocery money. Slavery is another example. Many black slaves lived on plantations and owed their existence to the master's provisions. Finally, some religious sects took communal possession of their devotees' earthly goods. Adherents felt they were beholden for all, and they paid all.

Not all these experiences were happy ones, but we should balance this tale by noting that thousands of workers feel they owe nothing to employers, or as little as they can get away with. These loafers and goldbrickers ride on the backs of other workers for as long as possible, then move to a different employer. Somewhere they gained the mistaken impression that employers owed them a living, and they owed nothing in return.

How much a worker is worth, and how much pay he or she receives, are functions of the life-work perspective described above. If a person feels that a job's monetary rewards should provide all of life's satisfactions, the worker may demand an unrealistic wage to compensate for imbalance in the life-work relationship. People with a good perspective on life and work have a better chance of settling on a reasonable wage, and paying what is due for it.

Some may imagine that achieving wealth through work is tantamount to accomplishing life's highest goal, but whatever your line of work, money and the lust for it can do you in. For instance, a Turkish wrestler named Ishmaelo came to the United States in 1897. After easily defeating the previous wrestling champion, he beat the current Greco-Roman champion, Ernest Roeber. Ishmaelo converted his winnings into gold coins which he kept night and day in a band around his waist. On his return voyage in 1898, the ship he was on collided with another near Nova Scotia and began to sink. Unwilling to discard the money belt, Ishmaelo went overboard. Though he was a good swimmer he could not stay afloat with the weight of the coins, and they carried him to the bottom of the sea.[77]

For workers, giving what is due includes two primary considerations: excellence and quality. Excellence is superiority, the faculty of surpassing. Quality is the degree of excellence or fineness, the grade of excellence. Usually a worker who gives what is due is an example of both. Many employers use observable, measurable performance standards to gauge excellence and quality, and an excellent worker who delivers quality work should come out on top. Problems develop if workers have no clear understanding of performance standards.

All kinds of prejudices and biases enter human judgment when these standards are applied since some people have preconceived notions about what one or another person can do. It reminds me of a joke about the work of nationalities in the hereafter. In heaven the police are British, the cooks French, the lovers Italians, and the Germans organize everything. In hell, on the other hand, the police are French, the cooks British, the lovers German, and it's all organized by the Italians. It is to be hoped that performance standards are applied without prejudice.

Our nation's current economic difficulties make it hard to rely on standards of quality and excellence. Excellence is no longer an unofficial guarantee of job safety, as many hourly workers and middle managers discovered in the 1980s. Money flowed from deregulated savings and loans into the coffers of junk bondsmen, who used it to "restructure" companies. Translated, that meant they caused fundamental changes; they sometimes closed U.S. factories, opened facilities outside the country, and robbed the company's pension plan to boot. Many workers found that quality and excellence meant next to nothing when Wall Street engineers came to town to restructure a company. It was disconcerting to see chief executives and others receive outlandish golden parachutes when they were also personally involved in the buy-outs.

The rapidly rising federal deficit also undercuts excellence as an unwritten job warranty. Increasing debt raised long-term interest rates appreciably, and long rates remained high in 1992, keeping corporate interest high. Another part of the financial disaster of the 1980s was the savings and loan fiasco. According to a recent study the bailout is expected to cost $1.3 trillion dollars, up to $15,000 per taxpayer (*Stanford Law and Policy Review,* 1990). The rising deficit and resulting trade imbalance made it more difficult to use traditional yardsticks in evaluating worker performance. Also, global markets were more competitive, a problem intensified by recession. Union difficulties compounded problems for many workers.

The average compensation of factory workers, engineers, teachers and chief executives changed at appreciably different rates between 1960 and 1990. Studies show that compensation for factory workers increased 393%, for engineers 402%, for teachers 524%, and for chief executives 926%.[78] In most companies executives received much higher percentage increases in compensation than workers, sometimes while their companies were losing money. Also, the sheer size of executive compensation seemed ridiculously unrealistic. For instance, in 1991 Anthony J. F. O'Reilly, chief executive of H.J. Heinz, received total compensation of $74.8 million, including $70 million from exercising stock options.

Executives argued that executive pay served shareholder interest. That it served the executives there is little doubt. After reviewing executive compensation in 350 companies in 1991, the *Wall Street Journal* reported that the top earner was Leon C. Hirsch of U. S. Surgical Corporation. Including stock grants and stock options awarded in 1991, he had earned $169.8 million for the year if he exercised available options in April 1992. Robert Goizueta of Coca-Cola received the largest stock grant in history, a one million-share restricted grant worth an estimated $60 million. Executives usually must hold restricted options for four or five years before exercising them.[79]

Returning to earth from the stratosphere of executive pay, we note that the nature of pay is changing for many workers as employers offer a cafeteria of benefits, each valued independently. They allow workers to pick among on-site child care, a week at a professional meeting, reserved parking spaces, on-site grocery and dry-cleaning services, fitness centers, and others. Naturally, not all employees choose the same benefits. For example, the selections of employees without children are different from employees with non-working spouses and children. Other companies make some benefits standard for all. One firm found that parents in the secretarial pool were concerned about children at home alone after school, so it allowed them to call home to check on the kids.[80] These changes in benefits may affect how workers pay what is due to employers since people are seldom motivated by money alone, and benefits often raise worker commitment.

Changing circumstances affect how we give employers their due. The employer faces new demands, there are shifts in performance standards, perhaps economic circumstances change nationally or internationally, the company hits a recessionary downturn, or employees gain new perspectives on life and, as a result, work smarter. These and other factors influence wages and the worker's contribution to productivity. Our society and economy's potential for change encourages workers to hope for improved conditions. Nineteenth century employment conditions no longer apply in most American companies, and social changes such as reducing sexual harassment make for healthier working conditions.

Changes on the Job

Changes in how you do your job can have many ramifications, depending in part on whether you initiate the change. On the one hand, change can heighten fears of inadequacy or of being fired. On the other hand, change sometimes brings a sense of relief, as Washington Irving said about shifting positions on a stagecoach seat. He wrote, "There is a certain relief in change, even though it be from bad to worse! As I have often found travelling in a stagecoach, that it is often a comfort to shift one's position, and be bruised in a new place."

An important question for employees is what to do when they cause a major mistake, since changes of some kind usually follow. Magazines and newspapers are full of incidents like the following examples. Contractors installed boilers and started fires after building the Howard Hotel in Boston, then discovered they had no chimneys. After workers hung Henri Matisse's *Le Bateau* at New York's Museum of Modern Art in 1961, it took forty-seven days before someone noticed that the painting was upside down. Early in the century Dan O'Leary of the old Port Huron baseball team came to bat against Peoria with the score tied. He hit what was to be his first career home run, but he was called out after rounding the bases. He had run to third, second, first and then home.[81] All of us can add our favorite stories.

The important question is, What happens next? A good answer is the "Captain Asoh story," which may be partly apocryphal although based on actual events. Captain Kohei Asoh was a Japan Air Lines pilot who landed his DC-8 jet two and a half miles out in the San Francisco Bay on November 22, 1968. Carrying ninety-six passengers and a crew of eleven, the plane was exactly aligned with the runway. It just came down short in the bay. Luckily no one was injured, and passengers rowed inflatable life rafts to shore.

Captain Asoh was a veteran pilot with more than 10,000 flying hours, so interest was high about how the accident happened. The National Transportation Safety Board held a preliminary hearing, presumably to set ground rules for later testimony about assigning blame. Private citizens, angry passengers, representatives of pilots, lawyers, newspaper reporters, and representatives of various governments were on hand. The first witness at the hearing was Captain Asoh, and the lead investigator opened with a question. "Captain Asoh, in your own words, can you tell us how you managed to land that DC-8 Stretch Jet two and half miles out in the San Francisco Bay in perfect compass line with the runway?" His reply was, "As you Americans say, Asoh screw up." With that the hearing concluded, with "details" to be clarified later.[82]

In unambiguous terms Captain Asoh told the truth as he knew it. According to reports, he flew for Japan Air Lines until retirement. Japanese organizations have "ceremonies" for individuals who made serious mistakes to apologize, and other members accept their apologies.

There is no room for deception in giving an employer what is due. The best way to deal with a mistake is to admit it and take action to foreclose future recurrences. The person who will not acknowledge a mistake is more dangerous to an employer than one who admits it and energizes himself for future excellence.

Correcting mistakes is one way of handling—or generating—changes on the job. Another is self-initiated innovation. Most employers look to employees for suggestions and innovations, and while some suggestions are rebuffed, others change the way companies do business. Some employees worry that innovative suggestions can result in being ostracized or fired for rocking the boat, but this seldom happens. Employees give what is due by suggesting new ways for handling tasks and details.

Work as Art

At its best your job is art, not science, whether you are an engineer or a stock clerk. An artist has complete mastery of materials and skills, along with a vision of what he wants to do with them. An oil painter, for example, knows all about mixing colors, using palettes and brushes, and the different textures of canvas. He has a firm grasp of dimension, perspective, the relationship between close and distant objects, and the details that go into the artist's craft. Ultimately the artist applies his vision to materials and skills and creates a piece of art.

That is an accurate portrayal of work at its finest. Work does not possess you, you possess it. You master the materials, crafts, and details necessary to do your job, and even more important, you impose a vision of how to use these tools to do your job well. You stick to the task with persistence, like Josh Billing advised his son: "Consider the postage stamp, my son. It secures success through its ability to stick to one thing till it gets there."

Work as art can never overrun your life since you have mastered your job's components and assigned work its fitting place in life. You have the confidence to give a firm response to any employer who says, "We want all of you!" You can skillfully describe your job as a piece of art, one among several in your life.

If your work is art you will know that Parkinson's Law does not apply to your job. It says that work expands to fill the time available. That may be true for a person who has not mastered craft and materials, but not for a work-artist; the vision you impose on your job's components, not work, expands to fill available time. To outward appearances you may look like a duck gliding gracefully across the lake's surface. With an artist's certainty you know that though it looks effortless, the duck's legs are paddling vigorously under water. You have done your homework with life goals and your job shows it.

Work as art includes good communication skills. These skills are invaluable for employees in Departments of Correction, which are administrative departments in many states. Using their communication skills, well-trained employees politely tell callers that no, the department does not correct errors in drivers license and birth certificates, or other mistakes. They explain that the Department handles prisoners and prisons.

Good communication includes a speaker and listener. We are generally better at initiating speech than receiving and understanding it, but work as art includes active listening. Active listening is not turning on a hearing aid but engagement. This process encourages other persons to explain exactly what they mean, and gives feedback to encourage deeper communication. The secret of good communication is positive affirmation, whatever form it takes.

To improve your communication skills on the job, I offer three foreign phrases so that you can say exactly what you mean. *Cavoli riscaldati* is an Italian phrase that means, "The attempt to revive a long-dead love affair; literally, 'to reheat dead cabbage.'" *Farpotshket* is Yiddish for "something that is all fouled up as a result of trying to fix it." Finally, *Schlimmbesserung* is German for "an improvement that makes things worse."[83] Sometimes the words will fit.

The accompanying table is a grammar guide for good written communication. Used faithfully, it can show that your job is art, not science, and that you have mastered important details of written communication.

GUIDE TO GOOD GRAMMAR
1. Verbs has to agree with their subjects. 2. Just between you and I, case is important too. 3. Make each pronoun agree with their antecedent. 4. Correct spelling is esential. 5. Try to not ever split infinitives. 6. Don't use no double negatives. 7. About those sentence fragments. 8. Join clauses good, like a conjunction should. 9. Don't write run-on sentences they are hard to read. 10. When dangling, watch your participles. 12. It is important to use your apostrophe's correctly. 13. Don't use commas, which aren't necessary. 14. A writer should not shift your point of view. 15. Don't abbreviate unless nec. 16. Check carefully to if you left any words out. 17. Last but not least, to coin a phrase, knock off the cliches.

To sum up, the employer-employee relationship is one focus in your struggle for life goals. It is not acceptable for an employer to claim all of you since you have the right to life goals, and that implies a right to life apart from work. Compartmentalizing life and work may seem to succeed for a brief spell, but the effort eventually collapses because the two are firmly linked. Burnout from work, for example, can infect all of life, and work problems seldom vanish on their own but must be faced head-on. Establishing goals in all areas of life is the best protection against an employer laying claim on your whole life. It is also the key to balanced living.

For most Americans, fitting life and work into perspective is a lifetime task. The ideal relationship is a symbiotic one since it involves unlike organisms. The best connector between them is self-responsibility; taking responsibility for work is the counterpart of taking responsibility for your life. Voluntary and involuntary job changes flow more easily when you take responsibility for life and work. In these and other transitions, new beginnings will follow endings and wildernesses if you are gentle with yourself. Taking responsibility is the essence of maturity in all phases of life, as Frank Crane says: "Responsibility is the thing people dread most of all. Yet it is the one thing in the world that develops us, gives us manhood and womanhood fibre."

Giving what is due on the job means working smart and meeting performance standards with quality and excellence. It includes handling changes on the job, taking the blame for your mistakes, innovating when possible, and using good communication skills. Your work becomes art when you master its crafts and materials and impose your vision on the job. As you succeed any wise employer will say, "We want more of you."

V
Pulled, Not Pushed

Earlier chapters covered a number of significant points about life goals. We discussed living the examined life, how to compose and envision goals, and how goals push us beyond ourselves and cost us time, money, and commitment. We saw that retraining the subconscious with new material is an integral part of forming life goals, and that the struggle for life goals puts life and work into proper perspective and leads to a balanced life. In this chapter our focus is motivation, and we will discover how life goals pull better than they push. They are tugboats, not bulldozers; pulling, not pushing.

From what I remember about physics, theoretically the same amount of energy can move an object by pulling or pushing it. A tractor can pull a 100 lb. block of cement twenty feet with a chain, or push it. Some people suggest that we also motivate ourselves and others equally by pulling or pushing. One maxim even advises, "Instead of giving yourself a pat on the back, try giving yourself a good shove."

There is no direct application of the laws of physics to human motivation. Motivation works best when it pulls you to action, not when you are pushed; life goals pull you to the future, they do not push. You frame the question of motivation with precision when you make "I" the subject of your life goals. "I" is not one of the twelve most often used words in written English,[84] but it must be the subject of every written life goal because without "I" your goals are empty bottles. How *you* get *you* to do what *you* want is pivotal. Pulling, not pushing works best.

In this chapter we examine motivation for sales and small business people. They offer a microcosms of the larger question of motivation since they struggle daily with self-motivation and persuading others to buy and work. For them, motivation and effective goals are do-or-die issues, and we learn from them.

Please do not skip this chapter if you are not active in sales or business. Isn't it possible that everyone works in these areas, whatever their station in life? We engage in a form of sales as we present ourselves to people each day, and personal and household budgets are businesses with profit and loss statements. Few people escape the challenge of negotiation in personal and family life, though they may not call it a sales tool. Stick with this chapter. Motivation is an important ingredient of your life goals and how you interact with others.

Motivation in Sales and Business

Life goals are good motivators since they lie ahead of us and pull us toward what we want with all our heart, mind, and spirit. They direct our mind's eye to the future's opportunities, and they yank us out of mindless preoccupation into the realm of new possibility. Life goals extract us from the clutches of a subconscious that replays old scenes and thwarts new skills and interests. They draw us out of ourselves and propel us toward new selves. Life goals stretch our minds and bodies to turn hopes into reality; they snatch us away from procrastination and deliver us from petty preoccupations. No wonder that we jump with anticipation toward a future that is vividly portrayed in our mind!

But what if life goals are pushers, not pullers? Then the following description applies. Life goals drag us down since they nip at our buttocks. They push us toward things about which we hesitate, and they elbow us in our preoccupation so that perhaps we notice a doorway down the hall. Life goals goad us into battling subconscious wishes to repeat the tried and true, crowding us out of ourselves in hopes that we find the new equally interesting. These goals prod us to think about our hopes, harass us to stop procrastinating, and smash our petty preoccupations.

Read again the two preceding paragraphs and you will appreciate the difference between motivational pulling and pushing. Life goals are great motivators, pulling us to a different outlook. They uncork our deepest hopes and explore new futures. That is why—and how—they pull us.

This truth also applies in sales and business since the nature of motivation is the same as for life goals. The future counts for people in sales and business, and the customer and client's future counts. Pull-motivation changes how they see themselves and their clients, and it gets the best results in motivating customers and employees. Push-motivation comes in a distant second.

Pulling Yourself

My understanding of human nature is that people like both pushes and pulls, with a natural predisposition toward pushing, but they come to prefer the motivational power of pulling the more they experience it. As we learn to motivate ourselves by pulling we change behavior and make choices different from the past. Pulling opens the future, and although it has boundaries the future offers options different than the past.

Pull-motivation changes the way you look at yourself. How? You are no mere object to be pushed from behind; something new and different can now attract you. The distinction is important, and this is the miracle of life goals. They give people a sense of self-worth that may have been lacking. They attract us and we deem ourselves attractive as a result. For some people it is a new way of seeing and understanding themselves.

The same is true for people working in sales and business. When the operative word is "pull-motivation" rather than "push-motivation," the future attracts them and they view themselves as appealing. Do not be surprised if sales and productivity increase as a result. Once learned, this secret of self-motivation is also a powerful tool in motivating others.

If you tell yourself not to do something in sales or business, your message usually reinforces the old behavior. A better approach is setting a positive goal that redirects behavior and pulls it in a new direction. Psychologists say that children respond to negative reinforcement by repeating the behavior. Frequently telling a child not to pick her nose reinforces the activity, and for a simple reason: negative comments bolster the behavior by drawing attention to it. An alternative is handing the child a tissue, and in time the nose-picking should stop.

Push-motivation also diminishes self-responsibility. Usually you can find someone or something to blame for what goes wrong, and somebody else can be the fall-guy. Negative behavior continues until you take responsibility for changing it with a goal that you want to achieve.

This circular process reminds me of a minister who moved to a "preacher-eater" church that had a bad reputation for devouring clergymen. While he was storing his things in the church desk, the newest minister found a packet left by the previous pastor. It held three sealed envelopes and a brief note saying that he should open the three envelopes when things got tough. After several months of turmoil the new pastor opened envelope One, which said, "Blame the last pastor." He did. Everything that went wrong was the last pastor's fault. Many members agreed and for a while the church was quiet. Then the members grew restless again and the pastor opened envelope Two. It said, "Blame the denomination." He did, and the people joined him in condemning higher headquarters. This worked for several months when things turned sour again. In quiet desperation the minister ripped open envelope Three. It said, "Prepare three envelopes." Yes, push-motivation has its drawbacks.

Pull-motivation works best since it surprises you. Surprise of surprises, *you* are ahead of you! You have taken responsibility for living life and achieving your goals, and you are pulling yourself. You no longer rely on sales managers and others to push you into an unknown future since you have preceded them, cutting your own path. Only you have the responsibility for reorganizing your life, and pulling yourself into the future is the way you do it. Unlike corporations, individuals cannot file for reorganization under Chapter 11; no bankruptcy court will give you months or years to reorganize yourself to face new circumstances. Time is short and you must act with conviction.

Nature recently taught me an important lesson about the role of motivation in adjusting to circumstances. A curved bill thrasher landed on a block wall by my door. This 11-inch bird had only one leg, but it did not lack the motivation to get to the feeder. Standing on one leg, the thrasher extended its long tail in the other direction for balance. There was a future out there and seed to find, and being one-legged was no deterrent.

David Stevens is a twenty-six-year-old television sports producer in Minneapolis. Eight years ago, he graduated from a small high school in Wickenberg, Arizona, where he played varsity baseball. At the coach's invitation, he returned to the school in 1992 to help coach the season's opener, and before game time he helped the team warm up by snagging ground balls and shagging pop flies. The opposing team gave the

Wickenberg players the once over, but their eyes lingered on David Stevens.

He stands about three-feet, two-inches tall and was born without legs. When playing sports he shelves his artificial limbs since they slow him down. He says, "I move along on my hands and lower body. I sort of swivel and roll and scoot right along. It works just fine." In high school he lettered in baseball, football, and wrestling, reaching the state wrestling tournament two times. While he was in college his adoptive parents died, but he pressed on. "The definition for *can't* is to not do something. I always thought I could at least try," he adds, attributing success to being his own coach over the years. "Many people didn't know what or how to coach me. But as the years went by, I got better and better." Wickenberg's coach says that Stevens should be measured by "the size of his heart—not his body."[85] His tenacity is a pull-spirit. Stevens shows that handicaps and circumstances, including those in sales and business, cannot deter a person pulled to a different future.

You and I have met salespeople who know the value of pull-motivation. They are educated and they have personalities, personal characteristics, and work habits that make them effective. Good salespeople are good communicators who show enthusiasm and conviction in their work. They are people-sensitive, need-sensitive, persistent, imaginative, and dedicated to growth. Their work habits show initiative, they respond quickly to customer demands, and they have the capacity to risk rejection.[86] These characteristics apply to good business persons too. Owners who lack them probably have grouches for customers and slouches for employees.

A *Wall Street Journal* article once described five "prerequisites" for good salespeople. They include believing in your product, believing in yourself, working on timing, developing a sense of humor, and realizing that "your customer isn't necessarily telling you what he wants." Writer Mack McCormack then told what it takes to be a "supersalesperson." He urged salespeople to "knock on old doors" since old customers are the best prospects. Making your obsession their obsession creates common ground emotionally while you cultivate interest and generate buying. Supersalespeople thrive in uncrowded territories, catching big fish in little ponds. They bring something fresh to every party, and their second visit maintains momentum with new information and new approaches since rehashing the first call is not enough. Supersalespeople back-pedal aggressively when necessary and are not afraid to say, "This is probably not right for you. Let's defer it for another time." Finally, they remove objections gently, without the customer noticing. Good salespeople engage in cultivating and educating, not in demolishing the customer's viewpoints.[87]

Supersalespeople have learned an important lesson from life's sales manual. It is that pulling yourself to a goal works more effectively than pushing. Once learned, you automatically use the process face-to-face with customers and clients.

Good sales and business people know about an Italian economist and sociologist named Vilfredo Pareto (died 1923), although they may not have read any of his books. He formulated the 80/20 rule, which throws a great deal of light on their work. Pareto's principle holds that significant items in any group are a small percentage of all items in that group. His was the idea of the "vital few" and "trivial many." While not one hundred percent accurate, the idea has great merit. For instance, in any discussion probably twenty percent of the participants contribute eighty percent of the comments, and eighty percent of a company's absenteeism may be due to twenty percent of its employees.

Salespeople may know that eighty percent of their sales usually come from twenty percent of the customers, but they may not realize that eighty percent of their success could result from using pull-motivation in twenty percent of their goals. They could probably increase effectiveness by eighty percent if they changed their method of prospecting a mere twenty percent by using pull-motivation. If they changed twenty percent of their dress habits they might influence eighty percent of the impressions they make on others. Many applications of the 80/20 rule are valid.

Fear of rejection is often a major hurdle in cold-calling on new prospects. As a result, some salespeople freeze in their tracks or delay cold-calling to a time that never comes. Fear of rejection can grow to enormous proportions and become a counter-motivator that prevents action. A salesperson can regain the initiative with a pull-motivator that controls this fear. One simple method is putting a rubber band on your wrist. When fear rears its ugly head, take the initiative, grab the rubber band, and snap it against your wrist. In the process tell yourself, "That is the worst that can happen to me, and it is over." Then let the pull-motivation of a friendly sales encounter entice you into dialing numbers or entering doors. By seizing control you pull yourself to a different future.

Since appearance is important, pull-motivation can also change how you dress for sales and business. Studies show that customers notice what salespeople wear and whether they "look good" in their clothes. Some people try to meet this challenge every day by asking what they should wear. A better way is to use pull-motivation by making your clothes compatible with your skin color.

Have you noticed that clothes of a certain color look glamorous on some people and ghastly on others? One reason is the skin's variations in hue. Blue-based (cool) and yellow-based (warm) subcutaneous skin palettes influence how you look in various colors. People generally fit into one of four color categories called winter, spring, summer, and autumn. Wearing clothes that match your palette enhances your face, making you look younger and more confident.[88] Dressing right includes more than color, but we can make a difference with the shades we wear. If pull-motivation is looking our best in sales and business, we relieve daily stress by "coloring" ourselves with clothes that match our complexion. Expending twenty percent of our effort here may take care of eighty percent of our dress problems and pull us into an exciting future.

One thing for sales and business people to avoid is pulling a con job on themselves. We need to recognize the racketeer's problem when he tried to hire a professional gunman with the promise, "We'll give you ten grand for this job, tax free." What do you think of the three men in Germany who mixed millions of gallons of cheap wine with sugar syrup and sold it as highly prized German wine? The men peddled eleven million gallons of the stuff between 1977 and 1982, labeling it top quality Rhine wine and duping official testers.[89] Perhaps they fooled themselves as well.

That is the con artist's nature, whether in sales or business. The first victim is the perpetrator himself since he pulls himself so forcefully into an illegal future that he sees it as legal. Sales and business people owe it first to themselves to ensure that their actions and procedures are legal, moral, and beyond reproach. Like all human tools, pull-motivation is susceptible to distortion and misapplication. The purpose of pull-motivation is changing self for legitimate purposes, not changing into a con artist.

Pull-Motivating Others

Pull-motivation also works better than pushing in motivating others. Offering future attractions moves customers and employees more effectively than threatening, and produces less tension.

We discover this truth as we work with life goals. They enable us to mold ourselves to new contours, and this alters how people see us. Our change produces changes in others because we change people by changing ourselves. For instance, consider a woman whose life goal is being more loving to her spouse verbally, physically, and emotionally. By changing herself she may see important changes in her spouse.

It is important to count the cost before committing yourself to a pull-motivation goal, whether a life or short-term goal. Part of the cost calculation is whether you want to influence others through this goal, and your answer may be the determining factor in whether you proceed.

The following table evaluates your commitment to life goal costs. Use it to evaluate your goal list. Choose one goal for the quiz, indicating your answer (one to ten) for each question. How you answer the last question is vital if you are considering goals in business or sales but less important for certain other goals.

COUNTING THE COST OF A LIFE GOAL									
Minimal, not very			Medium			High			
1	2	3	4	5	6	7	8	9	10
How important is this goal to you?									
How strong is your internal resistance to achieving this goal?									
How strong is the external resistance to achieving this goal?									
How much time, energy, and money are required for you to achieve this goal?									
What are your chances of achieving this goal?									
How much does this goal influence or change others?									

The Golden Rule says, "Do unto others as you would have them do unto you." Can we do less in motivating others? If pulling ourselves works best, can we achieve better results in motivating others by pulling instead of pushing? Do you not have more confidence when you see someone calling you from ahead than when you look back at someone pushing? In sales and business, people sense whether you are pushing or pulling yourself. If you are pulling, your pulling-self tows customers into the future, and they are more apt to follow.

One problem we face in motivating others is that we are too quick to categorize people. After classifying a person we recall how we motivated that group in the past, and then push like we pushed the group previously.

The classifications we use sound as odd as collective nouns for some animal groups. A murder of crows? A clowder of cats? A leap of leopards? A rafter of turkeys? A skulk of foxes? A peep of chickens? A knot of toads? A parliament of owls? A gaggle of geese?[90] What categories fit the people you meet in sales and business? Is it a snooze of old fogies? A whelp of teenagers? A mouth of young willow-snappers? A hulk of musclemen? A pocket of tightwads? Classifications are more useful for motivating people by pushing, not pulling.

Fear moves us to classify people into groups. Whether on a car lot or in a discussion group, we feel more at ease if we can pigeonhole people. This lets us relate to them on our own terms instead of pulling them along on theirs. Overcoming this fear is the beginning of wisdom in sales and business.

This fear is like a skeleton that frighten us. Just before Halloween Dr. Wayne Oates, a well-known counselor, took his four-year-old son to Caulfield's Novelty Shop. The show window featured costumes and a "for-real" human skeleton. The boy asked what the skeleton was, and Dr. Oates explained that we all have one inside to help us stand and walk and hold our bodies together. His son asked, "You mean I have one of those *things* inside me?" After his dad said yes the boy shook himself, drew into a knot, hugged himself with both arms and said, "Brrrr! That scares me!"[91]

Declassifying people and letting them be themselves is the first step in motivating by pulling, not pushing. When people can be themselves they tell you which categories they fit, if any. You may have to look your fear skeletons in the eye to do this, but you receive rich rewards.

Story-telling is an effective use of pull-motivation in sales and business, as in the rest of life. Good sales and business persons know the value of testimonials and stories because their plots declassify people by addressing the whole person. A good storyteller touches deep emotional chords while sharing a rational question that is worth considering. Stories also combine teaching and learning, which is the essence of sales and business ability.

Some salespeople do not know where to begin with stories while others do not know when to end. I file stories and real-life incidents in a folder, including personal experiences and others that are fictitious. I review the file while preparing to make a personal call, but how do you pick the right story?

A famous rabbi was known for answering every question with a story. Once a student asked, "Rabbi, how do you pick the right story for every occasion?" With an impish grin the rabbi replied, "That reminds me of a story." He told of a young soldier who stopped in a small village to rest his horse. While walking around a house he spied a wood fence with forty small chalk circles and a bullet hole in the center of each one. What amazing accuracy, he thought to himself. Every shot hit the bull's-eye! He asked who was the sharpshooter and discovered that it was a small boy. "Who taught you to shoot so well," he quizzed the boy? "I taught myself," the boy said. "How did you develop this skill," he continued? "Actually it is not very difficult," the boy answered. "First I shoot at the wall and then I take a piece of chalk and draw circles around the holes." The rabbi paused, chuckled, looked at his student, and said, "Now you know my secret. I don't look for a story to answer a question. I collect every good story or parable I hear and store it in my mind. When the right occasion or question arises, I point the story in its direction. I simply draw a circle around a hole that is already there."[92]

Good sales and business people know that every person they meet is a walking story waiting to be told. Some people's names have entered the language as words because of their life stories. Amelia Bloomer popularized bloomers after she first wore them in 1851. Irish tenant farmers ignored Captain Charles C. Boycott when he tried to collect high rents from them in the 19th century, and his name became a word. A soldier named Nicolas Chauvin suffered wounds seventeen times under Napoleon, and because he praised the French leader incessantly, "chauvinism" became a word for blind attachment. Rudolph Diesel invented a motor ignited by compression, the diesel engine. Other who lent their names as words were Braille, Lynch, Quisling, and General Ambrose Burnside (sideburns).

In sales and business it is never too early to ask people about their life stories and to involve the whole person by using stories. Getting people to tell their story is part of what we call pull-motivation. This process encourages customers to reveal themselves and their needs and wants. Since that is a prerequisite for sales, stories and testimonials are powerful sales tools.

Leadership is as much a part of sales and business as of life, and we use the term "leaders" to describe people we want to follow. The best ones have a vision of the future that draws us along as they guide. Business, sales, political, and organizational leaders lead best by pulling, not pushing.

An important facet of leadership is how you view others and interact with them. Sam Walton built a small-town five and dime store into a multi-billion dollar chain while calling Wal-Mart employees "associates." He was one of them, and they were part of what he was. That is the nature of leadership in the 90s; leaders pull people toward definite goals but remember that they are part of the crowd.

The day of the overpowering, dominant, know-it-all leader is over. General Dwight Eisenhower defined leadership as "the art of getting someone else to do something you want done because he wants to do it," and he was right. Our society no longer allows leaders to rely on coercion and authority. Now leaders must learn to make decisions, use influence, and project visions and hopes for change. True leaders use pull-motivation on themselves, and in the process they become pull-motivators for others.

Leaders recognize that things are complicated and they may not have all the answers. They rely on all available expertise, making leadership interdepartmental in nature. Leaders recognize that followers are taking the lead and making policy; they know like surfers that it is not always easy to catch a wave, but they help followers go where they want to go. Finally, leaders have a special obligation to cultivate optimism. As generalists they often see beyond the gloom and doom of experts and specialists, who can never know enough.[93] They know that experts make mistakes. In summary, leaders seek a consensus, make constructive use of ambiguity, and take the initiative while others get the credit. A Chinese public administrator put it well in the third century B.C. when he wrote, "Of a good leader, who talks little, when his work is done, his task fulfilled, they will all say, 'We did this ourselves.'"

Working with employees, sales colleagues, and organizations, good leaders carefully distinguish between people and the machines they operate. When industrialization swept the world in the 19th and 20th centuries many people mistakenly welded workers to their machines, at least psychologically. Eventually these views lowered sensitivity for workers, who were seen as mere cogs in the assembly line. Postwar industrial management in Japan and elsewhere recognized the fallacy of this approach. Productivity depends on "soft" human relationships, not on carrying out massive seven-year industrial plans. Treating people as cogs leads to a dead end, as we have seen in the collapse of Eastern European communism. Productivity depends in large part on personal goals and the goals of groups of workers; their sense of freedom contributes to the operation's well-being. In brief, productivity works best with pull, not push-motivation. Good business and sales leaders recognize that productivity planning that ignores the human spirit will encounter trouble.

Productivity is something like raising cows. Your success depends on the system in which you are operating. People joke that in socialism if you have two cows, the government takes both and gives you some skim milk. In Marxism, you are a capitalist if you have two cows. For the idealist, if you have two cows you imagine one is a bull and wait for the miracle that never happens. Under rugged individualism, if you have two cows that are dry, you sell them to a neighbor for double their value and then condemn the government for taxing your profit. Like real cow-raising, however, real productivity happens when people cooperate to achieve common goals and assimilate human freedom in their plans. That is pull-motivation.

Good sales and business people are first and foremost consultants because this approach puts a premium on pull-motivation. The key to sales, growth, and financial success is solving the customer's problem. A consultant gives no answer before he knows the question; neither does he offer meaningless advice. Sales ability at its best is consulting at its finest. A good salesperson discovers the customer's fleeting glimpse of a goal, hops onto it and tracks it, and then consults while the buyer pulls himself to that future. Good sales and business ability is problem-solving—offering solutions after unearthing problems. Poor sales and business people provide solutions to problems that people do not have, or try to fill wants and needs they cannot articulate. Poor sales ability is like the solar-powered nuclear fallout shelters peddled in the 1950s: "going solar" held little promise in the face of possible nuclear war.

People in sales and business face negotiations each day, just as bargaining is often part of family and organizational life. Too often we negotiate over positions, haggling until we do or do not reach agreement, but the best negotiation is a form of consulting. Here are four essentials of good negotiating:

(1) separate the people from the problem;

(2) focus on interests, not positions;

(3) generate a variety of possibilities before deciding what to do, and invent options for mutual gain;

(4) insist that results should be based on some objective standard or criterion, and use that to reach agreement.

In separating people from the problem it helps to acknowledge emotions as legitimate, not destructive. Put yourself in the other party's shoes, discuss each other's perceptions, and recognize the difference between your fears and their intentions. To focus on interests and not positions, identify interests by asking "why?" Look forward, not back, and be hard on the problem and soft on people. Find out what positions will satisfy the interests of both parties and what will be the consequences if you do what the other party seeks. In generating possibilities, avoid premature judgment, the "one answer," and an "either-or" mentality. To create options, separate inventing from deciding, brainstorm separately and together, look through the eyes of different experts, seek mutual gain, and dovetail differing interests. To base results on some objective standard, remember that it is costly for both parties to decide on the basis of raw will. What objective standards will settle a problem? Develop these criteria and test them with someone for fairness.[94]

Before any negotiation, sales and business people, spouses, and the rest of us should repeat the old rhyme,

Jack Sprat could eat no fat
His wife could eat no lean,
And so betwixt them both
They licked the platter clean!

Negotiations merge the divergent interests of people. After all, negotiating differences is not a process for assigning one party to heaven and the other to hell.

No one should underestimate the importance of the salesperson's first contact with a client. Customers indelibly record your first words and the first impression you make. Prepare carefully, since first impressions are not easily overcome. As lawyers say, this is time for evidence. Your introductory visit will show how much you value pull-motivation. Preparing a presentation book especially tailored for this buyer confirms that you are out front and leading, and the way you dress proves that you care enough to present the best possible image. Your first words reveal whether you are a pull-motivating consultant or a pusher answering unasked questions.

Salespeople should take "persistence" as their middle name. Some authorities suggest that up to seven contacts may be needed for most buyers to buy, so stopping at three is too early. If out-front motivation pulls people along to do their best, they will stick to the task as long as necessary. An old evangelist named Bud Robinson used this prayer daily, and with slight alteration it has the makings of the prayer of a persistent person:

O Lord, give me a backbone as big as a saw log and ribs like the sleepers under the church floor. Put iron shoes on my feet and galvanized breeches on my body. Give me a rhinoceros hide for skin, and hang up a wagon-load of determination in the gable-end of my soul. Help me to sign the contract to fight the devil as long as I've got a tooth—and then gum him until I die.

Christopher Morley said it well, "Big shots are only little shots who keep shooting." Persistence plays a critical role in closing sales since the buyer's act of commitment spells success in sales and business.

To close a sale and close it well, sales and business persons should cultivate their powers of observation. This little-used tool of human perception gives great insight into the buyer's perspective and readiness to consummate a purchase. The problem is that too often we are unobservant. For instance, have you noticed the religious symbol found on about 50% of all supermarket food items? The "U" with a circle around it shows that the item is "kosher" and contains no animal products. Some stock carries a "K."

Learning to be observant is a commitment to little things, but when tallied little things can give big signals. We learn this from a young man who studied Zen with a mentor for 25 years, and finally he told his guide that he was entering the world to become a mentor himself. Although he had reservations, the old master gave his blessing. After some years the young teacher returned to visit, and since it was raining he left his clogs and umbrella outside when he entered the house. The wise old man's first question had an odd ring as he asked, "Tell me, did you put your umbrella to the left or right of your clogs?" The young teacher's face grew red since he could not remember. Once more he became a student, practicing the art of constant alertness and observation for ten more years.

Observing body language can be helpful since it shows how people interact. Body language occurs in independent actions and in batches, with a group of actions usually providing the best information. Sales and business people learn much about themselves and their customers from closely observing body language. Videotaping sales encounters offers the chance to review and modify the body language of salespeople.

The seating arrangement of an office puts body language in furniture form. Relationships of space between people are important clues, and full body movements are valuable signals. Other signs are when a person folds his arms across the chest, crosses his legs, or extends fingers like a steeple (he may be showing superiority). Facial expressions can show smugness, anger, surprise, and sadness, and hand-to-face gestures may suggest interest (tugging on the ear to hear better) or lack of interest (putting a hand over the mouth, as if holding back words). A finger or object to the mouth may show a desire to interrupt or gain time for thinking, while a hand to the eye may indicate that the person does not want to see what you have. Hand-wringing implies anxiety, and this is a good time for the salesperson to offer relief with a story. Signals of boredom should never be taken lightly.

Closing the sale begins with your introduction to the buyer and continues throughout the relationship. It includes your alertness to small signals and your capacity to elicit positive answers to your many questions. Good closers show pull-motivation in action since they stand at the goal and pull the buyer closer at each step of the relationship. Other points are approaching problems from different angles and fearlessness in asking for the signature. Good closers already know what the hearing clinic at Northeastern University discovered, namely, that "no" is the hardest word to hear in the English language.

Good closers get excited when an objection accompanies "no." Most objections are handled best when they arise, but sometimes deferral is appropriate. Closers listen carefully to an objection before responding, and then restate it to see if they understand it. Their consultation has led them to conclude that the buyer wants or needs the item, so they understand objections as veiled questions. Since most objections relate to needs, price, and product quality, closers meet them by reselling benefits; offering a counterstatement of benefits is not disagreeing with a client. When handled appropriately, objections bring out the brilliance of pull-motivation in action because the essence of closing is weighing benefits against objections.

Sales and business concerns recognize the value of Pareto's 80/20 principle in much that they do. They want to learn which twenty percent of their closing methods land eighty percent of their contracts, and which eighty percent of their closing methods seldom pay off. Which negotiating methods (20%) lead most often to solutions and which (80%) are usually fruitless? Why do eighty percent of the salespeople stop too soon in their contacts with customers while the twenty percent who persist land the business? How can managers increase the number (20%) of salespeople who use pull-motivation on themselves and their clients? Why do pushers (80%) hit the jackpot less frequently?

Good sales and business people take full responsibility for the blather that too often fills encounters with customers. Nothing stifles sales like dullness. It gives the weary customer nothing to look forward to except the end of the presentation, and that seems light-years away. Boring talk, dull advertising, and flat sales presentations are not the customer's fault. When your motivation is pull-motivation you take responsibility for fresh, lively presentations.

People who make boring presentations remind me of the "Library of Babel," a grim tale by Jorge Luis Borges. The Library of Babel extended infinitely because it held all of the books and manuscripts that ever could be written. Librarians scurried from room to room looking at everything, but soon there was little joy in being in a library that contained all the books of the world, past and future. Why? No one knew how or where to find the books they needed. Furthermore, librarians and scholars became phantoms since they knew the library held all the books that could be written. What more could they do?[95]

Being boring is telling people what they either already know or do not want to know. It fills the airwaves with irrelevant data. Like the Library of Babel, a bore knows it all. He makes no connection with the living person who happens to be a customer, elicits and tells no testimonials or stories, and allows little opportunity for interchange. How do customers know they are in a bore's presence? When they count for nothing, their real wants and feelings are unexpressed and ignored, and the wait is as interminable as walking through an endless library. These customers have no doubt that colorless salespeople push instead of pull.

Pull-motivation gives freshness and vitality to advertising, marketing, and sales presentations. Customers are always front and center as we call them to the future, and we answer their questions and incorporate their real needs and wishes. We do everything we can to pull them forward since that worked well for us. Dare we do otherwise with them?

Pull-motivation works because it opens new possibilities. It changes how we see ourselves and how we see our customers; we are not objects to be pushed from behind, nor are they. Goals pull us like magnets, and we help customers find the same joy of fulfilling their needs, wants, and goals. Being in sales or business is not a pushing contest but a mercantile activity in which people find joy and fulfillment in the benefits of their purchases. Like life goals that open new futures, these goals unlock futures for the sales and business people who pursue them. They are the waves of the future for customers who want to look ahead at someone calling, not behind at someone pushing.

Business and Sales Goals

You may be surprised to see the resemblance between life goals and goals for sales and business. For success, both rely on a firm combination of thought and feeling. Thought alone seldom produces good action results while emotion apart from thinking can immobilize a person (although it may produce a catharsis). Fusing thought and feeling is the key to formulating and achieving life goals and business and sales goals. When we weld the two we create a dynamic unit where the whole is greater than its parts. We use visioning as the point of blending since seeing our completed goals in Technicolor intensifies the will to achieve them.

The best business and sales goals unite thought and feeling. Because they are well-formulated and "visible" to the minds and hearts of employees, they motivate to action. The Air Force Chief of Staff recently announced a well-formulated vision statement for the United States Air Force. It says, "Air Force people building the world's most respected air and space force...Global power and reach for America." This statement fuses thinking and feeling and builds toward action.

Formulating Sales and Business Goals

The Swiss psychiatrist Carl Jung described two primary ways that people "see" what they perceive and process as information. People who see in a "sensing" way pay close attention to the senses and attune themselves to sight, sound, taste, touch, and smell. Jung called "intuition" the second way of "seeing." It focuses on the big picture by combining many different impressions. People who "see" this way arrive at a hunch about how the facts add up. Both ways of "seeing" are equally valuable, but few, if any, perceive data both ways at once. One result is that two persons can witness the same accident and offer varying perceptions of what happened.

What is the relation between Jung's view and business and sales goals? His study helps us understand the importance of fusing thought and emotion when formulating these goals. Thought and feeling are probably the closest working equivalents we have to the two ways of "seeing."

Well-formulated sales and business goals speak to both kinds of people that Jung describes, the sensory-oriented and the "gut instinct, intuitive" person. Good sales and business goals provide the big picture along with sensory data, taking into consideration both those people who first see the forest and those who first see the trees. Welding thought and emotion is the closest parallel.

According to recent studies the human brain has left and right sides. The left side predominates in most people so they are right-handed and right-eyed. Even more importantly, the left side of the brain has major responsibility for logical thinking and reason while the right side is the emotive, intuitive, artistic, child-playful side.

Formulating sales and business goals should be a whole-brain activity leading to goals that appeal to the whole person. Number-crunching alone will not satisfy the right side of people's minds, so goals should also have playful and artistic elements to captivate the whole person. Fusing thought and emotion produces the best sales and business goals because employees and salespeople are intrigued by goals that cover the full range of human interest.

Personalities combine thought and emotion in goals in different ways, with every person contributing his wrinkle. For example, my father, who was a Chevrolet dealer in a small town, seldom expressed emotion, but one day I was startled to hear him say, "I am going to sell a car to Bud Smith." He did not say that he was excited about calling on Bud and selling the car. What surprised me was not his goal but the fact that he announced his goal to me, complete with Bud's name. He pulled emotion into his goal by announcing it to his ten-year-old son. The way he viewed it, that act cemented an emotional covenant between us and intensified his goal by marrying thought and emotion. Others wrap emotion into their sales or business goals in more expressive ways. They shake with excitement as they announce their weekly sales goal, visibly showing the role of emotion in their goal-setting.

Sales and business executives can learn an easy lesson about fusing thought and action in goals. It comes from a game invented in 1932 by an unemployed salesperson in New York City. The game appealed to thought and emotion, with a healthy dose of chance thrown in, although Parker Brothers first refused to market it because it took too long to play and violated fifty-two rules of good game design. Now there are world championships and players enjoy the game in fifty countries. People can clobber their best friends without damage. Sets are published in foreign languages and Braille, and on non-combustible paper for NASA astronauts.[96] The game is Monopoly.

What attracts people to Monopoly is the same thing that appeals to employees and sales associates in well-designed goals. The game is fun, takes skill (thought), and generates strong feelings of greed, success, and failure. And it acknowledges that chance plays a role in life (company computers show that Monopoly's most common roll of the dice is seven). This blending of thought and feeling attracts millions of players.

Since they combine thought and emotion, good sales and business goals are framed around customer benefits. Let's take an example. You are the sales manager for an automobile dealer and are responsible for formulating this week's sales goal. You compile two options. The first says, "At the end of the week we are celebrating the sale of eight new vehicles." The second says, "On Saturday we see eight satisfied and smiling customers as they drive their new cars shopping, visiting relatives, and going to the mountains." Which goal would make more sense if you were a salesperson in this agency? Which would motivate you more? Which merges thought and feeling more effectively?

Selling benefits is the common denominator in sales and business, so why should we ignore this fulcrum in constructing goals? Sales and business organizations tap a well-stream of vitality with goals that tout customer benefits since employees and sales associates are more apt to work for other people's benefits than for a number like "eleven units sold." Goals that incorporate customer benefits firmly connect buyers with the people achieving the goals. This process depends on people (sales people and customers) having common thoughts and feelings; without this commonality the opportunity for a sale diminishes.

Advertising and marketing goals should be formulated with the same precision. The best advertising sells benefits and not products, and marketing procedures have the same focus. These activities pay off when they ring the customer's benefit bell. A good measure of goal effectiveness is how well the goals incorporate customer value. In case it is necessary, Derby Brown gives us this reminder about the need to advertise: "The business that considers itself immune to the necessity for advertising sooner or later finds itself immune to business."

Effective marketing and advertising focuses on the customer and the product attributes that the customer wants or needs. Too often advertising touts attributes that are of little concern to customers. One way to stay on track is to ask customers about your products and services; customer focus groups can serve this purpose. Visiting competitors as a customer is an eye-opening experience for some, and contacting customers of competitors to see why you missed the sale is another.

Naturally, marketing and advertising are susceptible to misinterpretation. We exercise great care to ensure that sales slogans are not misunderstood due to cultural, linguistic, or economic differences. However, sometimes success evades even professionals. For example, the Chevrolet Nova encountered trouble in Puerto Rico since "No va" in Spanish meant "It doesn't go." "Body by Fisher" became "Corpse by Fisher" in Flemish, and General Motors had to return to the drawing board. Translation gave a new twist to the Pepsi slogan "Come alive with Pepsi" when it read in Chinese, "Pepsi brings your ancestors back from the grave."[97]

Again we can draw on Pareto's 80/20 rule in evaluating advertising techniques and sales and business goals. Which twenty percent of our goals draw eighty percent more cooperation from sales associates and employees? Why? Do we formulate eighty percent of our goals to land in employee trash cans? Which business and sales goals weld thought and emotion most effectively? Which advertising and marketing techniques do the same?

Operating procedures in sales and business are of more than passing interest. Among them are employee manuals, accounting procedures, purchasing policies, and the myriad standard procedures in organizations of all sizes. Is it time to review them to learn how effectively they weld thought and feeling? This is a relevant question since company "policies" are seldom designed as operating instructions for a machine. Policies are codified goal statements about how a company operates, and they usually include specific procedures. Many employees ignore them because they slight the people to whom they are addressed.

Another standard practice is using Boilerplate letters. This allows a secretary to respond to a customer's request or complaint by assembling selected paragraphs in a computerized letter. This procedure saves time and money, but customer relations agents and executives know that some customers demand personalized attention. In writing letters of complaint one writer always inserts what he calls the "Pullman paragraph" to shame companies into a personalized response. This is the paragraph:

> *I am reminded of the man who wrote a letter to the Pullman Company back in the 1940s complaining of bedbugs in his sleeping car. He received a very apologetic letter saying that this was the first they had ever heard of such a thing, and that all the cars were being fumigated as a response to his letter. Along with his letter was enclosed, by mistake, the original letter of complaint the man had sent. Written by hand at the bottom of the letter was: "Send this SOB the bedbug letter." I certainly hope that I will not receive a "bedbug" letter from you.*[98]

Like standard operating procedures, Boilerplate letters must be personalized.

Goal-Linked Action

Well-crafted business and sales goals are of little use without action. When goals fuse thinking and feeling well, chances are good that employees and sales associates will press toward action. Then, too, a goal with a finely-tuned balance between thought and feeling can prevent extremes on both sides.

Acting without thinking can nearly get you killed, even if you are a bona fide hero. Einar H. Ingman, a Medal of Honor winner, took command of a squad when its leader fell during the Korean War, and he added another squad when its leader was wounded. Spearheading the charge against a Chinese machine-gun nest, Ingman had an ear blown off when a grenade exploded a foot from his head, but he charged ahead and a rifle bullet hit him in the face. Dazed, he killed ten Chinese with bayonet and rifle, then staggered away and collapsed. He later said, "That bullet through my head kind of made me quit thinking."[99]

Many people have much less reason for not thinking than Corporal Ingman. Goal-linked action that is not well designed wastes energy since thinking is supposed to be a shortcut across intervening steps. Effective goals that combine thinking and feeling usually require additional thought to implement.

On the other side, good business and sales goals also teach us to avoid excessive emotion. Juxtaposing thought and emotion, they can check emotional excesses that might hinder sales. For example, language sometimes carries baggage that undercuts our sales efforts. In 1980 the U.N. General Secretary traveled to Iran to deal with the hostage crisis. On arrival in Tehran, he reportedly said, "I have come as a *mediator* to work out a *compromise*." Angry Iranians stoned his car within an hour after his televised appearance. In Iranian culture, "compromise" lacked any positive meaning, and the Farsi word for "mediator" meant "meddler."[100] Emotions ruled the day and undercut the effort.

A balanced combination of thought and emotion also molds good sales and marketing work. A salesperson filled with emotional vitality but empty of head generally wins few sales trophies. Similarly, a precise, logical description of a product may earn engineering awards but generate few sales. Like their sales colleagues, business managers mix thought and emotion well so the people they manage know they are people, not things.

Sales and business people regularly evaluate their actions to see how well they are linked with organizational goals. While management consultants collect millions for performing this essential task of review, local managers who do the job well can keep the money in-house for the bottom line. Usually the biggest problem in evaluation is the lack of clearly defined goals against which to measure activities. The critical question to ask is this: Why do we do this or that in sales or business if it has no direct link with an accepted goal? Ruthless pruning deletes activities that do not support goals.

Managers can also use the 80/20 rule to evaluate the success of various sales and business actions. The Pareto principle can help control costs (which operation produces the desired response and which does not?) and crop the bureaucracy's tendency to multiply. As they age most businesses tend toward top-heaviness, with an increasing number of managers and supervisors, but they find that adding managers does not necessarily increase productivity. If twenty percent of the managers do eighty percent of the work, what are the others doing? A study of the British Royal Navy early in the 20th century showed that the number of admirals always increased more rapidly than the number of seamen. That was true even when the number of seamen fell.[101]

Visioning leads to action in business and sales goals, just as in life goals. Visioning well defined, written goals unites thinking and emotion. You see what you are thinking about and have the added pleasure of joining emotion to goal achievement.

While some people in sales and business daydream more

than they vision, seeing the image of an accomplished goal is better than dreaming about what if and why not. A twenty-two-year-old German immigrant named Gerhard Mennen probably could not have started the Mennen Company with daydreams in 1878, when he owned a New Jersey drug store. After a singing banjo player on a horse and wagon warmed the crowd, Mennen told the people that his "sure corn killer" for feet was available at drug stores. In 1889 he introduced Mennen's Borated Talcum Infant Powder for use by mothers instead of corn starch and chalk powder. His shaving cream in a tube was a first for Americans in 1912, and soon the Mennen company became a sales giant. Visioning brings more results than daydreaming.

Many of the same techniques used for picturing life goals are applicable to business and sales goals. Meditating, self-massage, and pausing throughout the day with relaxation imagery can help in visioning goals. One writer recommends a special "creature" to combine thought and feeling when the time comes for you to review a goal-blocking problem.

Dr. Art Ulene says that both sides of the brain are the key in problem-solving, so he suggests that you create a "personal creature" such as a pet rabbit, monkey, dog, or other animal or bird. Give it a name, and when you meet a problem, vision yourself with your pet creature in the picture. Discuss the problem with your pet, but do not rely only on words. This form of guided imagery draws on the visual-imaginative (right) side of the brain and the verbal (left) side. You unleash both the brain's quick, visual power and its logical, rational side on your problem, and in this way arrive at solutions the verbal side would take longer to propose by itself. Some solutions might seem outlandish at first but later prove correct. Dr. Ulene insists that he has not gone "off the deep end" with this proposal.

> *By working on a problem with your creature-adviser, you are in essence bringing the visual side of your brain into the problem-solving process. The animal, of course, is nothing more than a symbol for your inner*

self, and talking to the animal amounts to talking to yourself, but on a brain wavelength you don't often use.

When facing a problem he says to himself, "Let's see what Corky [his creature-rabbit] says about this."[102]

Business and sales people cannot ignore the power of unconscious processes. So much mental activity occurs beyond the realm of consciousness that we need to tap that power. For instance, the president of a large industrial corporation faced a tough problem: he needed a new kind of furnace to melt magnesium, but he and his engineers did not know how to make it. One Sunday afternoon he was mulling the problem and wishing he had an engineer who could design the furnace when suddenly the plan he needed appeared before his eyes. He made quick notes and sketches and the next day gave the pages to his design man, who recognized the breakthrough design. When asked where he got the idea the company president said, "You wouldn't believe me if I told you." The employee insisted, so he finally told him the story. Then the designer said, "Well, I'll build it as fast as I can. I know it will work because that's the way I get all my ideas."[103]

Sometimes we can rely on unconscious processes to find new products and services. Some pan out and some do not, but the effort engages all our resources. Iowa farmer Joseph Connolly, known as "Head-On Joe," saw a vision of a new product that made him a millionaire. No one could stage a train wreck as spectacularly as he. Over forty years he demolished 146 steam locomotives in 73 shows with not a single reported injury among the hundreds of thousands of spectators. He copyrighted his "particular style of head-on collision as it pertained to train wrecks." In 1907, his most lucrative year, he staged six wrecks including one at the international fair in San Antonio. Locomotives whaled each other at speeds of a hundred miles an hour, sometimes pulling passenger cars that erupted in flames. In 1932, at his finale at Des Moines, Iowa, two trains roared toward each other down a thousand feet of new track. With the presidential election just around the corner, Connolly called one Roosevelt and the other Hoover.[104]

Harvard graduate Randall E. Wise proposes to equip the world's 1.2 billion egg-laying chickens with red contact lenses. He says red-eyed chickens fight less, appear happier, and spend more time laying eggs. A pair of twenty-cent lifetime lenses can save fifty cents a chicken.[105] Translating this vision into reality is a true marketing challenge.

The 19th century British prime minister Benjamin Disraeli said that "the secret of success is constancy of purpose." He did not tell us how to get constancy of purpose, but well-crafted goals create it in sales and business, as in life. Goals are powerful motivators since they pull us to the future instead of pushing us from the past. In the process we are empowered to reach new heights as pull-motivation changes our view of ourselves and our customers.

Sales and business people see themselves in a new light when looking from the perspective of pull-motivation. They celebrate goals they want to achieve with heart and mind, and they see clients and customers as people in search of product benefits. Stories and testimonials engage and pull customers toward a future of their choosing, and consulting is the watchword, not browbeating. Closing the sale starts with the opening bell as salespeople help customers describe the goals they want to achieve with their purchase. Sales and business leaders also motivate associates by pulling, not goading. Consciously combining thought and feeling, they formulate exciting goals and encourage and evaluate goal-linked action.

Visioning goals is a present-time experience that confers the motivation to achieve goals by linking thought and feeling. Combining thought and feeling is the key to motivation, so good goals incorporate the two sides of the brain. Goals forge a solid link between motivation and constancy of purpose, and that is why the best motivation for success comes from where you are going, not where you have been; from pulling, not pushing.

VI
Four Oars in the Water

The annual rowing contest between Oxford and Cambridge is a sight to see as sets of racing oars smack the water in unison, pushing the boats ahead with great speed. In the United States the Harvard-Yale rowing race began in 1852, and it is now the country's oldest intercollegiate bout, predating football by seventeen years. Unlike canoeists, these rowing oarsmen do not face forward. They look at the "coxswain" who sits in the back of the boat, steers it, tells the position of competitors, gives commands, and calls for spurts of energy. Only the coxswain looks ahead, peering toward the finish line.

Modern racing boats have two, four, or eight oarsmen (not six), each one grasping an oar with both hands. The objective is to get all of the oars in the water at the same time, and then out of the water at once. When this happens the team rows like clockwork to reach its goal. A team of four is headed for disaster if only two oars hit the water at once, with others following seconds later. The boat pitches and lurches and the oars may collide.

Marriages and families are like rowing teams since they, too, face trouble unless the team pulls in the same direction. Two, four, six, eight—all of the oars must hit the water at once for progress. While many things go into the composition of marriage and family, pulling together surely plays an important role, and that may be why soloists sometimes have trouble in these relationships.

No metaphor should be pushed too far, including this one, but one point remains. It is that the coxswain (remember him?) of every marriage and family is not a member such as father, mother, or husband, but the common life goals of marital partners and family members. Just as no oarsman is the coxswain, so no marital partner or family member dictates goals for all. Life goals that work in marriages and families are those that are negotiated and agreed upon by oarsmen who want all the oars in the water at once.

In these pages we will ask how life goals are applicable to married and family life (you may be involved in one but not the other, of course). After reviewing the complexity of married and family life, we will see that the two most important life goals are nurturing self-confidence and autonomy, and teaching and learning how to work toward common objectives. Marriages and families that pursue these life goals will have all four oars in the water at once, not one, two, or three.

Complexity of Marriage and Family Life

Part of the seduction of romantic love is that it oversimplifies things. Without a healthy dose of reality romantic love can make marriage look like an extended date. In this view a family is composed of parents and a gurgling infant or several toddlers, and they are taking a leisurely Sunday afternoon stroll in the park. But life experience and mature love teach us that marriage and family are complex. These social institutions are bound to be complicated since, as society's building blocks, many of the competing forces of society exist there in microcosm, or potentially exist.

The family has many tasks that contribute to its complexity. As economic units families address the issues of jobs and finances; they are also political units in which members exercise power internally and in the larger orb. As social units families socialize children and contribute to broader attitudes and values. Families instill cultural norms about how and what we learn, and how and what we appreciate, and they transmit religious beliefs and moral values from generation to generation. In the family we learn to express and repress emotions, and families teach us how to play and re-create ourselves. Taken as a whole, this is a large assignment for any family, while spouses in childless marriages engage in many of the same tasks on an ongoing basis.

Then, too, personal relationships within families are complex. Consider, for example, the ongoing relationships in a family that contains two parents and three children. **Figure 1** (see following page) depicts the interaction of one child (Number 1), both the child's direct relationships and those that the child monitors. The child has face-to-face relationships with each member of the family and perceptual interest in all the other family relationships, such as the interaction between the other two children and between mother and father. The child also has some understanding of the parent's marriage and what the family unit represents. **Figure 2** (see following page) portrays similar patterns for a mother/spouse.

With so much complexity it is clear that marriages and families are dynamic, not sets of unchanging relationships that are permanently set in cement. No wonder that Andr Maurois warns, "A successful marriages is an edifice that must be rebuilt every day." He could have said the same thing about a successful family.

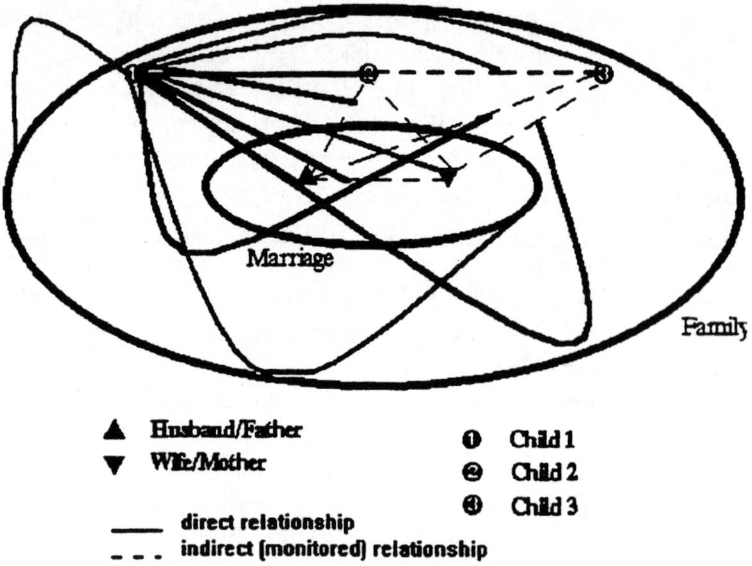

Figure 1—Family Dynamics of One Child (#1) Relating with Parents and Two Siblings.

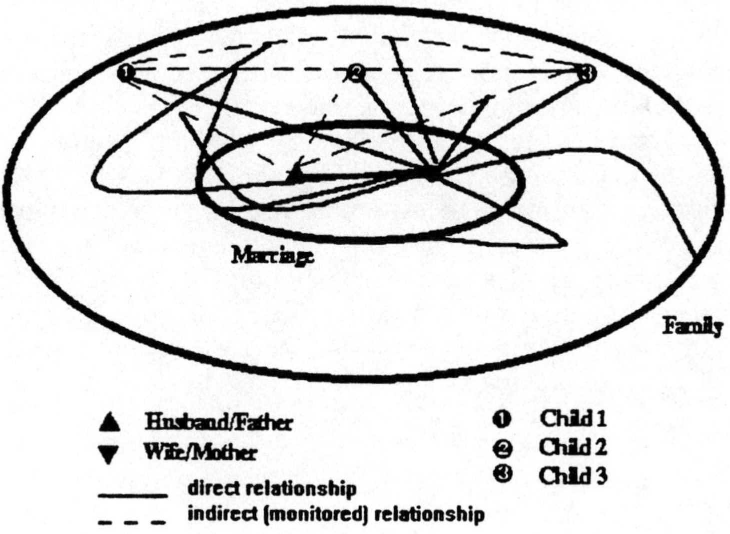

Figure 2—Marital and Family Relations of Mother/Wife Relating to Father/Husband and Three Children.

In rapidly changing circumstances it is absolutely essential to know what you are doing. Most would agree that it would be unwise to throw canoeists into the same boat with racing oarsmen. Similarly, if a person does not know what he is doing in marriage or family, how can he do it? The complexity can soon overwhelm him.

That is where the coxswain enters the picture. When marriages and families function with commonly agreed upon life goals, marital partners and family members know what they are doing, and they do it. A problem may baffle them for a while, but they soon take a cue from their coxswain goals and put all the oars in the water at once.

For marriages with children, the children's future is a strong incentive for common life goals. Parents with responsibility for turning helpless infants into productive members of society in a mere twenty years should remember what Ray L. Wilbur said: "The potential possibilities of any child are the most intriguing and stimulating in all creation." This challenge is worth thinking about since nearly every child has the potential of making history.

First Coxswain: Self-Confidence and Autonomy

Nurturing and developing self-confidence and autonomy is the single most important life goal (coxswain) for marriage and family. Marriage partners and family members set as a communal life goal that each member develops a strong sense of self-confidence and independence. Marriages and families succeed in direct proportion to how well they accomplish this goal day by day, but the task is never fully accomplished so long as there is a marriage or family to do it. With all the rowers facing in one direction the race is nearly won.

When arrived at by communal deliberation, this life goal helps clarify the definition and meaning of marriage and family. It also enables marriage partners and family members to communicate feelings in healthy ways. Positive growth in self-confidence and autonomy enriches marriages and keeps family life on an even keel, despite inevitable conflicts. When linked with the second life goal (teaching and learning how to work toward common objectives), this baseline goal helps people untangle the complexity that often undermines marriage and family.

Contemporary Marriages and Families

Our society is filled with muddled thinking about what makes up a marriage or family. The general tendency is to overload the importance of interactive feelings in both institutions. In other words, people try to measure the healthiness of a marriage or family by the intensity of feeling that exists between and among the various members.

Feelings and emotions are important, of course, but they cannot carry the full burden of personhood. Someone who is "pure feeling" can in an instant become almost no one when feelings are dashed. There is more to a person than feelings, and emotions alone can never be the foundation of a good marriage or family. If smashed feelings lead to a smashed marriage, the marriage was not well-based, and neither was the person whose feelings were shattered.

The best foundation for marriage and family are persons who are well-grounded in self-confidence and an autonomous spirit. Why? Because marriage is a social institution under which a man and a woman live as husband and wife by legal or religious commitment. A family is parents and their children, considered as a group. Individual people are the basis, the building blocks, for both institutions. Whatever else people try to do in marriage or family, whatever feelings and actions they generate, whatever interaction occurs—in all, self-confidence and a sense of independence are basic.

Marriage is a commitment of two individuals to each other, and this commitment has no termination point either in terms of time or totality of promise. Marriage partners do not commit themselves for a limited period of time, neither do they entrust only a portion of themselves to the other person. The commitment is timeless and total.[106]

Half-hearted "trial" marriages are a kind of self-deception because they give a sense of confidence, certainty, and commitment without its substance. In my book, a person who makes a marital commitment also makes a specific and total commitment to *this* marriage: *this* marriage will work because there are no alternatives. Intervening circumstances can affect this commitment and end the marriage, of course, but no partner should easily give up or give in.

To make this kind of commitment takes partners who are self-confident and who have a sense of autonomy. Both qualities flourish as the marriage matures since that is the partners' primary goal for self and other. Self-confidence instills self-confidence, and autonomy linked with timeless and total commitment provides a safe environment for strengthening each other's sense of independence. Louis K. Anspacher said it well: "Marriage is that relation between man and woman in which the independence is equal, the dependence mutual, and the obligation reciprocal."

This kind of marriage serves well as the family's basic building block. Marital partners who recognize the importance of self-confidence and autonomy have a head start on good parenting. Even when a marriage ends, these qualities are the primary life goal of a healthy family.

Families are important because through them society perpetuates itself. Fundamentally, families are the chief way our species procreates, nurtures infants, and guides them to maturity. Most childhoods are spent in a family of some kind, and the long-term effects of that experience are indisputable. William Wadsworth was right, "The child is the father of the man," and also the mother of the woman.

American families and households are in a state of flux today as social and economic forces draw new maps of family life. The most recent census confirmed trends that sociologists have been reporting for some time. The Census Bureau's study, entitled "Household and Family Characteristics: March

1991," offered insight into American households and families. The Bureau uses the term "households" for people living under one roof, whether members are family-related or not. The two kinds of households are family and non-family.[107]

Households are mostly smaller than a decade ago although the long-term slide in size has halted, at least temporarily. The average American household included 2.63 people in 1991 compared with 2.76 in 1980, and 3.01 in 1973. Lower fertility, more one-parent families, and the emergence of many non-family households caused household size to drop more substantially in the 1980s than the 1970s.

Only seventy percent of households consisted of families in 1991, while thirty percent were non-family households (persons living alone or with non-relatives). By contrast, eighty-one percent of households were families in 1970, and just nineteen percent were non-family households. In 1991 the United States had a total of 94.3 million households; of these, about 66 million were family households, and 23.1 million were one-person households (primarily women, at 60%). Married couples (with and without children) maintained 83% of the family households that were white in 1991. Married couples maintained forty-eight percent of family households that were black.

Only thirty percent of all households included one or more of the householder's children under age eighteen (compared with 45% in 1970). According to the Bureau's report, "the number of married-couple families who have not had children or whose children have left the home (27.8 million) is larger than the number with children present in the home (24.5 million)."

About twenty-nine percent of the thirty-five million family groups with children were single-parent families in 1991, compared with just thirteen percent in 1970. But while the growth of female-headed householder families continues, the rate of increase has slowed dramatically since 1980. The annual rate of increase of families without husbands or fathers has dropped from 3.9% in the 1970s to two percent a year since

1980. The rate among blacks has slowed from 6.1% to 2.9%. According to the report, most single parents are householders who own or rent their own quarters, but twenty-one percent live in a household belonging to someone else.

The diminishing size of the American family is no surprise, in part because some women delay child-bearing in favor of an extended career. Bearing and raising children while engaging in a full-time career is not easy. As Laurence Housman said half-humorously, "If nature had arranged that husbands and wives should have children alternatively, there would never be more than three in a family."[108]

Some quick facts about family and parenting throw a sharp light on these statistics about American families. *First*, nuclear families (husband, wife, and one or more children) are on the decline. Currently one in four families matches this description; by the year 2000 the ratio will be one in five. Gaining ground are childless couples, single-parent families, step-families, and unmarried couples with children. *Second,* the traditional family is fading, due in some measure to economic pressure. The traditional family is a married couple with father in the work force and mother at home. Only thirty-three percent of families fit this description, down from fifty-three percent in 1975. *Third*, step-families are increasing. More than five million couples have at least one child who is not related by blood to both parents. In 1987 almost half of all marriages involved the remarriage of at least one partner; one in five united two divorcees. Reportedly the majority child in 1990 was a stepchild.

Fourth, single-parent families are increasing, and they are poor. More than half the children living with their single parents officially met standards for poverty in 1987 (two of every three children in Black and Hispanic single-parent families). It is estimated that forty-two percent of white children and eighty percent of Black children will live in single parent households sometime in their youth. Twenty percent of all American children live in single parent households. *Fifth*, divorce continues unabated. Now each year one in two marriages ends in divorce. After divorce a man's standard of living increases forty-two percent while a woman's declines seventy-three. *Sixth*, latchkey children are on the rise as parents work. It is estimated that by 1995 two of every three mothers of preschool children will work outside the home. The number of latchkey children is estimated as high as seven million, about one of every four school-age children. *Seventh*, by 1990 the number of single parent and blended family households is reported to have been larger than the number of "intact" families. One in six babies is born out of wedlock, the majority to mothers in their teens.[109]

As if the situation were not muddled enough, some corporations and municipalities now recognize gay and lesbian partners and live-in straight couples as domestic partnerships. Included among them are the cities of Seattle (WA), Berkeley (CA), and Ithaca (NY), together with Levi Strauss and Lotus. In 1990, there were five times as many households of unmarried couples as in 1970.[110] Whatever the circumstances, nurturing and developing self-confidence and autonomy stands as the bedrock for marital (or pseudo-marital) and family relationships.

The absence of fathers in many families is a plague that will have grave repercussions in our society. There are many reasons for their absence, extending from bitter custody fights in which mothers do not want the fathers around, to fathers who pursue the siren call of individualistic self-actualization to the exclusion of paternal responsibility. Reportedly one-third of all American children are growing up apart from their biological fathers, and nearly one-fourth (about fourteen million children) are living in mother-only households. About one in six children who is living apart from his father sees him weekly; four in ten see their fathers less than once a year. For boys, one result of being fatherless may be rituals of masculinity based around gang violence.[111] "Paternity is a career imposed on you without any inquiry into your fitness," Adlai E. Stevenson said. While his remark is equally applicable to maternity, it reinforces the need for a solid sense of autonomous confidence for persons to serve as adequate fathers and mothers.

Traditionally, the family has fulfilled five functions. It ensures economic survival, provides protection, passes on religious faith, educates children, and confers status.[112] Much is changing. People can survive economically apart from the family as both men and women enter the work force. Government and police functions provide protection, and religious training has been delegated largely to religious institutions, and education to schools. Rarely today does the family confer status; it usually comes from work, possessions, and other sources. In our day families render a service more in terms of relations and relationships than in terms of function. People look to the family in seeking love and being loved; the family is provider of intimacy and trust.[113]

If anything, these changing traits of the family intensify the need to cultivate the primary family life goal, namely, nurturing and developing self-confidence and independence in individuals. Like many marriages, families often are consumed by privatism and individualism, a kind of psychological myopia that concentrates only on developing interior relationships. They lack the broader and necessary goal of preparing marital and family members to relate more effectively as human beings outside of marriage and family. Privatism and individualism show themselves in almost total and exclusive dedication to family and children, so that the people involved can draw more psychic energy out of the family. Love and marriage are seen as psychic attractions; they are not anchored in a pattern of role and of social institution, which seem foreign to many.[114]

Whether headed by a mother or father, single parent households face special challenges. For single parents who are African-American the responsibility is almost overwhelming, in part because racism and the skewed poverty of Blacks compound the follow-on poverty of most single parent households. Black children are three times more likely than white children to live in a single parent home.[115] Single parents have sole responsibility for the family's economic welfare, and for the socializing and educative functions of the family. Many times this responsibility overpowers individuals, and our society has been slow to help. Single parents with teenage children face a special kind of temptation, namely, to treat their teenage children as friends, colleagues, or counselors, as shoulders to cry on for emotional support. Teenagers are not members of a single-parent family to provide emotional support for the parent.[116]

Like the rest of us, single parents should heed the advice of an old Chinese proverb that hails the importance of example. "Not the cry, but the flight of the wild duck, leads the flock to fly and follow," it says. The single parent's best parenting skills and examples can flow from a sense of self-confidence and independence that is imparted to the family's children, teenage and younger.

Whatever its composition, the family is the seed plot in which the individual's sexual identity grows and develops. While everything is not sex, the development of sexual identity is an important contribution of the family. Nurturing self-confidence and autonomy is critical to that development. It enables us to escape the paradox that Bishop Fulton J. Sheen sketched when he said, "Sex has become one of the most discussed subjects of modern times. The Victorians pretended it did not exist; the moderns pretend that nothing else exists."

Many psychologists and psychiatrists hold that the basic outline of a personality is set by about age five. The first years of life indelibly stamp the years to come, at least in the dynamics of personality and psychological development, and sexual identity is an integral part of that formation. As women wrestle with the question of their role and the equality of females, they are engaging in a fundamental building of self-confidence and autonomy in the marriages and families of which they are a part. Similarly, as young girls and boys see their mothers and other females expanding horizons outside the home, they receive important signals for the formation of their own self-confidence and sense of autonomy.

This change in perspective about the roles of females can also have detrimental effects in marriages and families, depending partly on the capacity of males to expand their sense of masculinity to incorporate new developments. Self-confident and autonomous males should welcome the opportunity to expand boundaries that include a heightened appreciation of intimacy, a sense of women in the workplace as fellow-workers and not sex objects, and equal pay for equal work. Moreover, if both husband and wife work outside the home by choice or necessity, men need to find ways to take up their share of household chores.

This dynamic unfolding of female and male roles, evident in both marriage and family, emphasizes the importance of the chief life goal in both institutions. Nurturing and developing self-confidence and autonomy has long-range effects on the sexual identity of both partners and children.

For many observers there is little doubt that one of the family's important functions is to give children a firm sense of "home." "Home interprets heaven. Home is heaven for beginners," said Charles H. Parkhurst. A yearning for home seems to be an instinctual desire of children, and parents have the responsibility to ensure that they are not cheated or disappointed. An old Chinese proverb insists that "a hundred men may make an encampment, but it takes a woman to make a home." Few will argue that mothers have the special gift of making a home; a man can build a house but only a woman can make a home. Amid all the changes in American marriages and families, that is worth remembering.

Communicating Feelings

Communicating feelings effectively is a high priority in marriages and families. Since communication entails a sender and receiver, communicating feelings is a two-way street. As marital partners and family members grow in self-confidence and their sense of independence, emotions are communicated more freely and with greater reliability.

The capacity to express feelings and accept the expression of feelings happens best in settings of quiet confidence.

Confident people who have a firm sense of independence are well equipped to communicate feelings on both giving and receiving ends. A settled calmness permits them to exert a constructive influence, though the feelings of the moment may be inflammatory.

On the surface, communicating feelings may not seem like one of the most important lessons to be learned by marital and family members, but with its quiet results it outweighs many other lessons. Spouses, parents, and family members who communicate feelings effectively learn how to defuse potentially disastrous situations and prevent long-term damage. They are working behind the lines of anger, hate, sorrow, love, pity, and other emotions to allow mates and family members to vent feelings without causing destruction. A successful marriage is more than finding the right person; it is being the right person, behind the lines. The same is true for parents who work behind the lines.

This reminds me of a story told by Elmer Bendiner in his book about B-17 bombers during World War II, called *The Fall of Fortresses*. On one bombing run over the German city of Kassel, Nazi anti-aircraft guns fired vigorously at Bendiner's B-17. The firing itself was not unusual, but the craft's gas tanks were hit. Miraculously, the bomber made it back to base without a fire so the pilot asked for a bullet as a souvenir, and in the process he discovered that the gas tanks contained eleven of them. Not one had exploded although any one could have blown up the plane. During the examination authorities discovered that ten of the unexploded heads contained no explosive charge, but in the eleventh was a carefully rolled piece of paper with a note scrawled in Czech that said, "This is all we can do for you now."[117] Parents and spouses who communicate feelings well are like these resistors who worked behind the lines.

At an early age babies learn how their mothers communicate emotion. Recent studies show that the melody of a mother's speech is the key to conveying meaning, even before a child understands the words. What is called "parentese" gets a baby's attention, communicates, and teaches the language. Included in parentese are the melodies, long pauses, and word stretches that adults use to address infants. These melodic patterns are universal in all languages. Among them are a sharp, short staccato for warning (No!); a long, smooth, low frequency for comfort (Oooh); rising and then falling pitch for praise (Greeeat!); and a high, rising melody for calling attention to objects (Where's the buzz-a-BEE?).[118] Ed Howe once said that "families with babies and families without babies are sorry for each other." Maybe the reason for both of their opinions is the need to speak "parentese."

Listening to children—really listening—is no easy task by itself, and it becomes even more challenging when children communicate feelings. Parents who are self-confident and independent have a firm base for the task, and doing the task well engenders this important life goal in children.

Psychiatrist M. Scott Peck describes the challenge faced by the parents of a six-year-old who is apt to chatter almost non-stop. What should be their response? Dr. Peck offers five alternatives: forbid the talk; permit chatter but ignore it; pretend to listen with occasional responses; selectively listen (an alert form of pretending); and truly listen. He recommends a balanced use of all five, depending on circumstances. True listening requires total concentration; it gives concrete evidence of the parent's esteem for the child. Dr. Peck adds that "the need for one's parents to listen is never outgrown."[119] Listening well and the esteem that goes with it open follow-on opportunities for building a child's self-confidence and sense of autonomy.

Couples have the same challenge of truly listening. Shutting off communication, including the communication of feelings, is the opposite of confidence and independence-building. Spouses who cannot listen to one another are not communicating effectively, although external appearances may convince them otherwise. Listening is a discipline that a self-confident, independent partner exercises to help the other build confidence and autonomy. One way to ensure a fighting chance for true listening is talking by set appointment daily or weekly.

Many family maxims that work well no longer seem to apply when children hit the teenage years. Teens are betwixt and between, neither children nor adults—some would say not even human! This is a critical time for the life goal that lies at the center of marital and family life, and parents need a special dose of love and grace to instill self-confidence and responsible independence in a person who one minute acts like a responsible adult and regresses to a two-year-old's temper tantrum the next.

Parents can expend no more important resource on their teenagers than time. Teens need time to process emotions and ideas (the essence of adolescence), and they slowly work through various levels in doing so. Parents who do not spend blocks of time with their teens place them at a great disadvantage since few teenagers have learned how to give pointed business briefings. They do not look on their lives as a business but as a process that requires time. Like other children, teens want quality time when parents make no demands, when the focus is the relationship itself and not some kind of parent-inspired discussion of teenage responsibilities. Psychiatrist Ross Campbell recommends that adolescents need more time with the family, not less, even though they *seem* to want more time away. Communicating feelings is an important outcome of shared time, and communication in turn allows teens to work through their turmoil, discern and reaffirm values, and develop confidence and independence as individuals.[120]

Focused attention is a primary need for teens and children alike, and conversation is the medium. What Jean Paul Richter said about the long-range impact of fatherly conversation applies equally to mothers. He wrote that "the words that a father speaks to his children in the privacy of home are not heard by the world, but, as in whispering-galleries, they are clearly heard at the end and by posterity."

One critical part of communicating feelings is learning

how to express anger. Teenagers have no corner on this need for it is present in all the dynamics of married and family life. Very painful psychological problems can result from misdirected and unexpressed anger, including explosive and destructive outbursts, panic disorders, headaches, depression, and anxiety attacks. Self-induced physical ailments can also take root.

Many psychiatrists hold that anger is not a purely negative emotion but a warning alerting people that they are threatened and need to react. Anger is the psychological equivalent of pain, but the difficulty is that often it is not well expressed. Dysfunctional behavior such as screaming or bottling anger causes problems, not the original emotion of anger. Many people rise up to defend themselves in the face of a perceived threat or attack, aiming their responses outward and inward ("exploders" and "imploders"). Angry people are prone to view the world with fear and suspicion, seeing themselves as victims, and they also get hung up on the past. Some require long-range therapy, including skills in coping and problem-solving.[121]

Good parenting touches the problem of anger in two ways. One is learning how to manage one's own anger when children inflame it, and the other is teaching children to channel their anger. The goal of instilling self-confidence and independence plays a role in both.

When angered by a child it is important to isolate exactly why the words or behavior threaten you as a parent. The child (especially a teen) may be trying to deflate your ego purposely, and in this case your anger is a healthy warning about self-preservation. The key is how to express anger without being destructive to a budding teenager whose self-confidence you are trying to nurture. The old religious saw about "hating the sin and loving the sinner" has some applicability. Your best tact is to express displeasure with the child's specific actions or choice of words but not with the child or his personality. Tell why your feelings of anger arose as clearly as you can ("No one likes to be called a failure"), and if possible open discussion of life values to express your feelings vigorously but innocuously.

We follow the same approach to help younger children vent anger without becoming "exploders" or "imploders." Encouraging physical exercise as a legitimate "blow-off" can be beneficial. When children can name what bothers them clearly and verbally express their dislike of the threat, you are well on the way toward a constructive expression of anger. Anger as a form of self-preservation plays a pivotal defensive role. Expressing anger constructively is one of the most important contributions a parent can make in a family, and teaching children this lesson for life instills self-confidence and maturing autonomy.

What is true about anger in a family applies as well in marriage. Marital partners who are unable to express feelings of anger do not make a marriage so much as a chain gang, with one pulling the other. In good marriages partners express anger productively, and constructive arguing is accepted in the normal course. Poor marriages are like a battleground where battles are never fought, where confidence does not develop without testing, and where autonomy is only a word in the dictionary. For this reason, learning to communicate pleasant and unpleasant feelings is a priority in marriages as in families.

Traditional analysis can help in evaluating the communication of feelings. This tool dissects who—and which part of who—is saying what to whom—and to which part of whom. The hypothesis is that a "parent," "child," and "adult" is identifiable in each adult person, and expressions flow from any one of them. The person responding can replicate the pattern or follow a different one. If my "parent" says something to your "child" and your "parent" responds, chances are good that we are engaged in communicational misfiring. Over time, rhythms and patterns may develop that short-circuit the communication of feelings, affecting the confidence and sense of autonomy of marital partners and family members. We should add that some children become adept at appealing to their parents' "child," or needling the "parent" so that the "adult" does not participate in the interchange.

Photoanalysis is a second dipstick for measuring how feelings are expressed in marriages and families. It is the "study of photographs to arrive at personal and interpersonal insight." Robert U. Akeret calls photos "mirrors with memories" that can tell hidden stories. Reviewing pictures in the family album may help people discover relationships within the family and how family members communicate feelings in their poses, bodily distance, and facial images.[122] This can be more than a party game if family members talk about the pictures and how they portray the family's emotional ebb and flow. Unposed photographs and family videos can generate healthy discussion about the communication of emotions. Sometimes our society's technological emphasis makes a surprise visit in this arena. For instance, an admiring friend says to a mother, "What a beautiful baby you have there!" She responds sharply, "Oh, not really—you should see the video from the baptism!"

Another dipstick is the way family members and marital partners interact with pets. Dogs, cats, and other pets receive inordinate emotional attention in some marriages and families if the normal communication of feelings is short-circuited. In other cases pets participate like family members in the group's healthy expression of feelings. Sometimes the absence of a family pet hints at relative sterility in how feelings are expressed. In sum, the pet dipstick may help members raise the issue of communicating feelings with profit.

Positive Growth

Not all growth comes naturally in marriages and families, so there is place for intentionally nurturing the positive development of self-confidence and sense of autonomy. Life's rush all too easily blocks our efforts to cultivate this goal, or we put it off till later. Marcus Aurelius gives good advice to all spouses and family members: "Do not act as if you had a thousand years to live."

In 1983 two hundred Marines died in Beirut when a suicidal man penetrated the parameter of their building with a bomb. In the aftermath two military chaplains, a Jew and a Catholic, ministered to the living and the dead. The Jewish chaplain later reported two images that stuck with him:

> *One was a packet of three envelopes found in the building wreckage, tied together with a rubber band. On top, under the band, was a note which read: "To be mailed in case of death." The other was a Red Cross message, delivered the next morning (Navy families use Red Cross to communicate medical news from home). This message was a birth announcement, and we were to deliver the good news. Only now there was no father whom we could congratulate; no father to whom the news could be conveyed.*[123]

Time is always short, and today is always the day for nurturing positive growth.

Partners and parents have primary responsibility for ensuring positive growth in marriage and family. They edify each other and in the process bring their children to a fuller realization of self-confidence and independence. Theodore M. Hesburgh says that "the most important thing a father can do for his children is love their mother." Dorothy Canfield Fisher opines that "a mother is not a person to lean on but a person to make leaning unnecessary." Both are right since they are talking about the kind of love that helps other people stand on their own feet, confident in their ability and ready to spread this love in the whole family.

Loving criticism is part of a positive growth pattern in these relationships. Dr. Peck argues that "if they love their children parents must, sparingly and carefully perhaps but nonetheless actively, confront and criticize them from time to time, just as they must also allow their children to confront and criticize themselves in return." He continues:

> *Similarly, loving spouses must repeatedly confront each other if the marriage relationship is to serve the*

function of promoting the spiritual growth of partners. No marriage can be judged truly successful unless husband and wife are each other's best critics. The same holds true for friendship.[124]

Marital partners and family members are best friends who are unafraid of—in fact, who insist on—pointing out personal traits that need strengthening, actions that can be changed, and other areas. In a trusting relationship the self-confidence that discusses a shortfall can also engender self-confidence in the other. This is not the whole of love, but part of love. Quaker William Penn claimed that "she is but half a wife that is not, nor is capable of being, a friend." The same is true of a husband or a parent.

Genuine love does not mash two people into one, whether spouses, or a parent and a child. It is not narcissism. In genuine love "the distinction between oneself and the other is always maintained and preserved," and each person retains a totally separate identity. No great marital relationship develops when a person is terrified by basic aloneness and seeks a merging with another in marriage.[125] Genuine love reaffirms the basic goal of marriage and family, namely, building one's own and the other's self-confidence and independence. Marriage enrichment courses and retreats, couple communication seminars, and parenting courses and experiences are means toward this end. Finally, there is frequent physical expression of love when genuine love exists in marriages and families.

Parenting offers daily opportunities for nurturing positive growth in children and communicating feelings, though some parents may wonder how they got into the work to start with. A recent help wanted ad sums up the job:

Help Wanted. *Applicants sought for entry level position as contemporary parent. Experience helpful but not necessary. No degree required. Should possess necessary skills as educator, mediator, criminologist, sports psychologist, chauffeur and especially waiter, since substantial waiting is involved: up to 9 months prior to assuming duties, then every day thereafter for* *school buses, bathrooms, explanations, apologies, etc. Duties require 24-hour on-call status. Unlimited sick days (theirs, not yours), vacations (often running concurrently with sick days), and numerous fringe benefits (subject to your ability to recognize and appreciate them). On-the-job training and lifetime contracts available to those who qualify.*[126]

Perhaps a better description of the challenge was Franklin P. Jones' when he said, "Parenthood is the art of bringing up children without putting them down."

Like many marriages, families too can suffer from too much dependency, which dramatically affects the parenting. When a marital partner, parent, or child is overly dependent on another there is less likelihood that self-confidence and autonomy will flourish. Co-dependency often satisfies deep-seated psychological needs, and long-term counseling may be needed. In other situations of over-dependency, changing behavior and a conscious decision to nurture self-confidence and autonomy may be all that is needed.

Some parents react quickly and negatively when a child makes a dash for emotional independence or wants to demonstrate a capacity for psychological autonomy from his parents. Families have no right to demand a child's primary allegiance forever; that is unnatural. Using threats or guilt to maintain a dependent relationship between child and parent is not in the child's long-range interest, neither does it contribute to the parent's mental well-being. The psychological dynamics at work in a dependent marriage (dominance and submission) surface all too often in the parenting done by these marital partners.[127]

Healthy parenting encourages independence and a normal growth process that includes questioning authority. The primary life goal of marriages and families, namely, nurturing and developing self-confidence and independence, must be clearly asserted and *lived* when dependency or co-dependency is a problem. This positive goal encourages growth, maturity, and personal development. If society's primary seed plot, the family, fails to nurture these characteristics, they have a harder time flourishing in the rocky soil of later life.

The teenage years offer parents their greatest opportunity and challenge to live out and impart this fundamental goal. One authority asserts that teenagers are "the most vulnerable person[s] in our society" because they have the deepest need for love. That need for love gives parents the opportunity, at one and the same time, to deepen feelings of dependency or to encourage the development of self-confidence and sense of autonomy. The paradox is this: a great many teenagers feel they are not loved while parents think they are conveying love.[128] Logically both cannot be right. The problem is that teens look for the conveyance of unconditional love through their parents' behavior, meeting of the eyes, and physical contact. Parents are more inclined to think that it is sufficient to provide the necessities of life and the normal "loving" patterns used with younger children, along with "extras" like pizza and movies. The adolescent's deeper yearning for love requires, paradoxically, deeper expressions of love by parents, along with encouragement to develop self-confidence and autonomy. It is a tricky assignment.

Unconditional love of a teenager tests parental mettle. It means loving a teen "no matter what the teenager looks like; no matter what his assets, liabilities and handicaps are; no matter how he acts." It is an ideal to be worked at, but never ignored. Saying "I love you" is not enough. Teens look for behavioral reinforcement of your words so that what you do says "I love you" loudly and clearly. Loving, consistent eye contact sets the communicational channels abuzz, but more, it offers emotional reassurance to the teen. Touching, hugging, and other bodily contact provides further proof that your words are true.[129]

Of course, these patterns should be a continuation of parenting habits used with younger children. Parenting's primary purpose is to enable children to mature into independent creatures who are at home in God's world. Like the mother bear who walks off and leaves her cubs—though perhaps not as suddenly—parents look toward the day when they can rest from their labors. The fruits of their work are persons who are self-confident mentally, psychologically, spiritually, and socially, and persons whose sense of independence and autonomy is as firm as granite.

It remains for a French priest, who has no family, to portray the parenting assignment for us in unforgettable terms. Father Jean Sullivan issued a clear challenge in his book entitled *Morning Light*:

> *If you are a father or mother, be one as briefly as possible. Don't need your children in order to exist....Let the time come quickly when they choose you. Let your plans, worries, and good advice perish with you. Not all of you will see the year 2000, but your children will be in the best of health. To turn them into carbon copies of you is to assassinate them....*
>
> *The family seizes the individual and never leaves him alone, just like the society that overwhelms him. Its basic aim is to hem him in, enclose him in its ghetto, to integrate him. But if he is to give life to society and prevent it from petrifying, it is important that he become joyously himself.*
>
> *The family sometimes can become more than a hot-house of prejudices and slavery. Ties of spirit can become stronger than those of blood. That is its specifically Christian goal. In any case, the person who wakes up will sooner or later choose his own family, from which his relatives are not necessarily excluded.*[130]

In view of this sobering statement it is any wonder that someone asks, almost facetiously, "Have you ever noticed that parents of grown-up children are at any moment only as happy as the *least* happy offspring?"

Oarsmen keep an eye on the coxswain so all the oars are in the water at once. For oarsmen and oarswomen in marriages and families, the most important coxswain is nurturing self-confidence and a sense of independence in spouses and family members. This bedrock goal is even more important in a day when American families and marriages are reeling from many changes. This life goal is a pivotal part of communicating feelings, including feelings of anger, and it makes a mighty contribution to the parenting of teenagers. Nurturing positive growth in these traits pays rich dividends to spouses, parents, and children. This coxswain goal encourages us to strive toward genuine love in marital and family relationships (including constructive criticism), nurtures independence in children and teens, and opens the way for parents to love their teens unconditionally.

Coxswain Two: Working Toward Common Objectives

Marriages and families serve an important educative function as the smallest working social units in American society. Assuming that adults and children learn best in small groups, marriages and families can be hotbeds of learning. A second feature of the small group is that it function best when its members are working toward common objectives and pulling toward the same ends.

Taken together, these features help us understand why the second coxswain for marriage and family is teaching and learning how to work toward common objectives. Oarsmen, oarswomen, and oarschildren in families and marriages will look often at this coxswain for instruction on getting their oars in the water at once. As educative units, marriages and families encourage members to teach and learn the importance of working toward common objectives. Functioning as social units, these members come to understand the substance of what they are learning by doing it, namely, working toward common objectives.

In sum, effective marriages and families create mechanisms for cooperative planning and goal-setting, overcoming problems, and instilling and practicing religious and moral values. This is how to put two, four, or eight oars in the water at once, and to get somewhere when the oarsmen do.

Cooperative Planning and Goal-Setting

Not all life goals are solo activities. Some are created in common with others and achieved with their cooperation. Surely this is the case for goals in marriages and families that are bound by mutual respect, love, encouragement, and cooperation. Independence and autonomy (our first coxswain) flourish in marriages and families not for its own sake, but for deployment and cooperative use with others. This completes the great cycle of growth and learning that marks marriage and family as society's building blocks. At the foundation they contribute to personal growth in independence and autonomy, and they also nurture the cooperative spirit that is a mark of humanity and of human endeavor in the world at large.

In families, as in marriage, it is sometimes easy for members to slide into independent and autonomous spheres where only a common address binds the members together. As good leaders, parents and spouses will find ways of involving other members to the extent of their ability. To do the job yourself is the chicken's way out, as this parable shows.

Once the Little Red Hen owned a wheat field. "Who will help me harvest the wheat?" she asked. "Not I," said the pig, "I don't know how." "Not I," said the cow, "I'm too clumsy." "Not I," said the dog, "I'm busy with other things." So the Little Red Hen did it herself. "Who will help me grind the wheat into flour?" she asked. "Not I," said the pig, "I'm not trained for that vocation." "Not I," said the cow, "for you can do it more efficiently." "Not I," said the dog. "I'd love to but I am involved in some matters of greater urgency. Perhaps another time." So she did it herself. "Who will help me make some bread?" asked the Little Red Hen. "Not I," said the pig, "nobody ever taught me how." "Not I," said the cow, "you are more experienced and could do it in half the time." "Not I," said the dog, "I've made some plans for this afternoon but I will help you next time." So she did it herself. That evening when the guests arrived for her big dinner party the Little Red Hen had nothing to serve except bread. She had been so busy doing work that others could have done that she had forgotten to plan the main course, prepare a dessert, or even get out the silverware. The evening was a disaster, and she lived unhappily ever after.

Cooperative planning and goal setting underlie many of the traits of healthy families because these families are active, vibrant social units in which members show care and concern for each other in tangible ways. Dolores Curran identifies fifteen traits commonly found in happy, successful, and healthy families. The traits include communicating; affirming and supporting; trusting; respecting others; sharing time; teaching morals; fostering responsibility; enjoying traditions; respecting privacy; sharing religion; valuing service; and getting help. A researcher named Nick Stinnett studied 3,000 families and found that strong families (1) are committed to the family; (2) spend time together; (3) have good family communication; (4) express appreciation to each other; (5) have a spiritual commitment; and (6) are able to solve problems in a crisis.[131]

When the second coxswain is a family's major goal, the family moves as a unit toward whatever common objectives are needed for the time. The mechanism may be as formal as a family council or as informal as TV-room conversation. The subject can vary from the summer vacation to a child's problems in school. What is clearly evident is a sense of mutual respect and caring that is not satisfied with words and feelings alone, but presses ahead to formulate a commonly acceptable plan of action to face the challenge.

Families in which caring is a daily motif seem to be most adept at moving under this coxswain's encouragement. Family members set a priority of loving those around them and express positive feelings toward each other; they show love and affection by acts of kindness and touching. They listen to one another, respond rather than react, offer helpful feedback, and share pain and hurt. They show mutual respect for family traditions, rituals, and history, and share religious faith openly. When facing difficulties that require professional assistance they readily turn to clergy, counselors, and others for help.[132]

Marriages that work toward common objectives show many of the same traits. Partners teach one another and learn from one another how to show a united front when necessary, work through differences toward shared objectives, encourage each other in new efforts, and package their mutual caring into common purposes. Peter De Vries warns us that good marriages mature over time, like good wines—or good bonds: "The bonds of matrimony are like any other bonds—they mature slowly." Part of that maturation is learning how to teach—and learn—so that the other partner moves with you toward mutually agreeable objectives.

In marriage and family, traditions can serve the important function of cementing renewed commitment, but, like all human ritual, traditions can become hollow and meaningless. In one central European town the people, especially the older ones, made the sign of the cross when they passed a certain stone wall. A visitor asked why they were doing this since he saw only a wall, but no one could give a satisfactory answer. His curiosity raised, the visitor approached the wall and began chipping away at the paint, whitewash, and dirt, and there underneath many layers was a beautiful mosaic of the Virgin Mary with the Child. Earlier generations had a good reason for making the sign of the cross, but succeeding generations had forgotten.[133]

Family traditions of births, birthdays, anniversaries, religious and secular holidays, marriages, deaths, and other occasions are opportunities to scratch off the whitewash and discuss the tradition in depth. What did it mean seven years ago when Bob came into our family? What does it mean now? How has this child changed our family and contributed new graces? In families we ignore too many good chances to examine our commonality and our need for common objectives when we fail to scratch our traditions for the reality beneath them. Couples have that same opportunity in marriage. Talking about the first date, the honeymoon, the first child—most marital partners share these traditions in common, and reaffirming them reinforces the willingness to build common objectives in the marriage.

In marriage and family alike, creating new traditions is part of the process of distinguishing this family or this marriage from all others. Why not consider a family tradition of exchanging a Christmas gift in July instead of during the hectic days of Christmas? Variety is the spice of life, and also the spice of families and marriages that establish new traditions.

The question of "family destiny" arises when we consider the family objective of working toward common objectives. It is a complex issue since children unconsciously "catch" so much while they are raised in a family. Apparently some executives avoid certain career advancements because they have reached a "comfort zone" set in their mind by the family. Basically, the theory of family destiny says that

> *the choice of career and level of motivation is absorbed during childhood; that parents and home environment leave an indelible imprint upon the subconscious, determining, often extremely precisely, the path upon which an executive will embark, the level of society to which he will gravitate, and the destination at which he will feel that he has arrived.*

Geography, sex, place within the family unit, name, religion, education and familial expectations are largely fixed in childhood.[134]

Few would deny that families are a major influence in how children move into society, pursue careers, and press on with their lives, or that family destiny is an important factor in the lives of people. But the more important question here is whether family destiny is a subject open for discussion and resolution in the family, and whether family members can contribute to the formulation of a common "family destiny" theme. If parents pull rank and put this subject off limits, they abdicate their responsibility to both of the coxswains we are describing.

In summary, it is rather complicated to say that marriages and families that teach and learn how to work toward common objectives are more apt to be effective social units. Let's merely say that marriages and families that fly together get farther. We can learn a lesson about this from geese heading south. By flying in a "V" formation a flock of geese adds at least 70% greater flying range than if each bird flew alone, according to scientific studies. If a goose falls out of formation it feels drag and resistance and hurriedly returns to the formation, taking advantage of the lifting power of the bird in front. A tired goose rotates to the back of the wing and another goose flies point. The geese that are behind honk to encourage those up front. Finally, if a goose gets sick, falls out, or is shot, two geese follow it down to help protect the fallen comrade. They remain with it until it is able to fly or is dead, then launch again.

Overcoming Problems

Modern marriages and families have many kinds of problems, some of them (such as AIDS) new to the human race. Three pivotal areas where problems arise are quarrels, parental discipline, and finances. In these, as in all problems, marital partners and family members are battling the will to fail. Up front and out loud we need to admit that there is a mean streak in human nature that likes to see failure, propels people toward failure, and maliciously enjoys its fruits. But openly admitting that the will to fail exists is not the same as giving in to this distorted bent toward ruin. Family members and marital partners overcome problems—and the will to fail—by focusing on the second major coxswain, working toward common objectives.

Herbert Samuel warns that it "takes two to make a marriage a success and only one to make it a failure," and quarreling is one way. According to Elbert Hubbard, "Every quarrel begins in nothing and ends in a struggle for supremacy." The difficulty is that "people generally quarrel because they cannot argue," as Gilbert K. Chesterton warns.

Learning how to fight cleanly is not limited to boxing. Partners in any successful marriage have learned the ropes. They recognize that differences arise and must be worked through, but they are intent on discussing the problem in ways that do not degenerate into a knit-picking quarrel. Arguing cleanly means not dredging up past subjects, not impugning motives, not attacking the other party personally, and not going for the jugular. Clean fighting—constructive arguing—has as its goal that both partners are standing when the fight is over, that anger is vented properly, and that the intellectual and psychological ramifications of various positions are discussed openly and without rancor. When constructive and successful, marital and family arguments clear the air and renew strong feelings of connection and relationship. The objective is to overcome the problem with as rational a discussion as possible while appreciating differences of opinion and emotional involvement.

Urban legends floating around the country often focus on the unfaithful spouse or philanderer, or on the unjustifiably suspicious spouse, as a marital problem. These legends carry implied teachings as they are told from one person to another. The legend of the Solid Cement Cadillac usually describes a cement truck driver who, while in his neighborhood, decides to stop by the house for a mid-morning cup of coffee with his spouse. As he drives down his street he notices a flashy car parked in front of his house, and so he unloads tons of cement into the parked car. In some cases the dealer was delivering a new Cadillac just for him, paid for by his wife's hard-earned savings (or won at a raffle); in others it was the car of the unfaithful spouse's lover. In another legend, called the Philanderer's Porsche, a wife sells her husband's high-priced sports car for a paltry sum. Answering the disbelieving buyer's query as to why the price is so low, she replies that her husband "ran off with his secretary a few days ago and left a note instructing me to sell the car and the house, and send him the money."[135]

While a Japanese proverb warns that "all married women are not wives," the same is true of all married men being husbands. Spouses daily engage in conversation and action that give the lie to the lifelong commitment they make to each other. The problem is exacerbated, sometimes beyond repair, when one or the other engages in extramarital sexual relations, but at such a time of testing a partner needs to show extreme care in how the black sheep is taken back into the fold.

There is little to be gained by the "innocent" party continuing to harp on the affair. What is more important is to gain an understanding of the dynamics and causes that led up to the break of commitment; marriage counselors and clergypersons can often provide help in this pursuit. Interpersonal relationships are complex, especially those between two people who pledge their trust in marriage. The period after an affair can be one of growth, maturation, and change if partners move together towards these goals. Teaching and learning from one another, it is possible to step to a higher plateau of marital fidelity after a major misstep. This kind of experience holds aloft the importance of forgiveness in marital and family relations, just as it tests the fabric of forgiveness for strength.

Another challenge in most families is child discipline. Since lack of discipline and spoiling sometimes forge an unhealthy alliance, parents should be alert to signs of overindulgence. Approaching child-rearing on a purely democratic basis may be appealing, but it flies in the face of a child's psychological need for boundaries. A spoiled child can be bossy, disobedient, and rude, and may use tantrums and complaints to get its way.

The key to discipline is a common approach toward a mutually agreeable goal. The goal is behavior that is acceptable to both parent and child. Most parenting authorities suggest that the best results come from focusing on only a limited number of behavioral problems at one time, not trying to change everything at once. Parents carefully explain the rules and the consequences that will follow if they are broken. Just as important is the consistent enforcement of family rules so the child learns that punishment is a demonstration of parental disapproval (warn only once, do not negotiate). Parents recognize that changes in behavior may be slow in coming and that the child will continue testing the rules; be prepared for a tough time, but hang in there. All discipline should be aimed at specific behavior and not at the child per se. There is some truth to the old adage, "Spare the rod and spoil the child," as Edmund Spenser says so well in his commentary on nature's discipline: "A stern discipline pervades all nature, which is a little cruel that it may be very kind." Failure to apply this truth in parenting sets a child up for further disappointment down the road.

Teenagers present special discipline problems for many parents. All too frequently teens affirm the claim of Peter De Vries that "there are times when parenthood seems nothing more than feeding the hand that bites you." Since teenagers are trying to resolve what one authority calls "all conflicts they have previously experienced in their lives, especially with their parents," it is not surprising that mood swings and regression make discipline—let alone parenting—difficult. The best tact seems to be to track the teenager's moods and relate to him or her in the prevailing mood of the time (such as a two-year-old's temper tantrum). The parent's emotional self-control is pivotal, and this practice may become easier if a parent recalls the family's primary objective of developing independence and autonomy in each member.[136]

The key to disciplining teenagers is wrapped in a statement by Cyrus H. Curtis, who says, "There are two kinds of men [and women] who never amount to much: those who cannot do what they are told, and those who can do nothing else." Teens have to learn to do what they are told and also to do what they are not told. They are developing freedom and autonomy as persons and they are also living in a family unit—and broader society—that is working toward common objectives. While these objectives may lack explicit behavioral boundaries, defining the boundaries is part of maturing. In sum, parenting and disciplining teenagers involves holding up before the young person both coxswains of family life.

One way to impact teens is to create a significant emotional event when certain actions clearly need correction. Parents must show that they are directly involved in seeing through to the end the specific change of behavior that is required, and they must show an evenhanded and fair spirit in the conversation. They describe in detail the behavioral changes they expect to see and the consequences that will follow without the changes. Most importantly, they impart to the teen full responsibility for making the changes, explicitly describing what is expected. In the whole experience parents will show their love and care for the teenager, but they do not avoid their responsibility for pointing out the need for change and the desired behavior. Such a significant emotional event can have long-lasting consequences if parents follow through, encourage, and sustain the teen with reinforcing praise and love.

Of course, over a lifetime marriages and families change appreciably, and problems with teenagers can appear more or less serious in the light of later developments. As couples and parents, mid-year couples face different challenges than young couples with toddlers, or retired couples. Taking care of aging parents or relatives can add stress to marriages and families. Through it all the importance of praising partners and family members cannot be underestimated. "I can live for two months on a good compliment," Mark Twain bragged. Sadly, some children and marriage mates go longer than that without a compliment of any kind.

A final set of problems revolves around family finances. In many marriages one sure sign of trouble is constant reference to "my" and "your" money. The wide use of prenuptial agreements has compounded the problem for some. Commitment that extends only as far as the end of my bank account is hard to defend under fire. While of course there are legitimate reasons for separating spousal finances, including inheritance tax, in general this approach gnaws at the essence of a marriage.

Family budgets are a necessity in our day, and both parents or partners should be involved in the budget process. The key question is what this marriage or family is trying to accomplish with its commonly agreed on objectives. This, our second coxswain, sets the tone for major financial decisions. Taking this approach, there is little room for a lone ranger's unilateral decision about family finances.

When divorce plunges its dagger through a marriage, finances often become the bitterest point of contention in litigation. This is not surprising since finances probably contributed to the divorce decision. When children are involved, the second coxswain must continue to guide the interaction of the divorcees as much as possible. After all, you are going to be divorced from this person the rest of your life, and you are short-sighted to make your children pawns in a power struggle. For their sake alone divorcees should attempt to be civil and courteous in arranging and fulfilling obligations about visitation and support. As long as the children remain dependent on the divorcees, the separated partners should be teaching and learning how to work toward common objectives for them.

The key to solving problems in marriage and family is arriving at cooperative objectives that overcome problems. Partners and parents who follow this approach teach—and learn themselves—how to look beyond immediate irritations to their common goal. This process allows them to argue constructively without quarreling, to discipline children and teens so they develop their independence and autonomy, and to work through financial challenges on the way to accomplishing clear objectives.

Religious Faith and Moral Values

One interesting thing about life is that in many families "old sayings" from earlier generations are often repeated. Charles Schulz of *Peanuts* fame reports that his mother was fond of saying, "You'll never miss the water 'til the well runs dry." Whenever the family returned home, invariably as the car pulled into the driveway she would say, "Home again, Finnegan!" His grandmother's favorite saying was, "When your children are young, they step on your toes. When they grow up, they step on your heart."[137]

Family "sayings" are sometimes unofficial codification of values, or at least they point to an ethical and moral value structure. Families function less efficiently without a set of common values. A lack of moral boundaries usually leads not to freedom but license, and the difference is important. Responsible freedom is the exercise of choice within an accepted value structure.

The most important common objective toward which a family or marriage can strive is the inculcation and acceptance of religious faith and moral values. The stock of religious faith and values fluctuates widely over time, of course; in recent decades our nation has seen a realignment of values and a general softening of allegiance to religious faith. But baby boomers, who are now parents, are showing renewed interest in both. They have discovered that children ask about good and evil and about God and man, and many of them are now scrambling to equip themselves to answer. In the process they are discovering anew the importance of religious faith and moral values in family life and in their own lives.

We should not underestimate the importance of religious faith in American life. Millions of people attend churches and synagogues regularly, contributing billions of dollars to the land's religious institutions. About fifty percent of Americans are regular attenders at worship. In addition, consistently since 1976 pollsters from the Gallup Poll and other organizations have found that a third of all Americans report that they have experienced a powerful religious awakening, what a 1988 question called "a religious or mystical experience, that is, a moment of sudden religious insight or awakening."[138]

When parents and partners in families and marriages openly discuss religious faith and moral values, they are moving both institutions toward a very important common goal. Naturally, families and marriages can exist apart from religious faith and a conscious moral framework. But since personal qualities such as truthfulness, faithfulness, and a forgiving spirit are often found in both institutions, consciously cultivating religious faith and moral values should contribute to the health of marriage and family.

The long-range impact of religious and moral training in the home is clear. While religious faith usually matures as life progresses, and while some moral issues take on a complexity that they did not have earlier, the bedrock of faith and morality laid down in childhood is often an important touchstone as children become adults. When parents work with children to nurture a common religious faith and value structure, probably as much is "caught" as "taught." What this endeavor shows children is that religious faith and moral values are important for living, and surely families may want to consider this goal as a common objective.

The religious and moral values of forgiveness and love play a central role in family life and in the common pursuit of faith and values by the family. People learn first, and perhaps best, how to love and forgive in marriages and families. The best gift that parents can bestow is a good example of love and forgiveness in action. When this happens a family is well on its way toward its common goal of inculcating religious faith and moral values.

Parents use churches and synagogues to help them in their task, but theirs is the primary responsibility. Prayers, discussions, faith practices and traditions, and other methods can focus attention on religious faith and ethics in the family.[139] Family life presents daily opportunities for broaching questions of responsibility to others, trust and reliance on God, moral factors in decision-making, and many other areas. Most parents find that they plumb anew the depths of their own religious faith and value structure as they make conscious efforts to share their beliefs and convictions with children.

Any family will make progress with four oars in the water at once. The same is true for a marriage with two oars. The key is knowing what you are doing and where you are going.

Marital and family life is complex today, but in both institutions two goals are primary, namely, nurturing and developing self-confidence and independence, and teaching and learning how to work toward common objectives. These goals are aimed at individuals who, working together, make up the social institutions of marriage and family. To the degree that these goals are accomplished, individuals find strength to face the world's onslaughts while at the same time learning the need for and benefits of cooperative endeavor.

Parents who understand their role will immediately recognize the truth of Rig Lardner's comment, "The family you come from isn't as important as the family you're going to have." Instilling self-confidence, independence, and a willingness to work toward common objectives is the greatest gift they can give their children. As children extend these important qualities to all areas of life, including its social, economic, psychological, and spiritual dimensions, they will look ahead to the families they will have and the way of living that they will transfer to their children.

The challenge is just as important for marital partners. In the dependent relationship that we call marriage, partners nurture their mate's self-confidence and independence as they grow in their own, and they willingly settle on common objectives for the marriage. A truly dynamic and healthy marriage exists in a creative tension between individualism and mutuality; in this environment disagreements are occasions for growth, not stifling or throttling another.

VII
Don't Roll Up Your Sidewalks

Rolling up sidewalks at 9:00 P.M. is a daily activity in Sun City, Arizona—that is, if you believe what some non-residents say about this retirement mecca. Stories abound about how residents stop all travel and bed down for the night long before the 10:00 o'clock news. The popular myth is that people in Sun City and Sun City West are inactive, immobile, and do nothing but rest from life. Some outsiders call the towns "God's waiting room."

Residents have the last laugh, literally. Retired podiatrist Milton Gross organized a Joke Telling Club after discovering that none of the 225 clubs meeting in the area's recreation centers featured jokes. His wife says of him, "He was such a quiet man once." Jokes focus on the fun and foibles of getting old, among other things. One man told about an ad in a newspaper that read, "Elderly man who likes smoking and drinking wishes to meet elderly woman who likes smoking and drinking. Object: Smoking and drinking."

Another joke-teller said that leaving a store he came upon a little old man who was crying and he asked, "Dad, why are you crying?" The old man answered, "I was married to this woman for thirty-one years. She was a lousy cook and housekeeper, and sexually she was a cold banana. We just didn't get along at all. Then she died. I married the nicest woman. Oh, we get along beautifully! She's such a good cook, good housekeeper, and we're so compatible." So the man asked, "Then why are you crying?" The old man answered, "I forgot where we live."[140]

This chapter is about the whole of life and how to keep from rolling up your sidewalks too early. We will discuss how life goals make it possible for you to seize the future (it is all you have, whatever your age). Life goals are vehicles for pursuing old and new interests. They help you endure life's little bumps and persevere through the big ones. Finally, they allow you to plan beyond life.

Using the imagery of sidewalks, we talk about stopping the sidewalk-rollers, and about cobblestones and wandering sidewalks, sidewalk cracks, and the end of the trail. Sidewalk-rolling is a perennial temptation for people in the sunset years, so they are our sidewalk engineers for this journey down life's paths.

Roll Back the Sidewalk-Rollers

There are sidewalk-rollers and then there are sidewalk-rollers. Rolling up your own sidewalks to get to bed early is one thing, but suffering at the hands of other sidewalk-rollers is quite another.

Our society loves passive, don't-rock-the-boat kind of people. After all, do we want someone who thinks for himself operating a nuclear plant, assembling automobiles, or sitting on our board of directors? Should we expect something different from retired people than we expect from most of the passive people in our society? Every day people have sidewalks rolled up right in front of them and what do they do? They mutter, "That's life. That's the way the ball bounces." Why should people entering retirement years want—or find—anything different?

All kinds of gimmicks sidetrack us too easily from the freedom that is ours. Renting a video movie is quick, painless, and cheap; viewing it passively in the comfort of home saves gas and money. So why not take the easy way and deprive ourselves of free choices that may lead down new paths? Commercialism can cut our freedom so deeply that it bleeds to death. As years of conditioning take their toll, some retirees find it easier to roll up sidewalks than to pursue new paths.

American society cultivates a distorted image about retirement. It teaches that retirement is the end of work-life and a time for rolling up sidewalks on much that is important. Our MTV-saturated society wants us to think that retirees should have as much freedom and independence as the rest of us—that is, as little as possible. We are supposed to remain passive and pliant to the influence of others.

Our culture gets a solid "handle" on retired people through myths about aging, a process that presses seniors into a common mold and denies the freedom that is theirs. We hear that elderly people are susceptible to acute illness. Is there any question that people decline rapidly after age sixty-five? Or that older people cannot cope with mental activity since their brains deteriorate? The myth-holders should have presented their claims to judges who awarded Mother Teresa the Nobel Peace Prize in 1979, and someone should inform her and her Sisters of Charity of these myths about aging. Surely they should tell the poor people in Calcutta and around the world that she is the one who needs help.

These are attractive myths, but here are the facts. A person over sixty-five has an average of 1.3 acute illnesses a year compared with 2.1 for people of all ages. Also, Duke University studied a group of people over age sixty-five and found that half of those returning for periodic checkups had no detectable physical decline over periods ranging from three to thirteen years. Finally,

> *mental disorders previously absent are not likely to occur in old age. True senility is uncommon, and only one percent of the elderly are likely to become demented. The much-touted loss of brain cells is a natural process common to every human being.*[141]

One cliché turns out to be true. People mellow with age as small problems become minor annoyances and big problems get smaller. Dr. Steve Roose of the New York Psychoanalytic Institute says research shows that the middle years reduce anger, anxiety, and impulsiveness as brain functions change.[142]

Life expectancy tables force us to face passivity and aging head-on for if we like to roll up sidewalks at age thirty, what lies ahead for us at seventy? In 1890 we would not have worried much since a man's life expectancy was forty-two years and woman's forty-five. Average life expectancy in the United States has almost doubled in a hundred years. The following data from Metropolitan Life Insurance illustrates current life expectancy from birth through age eighty-five (all figures are approximate).[143]

One way of stopping sidewalk-rollers at any age is to see in our minds how things can be different. That process is visioning life goals. Whatever your age and life expectancy, imaging life goals and positive self-talk can help you avoid the Seven Last Words of a Non-Growing Person: "*I never did it that way before.*" We change habits and attitudes about the future by visioning a different future.

Do you tell yourself you cannot do something or make certain changes, or that you cannot stop the sidewalk-roller wherever you are in life? When you do, remember that many people have been wrong about predictions like these. Even admirals make mistakes. Two years before Pearl Harbor U.S. Navy Rear Admiral Clark Wood declared, "As far as sinking a ship with a bomb is concerned, you just can't do it."[144] He probably would have said the same about stopping sidewalk-rollers!

AMERICANS LIVING LONGER

YEARS TO LIVE

WOMEN = O
MEN = X

80	O								
	XO								
70	XO								
	XO	O							
60	XO	O							
	XO	XO	O						
50	XO	XO	O						
	XO	XO	XO	O					
40	XO	XO	XO	XO					
	XO	XO	XO	XO	O				
30	XO	XO	XO	XO	XO				
	XO	XO	XO	XO	XO	O			
20	XO	XO	XO	XO	XO	XO			
	XO	XO	XO	XO	XO	XO	XO		
10	XO	XO	XO	XO	XO	XO	XO	XO	
	XO	XO	XO	XO	XO	XO	XO	XO	XO
0	XO	XO	XO	XO	XO	XO	XO	XO	XO
	Birth	**15**	**25**	**35**	**45**	**55**	**65**	**75**	**85**

CURRENT AGE

When Life Goals Go Flat

Sometimes after we achieve a goal what remains has a flat taste, like day-old cola. This can happen when we make important shifts in lifestyle or life-direction, or after a major accomplishment such as reaching retirement. Will Rogers reminds us at times like this, "Don't try to heat an oven with snowballs."

Life goals can go flat when extenuating circumstances *force* us into goal evaluation. Usually it is easier and more fun to initiate your own changes. Forced change is like having a molar pulled without novocaine, and rebellion is a natural reaction when compulsory change is thrust on us. The future is all we have, and it seems less inviting if someone has already spelled it out in detail.

Making decisions about life is critical work since these decisions affect the future that life holds. For example, among critical decisions are those about retirement and expanding life horizons, and some people want other, wiser heads to make these decisions for them. In his cartoon "Ziggy" once asked an old sage on the mountain, "What is the meaning of life?" The sage replied, "Keep breathing as long as possible."

For us all, including people nearing retirement, the most critical decision about the future is our decision about the future itself. The sage's "Keep breathing as long as possible" is one option among others. If it is our future's only focus, it shows that our basic plan is reliance on self-preservation to overcome fear, and the rest of the future is largely irrelevant. There has to be more to the future than "keep breathing."

Our perception of time is closely related to our view of the future. We agree that sixty minutes make an hour but differ on how long an hour is. This experiment with friends makes that clear. Set an alarm clock to go off in an hour and hide it, then start visiting to see how long it takes for each of you to time an hour without referring to your watch. The alarm clock tells the chronological truth, and you tell the perceptual truth about time and the future.

Time "stands still" and "flies," and we apply similar filters in our view of the future. How we think about the future, the time to come, affects our decisions about that future. Sometimes life goals go flat when the future looks flat. The following worksheet will help you understand your view of the future as you answer each question.

ATTITUDES ABOUT THE FUTURE		
	Circle one	
Thinking about the future, I feel what is coming will be mostly	GOOD	BAD
When I think about my ability to influence or change the future, I feel that	YES, I can change it	NO, I cannot change it
Based on my answers, my basic attitude toward the future seems more like (choose one)		
A. Here comes the future and I can make it better.		
B. Here comes the future but it unfolds by itself and I cannot change it.		
C. Here comes the future and although it is bad, I can make it better.		
D. Here comes the future; it will be bad and I cannot do anything about it.		

Many people in the United States are more pessimistic about the future than they used to be.[145] We cannot ignore our nation's major problems and the world's ills, including racism and poverty, but as individuals we still have some influence and control over our futures. The people who are sidewalk-rollers prefer that we have a negative view of the future since it serves their purpose. It is our task to know what things we can change and to do so; many people waste time and their life trying to change what they cannot change.

Do not be surprised by a grim future if you merely repeat the past. When goals go flat it is time to give your eyes something new to look at, a vision of your future. Turning your mind's power loose on a different future takes energy but rewards are great. Life goals are for visioning. They cannot go flat if your eyes see them vividly, and they bring a future that holds excitement.

Retirement Planning

Planning for retirement is a lifelong process that begins with a person's hopes and dreams for freedom to do what he or she wants toward the end of life. Retirement planning ends when these hopes and dreams end, sometimes before retirement begins. This planning is a major weapon for use against sidewalk-rollers.

Retirement usually causes a major upheaval in lifestyle, so planning is important. People who went to work regularly for forty years suddenly have the leisure of staying in bed; homemakers accustomed to peace and quiet have another body rattling around the house. For many retirees the haunting question each day is what to do today? We should never be in the situation of a man who was asked what he did and replied, "Nothing, I'm retired."

Planning life goals for retirement creates new hubs for daily living. Life goals help us focus on what we want to do to fill our hours with meaningful activities and experiences. The time and effort needed for planning pays off since there is more ahead.

Before Columbus' famous voyage most people believed that the world ended in the Atlantic, just past Gibraltar. Spain proudly claimed to be the westernmost part of the earth, lying at world's edge, and the motto *Ne plus ultra* ("There is no more beyond here") adorned the Royal Coat of Arms. After the discovery of Columbus the royal motto was meaningless in its old form so an advisor recommended that Queen Isabella drop the *ne* (no). Her Coat of Arms then read, "There is more beyond here."

Retirement planning does the same. It says there is more of life around the corner. New routines and exciting experiences replace the workaday world that retirees leave behind. Retirement is a third career, after early life and education, and raising a family and earning a living. Those who pass up pre-retirement seminars and workshops ignore training for that third career.

We live in a new age when retirement planning is a necessity. Through most of American history one in ten people could expect to live to age sixty-five, but now almost 80% of Americans will live past sixty-five, with 3,000 people retiring each day. Estimates are that by the year 2040 over eighty-seven million people will be older than sixty-five. Baby boomers born between 1946 and 1964 (one third of the nation's population) will start reaching retirement age in

2011, bringing great changes to American demographics. A female at age sixty-five can expect to live 18.6 years and a male 14.6 according to life insurance statisticians. Even now the government sends Social Security payments to 7,000 people who are above the age of 100.[146]

As we plan for retirement, whatever our age, some of us may expect something for nothing. We hope to arrive at the gold watch with little exertion along the way. We want to believe what Mark Twain said: "It is better to have old, second-hand diamonds than none at all." As if they grew on trees!

Expecting something for nothing in retirement reminds me of an urban legend that floats around the United States. Maybe you have heard it. It goes like this. Someone reports that a friend in Los Angeles (or somewhere) told her she could buy a $40,000 Porsche sports car for only $500. The reason for the low price was that the car sat in the desert for a week with a dead man inside and the dealer could not remove the smell of death.[147] This legendary "death car" is one of the few things you can expect for almost nothing.

Financial planning for retirement is like all planning: it takes time, effort, and consistent visioning of goals. It is essential to begin with a realistic basis, and that means eliminating financial myths about retirement. Here are five of them.

First, "I will not need as much money in retirement as I do now." Most financial planners say you need seventy percent of pre-retirement income to maintain your lifestyle. Second, "Social Security will cover my retirement." In 1990 the average recipient collected $602 per month, amounting to thirty-eight percent of the per-capita retirement income. "My company pension will cover my retirement needs" is the third. That depends on how well your company invests pension money, whether the company exists when you retire, and who might rob the pension bank through restructuring. Some people do a poor job of investing their own pension funds if given a choice. Myth four is "Medicare is the only health insurance I will need to retire." Medicare commences at age sixty-five and typically pays only fifty percent of medical expenditures. Last, "I can put off retirement planning until I am in my fifties." Time is your best friend for accumulating retirement diamonds. If you want a million dollars at age sixty, contribute $2,715 a year starting at age twenty. At nine percent annual return you will have it, minus Uncle's tax bite.

Here are some interesting facts to use in retirement planning. With today's life expectancy, people retiring at age 65 will live fifteen years without a paycheck. What happens by age sixty-five for each hundred people who begin their careers? Twenty-five are dead. Twenty have annual income under $6,000. Fifty-one have annual income between $6,000 and $35,000 (the median for this group is about $8,000). Four of the one hundred are financially successful with annual income above $35,000. These people did not plan to fail. They failed to include retirement planning in their life goals, and then vision and execute their financial plan.

Planning to retire at sixty-five or earlier is one thing, but retiring out of necessity is another. That happens more often than we think with disability as the major cause. Insurance agents stress the need for disability insurance to supplement the generally small protection offered by employers, and here is why. At almost any age the odds of disability are greater than the odds of death. At age thirty-five the odds of becoming disabled are three times higher than dying in the next fifteen years. This table from a major disability insurer tells the tale.

DISABILITY AND DEATH

Age	Chance of Disability in 15 Years	Chance of Death in 15 Years	Chance of Disability in 30 Years	Chance of Death in 30 Years
20	1 in 10	1 in 35	1 in 3	1 in 10
25	1 in 8	1 in 29	1 in 3	1 in 8
30	1 in 6	1 in 22	1 in 3	1 in 5
35	1 in 5	1 in 15	1 in 2	1 in 4
40	1 in 4	1 in 10	1 in 2	1 in 3
45	1 in 4	1 in 7	1 in 2	1 in 2
50	1 in 4	1 in 4	Virtually certain	Virtually certain

Here is a startling fact. Fifty percent of all persons who are age twenty-five will experience disability of at least three months duration before reaching age sixty-five. The average duration of disability for people in this group is almost four and one-half years. People who are disabled more than three months have a high chance of lifetime disability. At age twenty-five that probability is 25%, at age thirty-five it is 8%, at age forty-five it is 33%, and at age fifty-five it is 40%. In sum, about 13% of twenty-five-year-olds will have a lifetime disability before age sixty-five. Forced retirement arrives earlier than expected for some.

The probability of disability increased as medical science reduced the death rate from four major diseases. The period between 1960 and 1979 saw dramatic decreases in deaths from hypertension (-73%), heart disease (-29%), stroke (-48%), and diabetes (-27%). The total death rate from all four fell by thirty-two percent. On the other hand, the four diseases raised disability by a total of 55%. This period saw a rise in people disabled by hypertension (+70%), heart disease (+44%), stroke (+36%), and diabetes (+36%).

Planning for voluntary or involuntary retirement is a lifelong project that includes financial and disability strategies. Financial counselors and others can offer guidance, but the responsibility for setting goals and executing plans is yours. For help I offer this tongue-in-cheek economic forecast, which applies to any decade between now and the year 2050. "Besides war or peace, you have almost nothing to worry about. Naturally there will be adjustments and some businesses will disappear, but when viewed from a broad perspective this is a healthy thing. It reduces competition. Most indications are that people will continue eating, drinking, sleeping, and having babies throughout most of the decade. Don't sell America short. If you take a gamble and lose anyway, remember that I told you so."

When you retire with wealth remember this old Chinese proverb. "Though you dwell in the heart of the mountains, you will have many distant relatives if you are rich." And what about the following categories—do any of them fit your financial condition?

If a man runs after money, he's money-mad; if he keeps it, he's a capitalist; if he spends it, he's a playboy; if he doesn't get it, he's a ne'er-do-well; if he doesn't try to get it, he lacks ambition. If he gets it without working for it, he's a parasite; and if he accumulates it after a lifetime of hard work, people call him a fool who never got anything out of life.[148]

Retirement planning may not seem worth the trouble with everyone complaining about your money, but when retirement comes you will know your visioning was the key to success. You used life goals to seize the future and make it happen. Each day of retirement planning is another day devoted to rolling back the sidewalk-rollers.

Another phase of retirement planning touches on your values. This is not a venture you suddenly undertake at age sixty-four since clarifying values is a lifelong pursuit. But it is also an important part of retirement planning. Retired people have more time to do what they want to do, to do things that count. Figuring out what counts can be a challenge, as Robert Frost taught us in his short poem, "Precaution."[149]

I never dared be radical when young
For fear it would make me conservative when old.

Not taking positions or holding firmly to values makes it easier to avoid life goals that carry out values.

At any point in life you can use the following survey of values to decide what counts for you. The survey has two sides. First are what you consider the most desirable "end" values, or Life Values. Second are the personal values you consider most important for conducting life. Choose a number between 1 and 18 for each of the Life Values (no two numbers alike), and do the same for Personal Values. In each set the most important value is numbered 1, the least important 18. Fill in all the blanks.[150]

Life Values

____ A comfortable life (prosperity)
____ An exciting life (stimulating, active, creative, imaginative life)
____ A sense of accomplishment (lasting contribution to something important)
____ A world at peace (free of war and conflict)
____ A world of beauty (beauty of nature and the arts)
____ Equality (fellowship, equal opportunity for all)
____ Family security (taking care of loved ones)
____ Freedom (interdependence, free choice)
____ Happiness (contentedness, well-being, relaxation)
____ Inner harmony (freedom from inner conflict, feeling your life is going in the right direction)
____ Mature love (sexual and spiritual intimacy)
____ National security (protection from those who encroach)
____ Pleasure (enjoyable, leisurely life)
____ Salvation (eternal life, religious faith)
____ Self-respect (self-esteem, feeling good about yourself)
____ Social recognition (honored, respected and admired)
____ True friendship (close companionship)
____ Wisdom (mature understanding of life)

Personal Values

____ Ambitious (hardworking, aspiring)
____ Broad-minded (open to new ideas, experiences)
____ Capable (competent, effective in whatever you undertake)
____ Cheerful (joyful, spontaneous)
____ Clean (neat, tidy)
____ Courageous (standing up for your beliefs, taking necessary risks)
____ Forgiving (willing to pardon others)
____ Helpful (working for the welfare of others, dedication to something outside yourself)
____ Honest (truthful, sincere, person of integrity)
____ Imaginative (daring, creative, innovative)

____ Independent (self-reliant, self-sufficient)
____ Intellectual (reflective, intelligent)
____ Logical (consistent, rational)
____ Loving (affectionate, tender, give and receive love)
____ Obedient (loyal, respectful, dutiful)
____ Polite (courteous, well-mannered)
____ Responsible (dependable, reliable)
____ Self-controlled (self-disciplined, restrained, hold back emotions when necessary)

The important question is how well you put into practice the life and personal values on the top of your list. For a person nearing or entering retirement this question can lead to solid planning and action. You can formulate goals that incorporate the life values most important to you, and other goals around personal values that you want to display in your retirement years. Visioning these goals will lead to action, and soon you will be counting the fruits of retirement planning.

Here are two other valuing exercises useful throughout life, and especially in retirement planning. The first is to pick the three or four places on earth that are most important for you personally. Why are they important? Are they worth re-visiting? Should that become a life goal? Second, what three or four objects are your most valued possessions? Why? What do they say about the personal and life values you selected above? Should you make them part of your goal matrix in some way?

Planning for retirement also involves blueprinting a longer life. We do that when we plan tomorrow, for tomorrow is all that we have. A longer life means more time to accomplish our life goals.

In one word the simple prescription for a longer life is activity. That means physical activity, intellectual stimulation, and social and emotional involvement. People who keep moving physically, intellectually, socially, and emotionally will have longer lives, with fullness thrown in for good measure. Falling down in any area will shorten the quality and perhaps the length of life.

We like to joke about how old people rely too much on momentum to get going. A one hundred-year-old rabbi celebrated his birthday in New York's Queens eight years after retiring from rabbinical work. People told him to keep his remarks short at the party, but he wanted to thank everyone on hand. His biggest problem was getting around. His daughter told about helping him one time and later he shouted his disapproval for a full hour. "I don't want it," the rabbi said about help in getting around. "I have one hand on my cane, and I wave this arm and I get momentum and I go forward."[151]

If needed, start waving your arms right now for locomotion and activity. The secret of a long, full life is moving physically, rearranging brain neurons intellectually, exchanging niceties socially, and involving yourself with others emotionally. Just ask the rabbi about locomotion. It is never too late to start and always too early to quit. Ninety-year-old Walter Heck of Florida has a passion for exercise. He says that sometimes "you can hear the bones crack," but he swims regularly and joins in calisthenics classes in and out of water.[152]

To sum up, there is an easy way to tell whether you have to battle sidewalk-rollers each day and continue retirement planning, even if you are retired. Here is the test. Pinch yourself to see whether you are alive. If your ticker is ticking you still face the challenge. If you are breathing, you can use life goals to seize the future. That is all you ever have, whatever the age.

I used to tell my eighty-five-year-old mother that if God wanted heaven to be her only goal she would be there already. The same is true for all of us. This side of the Great Divide, one constant life goal is pushing back sidewalk-rollers that want to terminate your goals and put you to sleep before bedtime.

Cobblestones and Wandering Sidewalks

Europe's cobblestone sidewalks have a novelty of their own. These old paved walkways show a new side of life to traveling Americans, and people who are used to cement find that something old can be new and exciting. No less interesting are the new-style wandering sidewalks found in some cities. They meander through parks and along trafficways, bringing refreshment and renewal during long walks. They invite you to join their gentle weave from side to side, and after walking their paths you may experience a letdown on straight sidewalks. Wandering sidewalks show how variety can overcome the staleness of a life.

Variety and something new make a powerful combination, and that is why brides wear something old and something new. Living life before and after retirement is much the same. It is a process of change, growth, and learning; of combining old and new.

Old and New Skills and Abilities

Like the rest of life, retirement combines variety with the mundane, old skills and new interests, old habits and new conventions. Retirement's sidewalks are linked with yesterday's, taking up where they end. Sometimes they are cobblestones laid out in new patterns, and sometimes they are meandering sidewalks that apply old interests and skills in new ways. Life goals are vehicles to pursue these old and new interests.

Businesses today want a precise mission statement that describes what the company stands for. I value the personal creed as a vision statement for life. While a personal creed may change often, it embodies a person's old and new interests and tells how they apply to life.

Try composing your personal creed right now. Take a blank sheet of paper and write "I believe" on every other line, then fill as many lines as possible by completing the line. "I believe every person has a right to his own opinion." "I believe big government gets in the way of the small businessperson." "I believe that dogs are smarter than cats and should receive better treatment." Whatever your beliefs—and let's hope most are serious in nature—put them down, including religious faith and values. Then change the list as necessary, add belief statements you missed the first time, and sign your name if this is your *credo* about life.

This simple exercise encourages you to apply skills and abilities in new environments, and to develop new skills and abilities in old surroundings. Do you believe what you wrote? Then what life goal(s) can move your personal creed from contemplation to reality? Will you pound your creed until it speaks in the world of action?

In retirement people have the luxury of time to give flesh and bones to their personal creeds. One way is constructing a hundred Round Tuits and using one a day while they last.

You do not recognize Round Tuits? They are the things that you always wanted to do but never got "'round to it." Now with time available all you need is the Round Tuit that you lacked. You can use the tops of cans or cut them from wood or paper. Write with a magic marker the things you wanted to do for so long, and then do them. Your personal creed can help you assign Round Tuit priorities. I can see you now. You are sitting with stacks of Round Tuits, laughing as you accomplish one, then another after waiting forty years to get around to it. When will you start?

Whether you rely on Round Tuits or other methods, all your plans will come to nothing without action. Unless you take action you will not use old skills in new circumstances, or develop new skills in old surroundings. Dreaming of cobblestones and wandering sidewalks is not walking on them. Samuel Johnson described the difference between growling and barking in retirement: "Don't think of retiring from the world until the world will be sorry that you retire. I hate a fellow whom pride or cowardice or laziness drive into a corner, and who does nothing when he is there but sit and growl. Let him come out as I do, and bark."

Your life goals are vehicles for pursuing old and new interests. You assemble the two puzzle-pieces of creativity when you dream creative thoughts and then do something tangible and visible. It is important to remember that people do not have the "special gift" of creativity; they develop this gift by marrying hard work to life goals. J. Robert Evans reminds us that "productive creativity is neither kooky nor mystical." It is a process, a "series of events and a way of doing things that leads to a desired result or product."[153] Take Thomas Edison, for instance. Other inventors had ideas about how a light bulb should work, but he alone turned thought into reality with a working bulb. His creativity linked a dream with hard work, and the result was the first incandescent.

Retirees, like the rest of us, have to make the first effort to use old skills and abilities as they pursue interests old and new. One author puts it well:

> *I also know that no one will come to my door to invite me to become master of my work and my life. It is something I must initiate on my own. Have you ever seen a leaf in search of a tree, or a twinkle in pursuit of a star? It is equally absurd to envision rain hunting for a cloud or fragrance in quest of a flower.*[154]

Waiting for a world of new interests to fall from heaven in retirement is like waiting for lightning to strike when the sky is blue.

People build cobblestone walks and wandering sidewalks as they develop new interests and channel old interests into new pursuits. Their paths result in many interesting journeys. For example, some people have the gift of visiting and others the gift of letter-writing. What about using these interests with prisoners?

Joyce Page has taken up the challenge at the St. Louis County Correctional Institution almost every weekday since 1979. She spends her lunch hour with prisoners, eating a peanut butter sandwich, holding a worship service, singing, and discussing life and the Bible. "It depends on their needs," she explains. Why during lunch? She has no time after work. She is raising six of her own kids as a single parent.

A ninety-one-year-old retiree named Myrtle Howell reaches prisoners all over the country with her letters. She has corresponded with hundreds, as many as forty at once. The project began with her letter to "Any Inmate" in the Atlanta penitentiary. When Charles Colson of Watergate fame visited her in a Georgia nursing home he saw stacks of prison mail on her tiny desk. He thought to himself, "This woman is not preparing to die."[155]

Acting on interests old and new can surprise retirees and others. Eleanor Hyndman took up karate with her grandson at age seventy-eight, saying it sharpened her mental abilities and increased her self-confidence. She soon moved from the orange to purple belt and won a gold medal in her division.[156]

Hobbies connect the sunset years with life before retirement. Some are old interests that carry forward to a new age while others blossom in retirement, when time and money are available. Retirement often extends for fifteen or twenty years, and this is more than enough time to grow a hobby or three.

> *Among other things, you could master another language or two; raise funds for a favorite charity or your alma mater; become a lawyer or legal aide; a "grandperson" to a lonely child; an expert on local history, world history, eighteenth-century French history; brush up on your musical talents, form a musical ensemble; write a novel, contribute a column to the local newspaper; become a good real estate agent; turn to carpentry...the list is endless.*[157]

Pets also can be a diversion. Part of living is sensing living things, so gardening and cultivating indoor plants are old interests for some and new ones for others.

For many retirees, having a second career (after making a living) is a life goal for pursuing interests old and new. Second-career people retire to build the cobblestone walk or meandering sidewalk they always wanted to build. Grandma Moses (Anna Mary Robertson) began painting at seventy-two and was still working at one hundred. Colonel Sanders started a fried chicken business at age sixty-six and Noah Webster was seventy when he compiled his dictionary. Sometimes careers extend long into life. Winston Churchill wrote a major history of the English people at age eighty-two. Goethe finished his *Faust* at eighty-one, and George Burns charms young women in his late nineties. I have considered a second career writing obituaries in Florida and Arizona's retirement towns. Wouldn't this be a snappy business jingle for a TV commercial? "You live your life—We write the happy ending!"

In the nineteenth century, when most women were greatly underestimated, Dorothea Dix changed the treatment of mentally ill people almost singlehandedly. She started her campaign at age forty-five. Storming from state to state, she unshackled insane people and led them from dark, filthy dungeons into more respectable treatment. She would not believe the jailer who told her that two inmates in an unheated cell "can't feel the cold" with their minds gone. When she died at eighty-five she could claim responsibility for more than a hundred modern asylums and hospitals in America.[158] Her career extended late into life.

One big mistake sometimes made in retirement, as in other phases of life, is over-reliance on a single goal. You probably have met retirees who say they are going to travel, and that is all they intend to do. Travel is an important part of life (see below), but seldom can it serve as life's end-all. Neither can gardening alone, or any of hundreds of other interests and hobbies. American novelist Ellen Glasgow said it well. "The only difference between a rut and a grave are their dimensions."[159] Loading all retirement interests into one basket creates the potential for boredom that single-track people suffer throughout life. The key is having life goals for old and new interests.

Pope John XXIII provides an illuminating example. When he was elected in October 1958, the short, fat Italian was supposed to be a "caretaker" pope. Would it not have been enough if he had plowed ahead with single mind, caring for the institution? Had the church elevated him for any reason besides preserving the papacy for his successor? What more could one ask of a prelate just short of his seventy-seventh birthday?

Perhaps it was an unconscious life goal that lay submerged for years. Anyhow, the idea of an ecumenical council suddenly appeared in John XXXIII's mind and became his consuming goal. Hear him tell how he distinguished between a rut and a grave in these words:

> *Without any forethought, I put forward, in one of my first talks with my Secretary of State, on 20 January, 1959, the idea of an Ecumenical Council, a Diocesan Synod and the revision of the Code of Canon Law, all this being quite contrary to any previous supposition or idea of my own on this subject. I was the first to be surprised at my proposal, which was entirely my own idea.*

Pope John called it a grace that he accepted "certain ideas which were not in the least complex in themselves, indeed perfectly simple, but far-reaching in their effects and full of responsibilities for the future."[160] More than that, the ideas could be carried out.

John XXIII turned the papacy into a second career. His goal was not to be a caretaker for life but to show the ecumenical nature of the whole church, including the "separated brethren." He used a life goal to pursue old and new interests, and the world of faith has not been the same.

Moving

Where to live is a lively question for retirees, but they share this concern about moving with most Americans since on average one-fifth of us move every year. With a population of 275 million that comes to about 55 million people annually. We average fourteen to fifteen moves in a lifetime, so several residential changes in retirement fit the pattern.

Finding the right place to retire is another way of asking, "How will my life goals pursue old and new interests?" It is the same question that people ask before moving north at age thirty-five because they like skiing and shoveling snow.

It is wise to consult others about where to live in retirement, but beware of pompous pronouncements. When someone absolutely, positively knows where you should retire, chances are good that the opinion is suspect. That is like an Associated Press declaration in 1954 that said, "The Leaning Tower of Pisa leaned 6mm. (.236 inches) thus far this year. Experts said if the present rate of lean continues it will collapse in about 400 years." I am sure the inhabitants of Pisa were very worried with this news.

Cowboys in the Old West gave some good advice about where to retire when they said that "a stone stops rollin' when it finds the kind of moss it wants to gather." Your retirement home should fit your lifestyle like a glove. Like much of life, retiring is about making cobblestone walks and wandering sidewalks. Where you do it depends in large part on how well your life goals can pursue old and new interests.

Daily Success

An older woman once told me, "Always be planning something." These words apply at age twenty or eighty because life without plans is a rolled-up sidewalk. A successful life revolves around successful days, and if we plan successful days they become successful months and years. We find little trouble planning and enjoying successful days if our life goals pursue old and new interests.

Say you have done all the right imaging of your life goals. You engage in positive self-talk and feel good about life. What have you done? You have laid a firm foundation for the attitudes and habits that move you where you want to go. What comes next? How can you give your subconscious a helping hand in moving toward that life goal? How can you put attitude and habit into practice so that you act? In brief, how do you lay the first cobblestone? The answer is a daily success. The answer is behavioral modification, your modification of your behavior. Both are true.

Only you can change you, and the best way is to start changing. Perhaps you are willing to pay $7,500 for a psychiatrist to help you discover why you have trouble meeting people, and it may be worth it. But maybe you should modify your behavior bit by bit so you begin meeting people.

Over the years I have counseled individuals with a variety of problems. Many just needed someone to help them understand their problem and reaffirm their strength to do something about it. Those with clinical maladies received long-term care with a psychiatrist or psychologist. As counselees grew more comfortable with me they stopped talking about little problems and got around to the "biggie" that bothered them. They had been testing to see whether I was ready to listen, and some expected shock, horror, or rejection when they discussed the real problem.

In later sessions I generally offered a choice of two or three activities for them to take control of their problem. Usually the counselee accepted the challenge and we made a pact to "see how it went" with their action, which involved modifying behavior. For example, one woman agreed to count aloud to twenty before snapping back in anger at her husband, and this modification of her behavior became part of the solution. In the process most counselees saw their problems more clearly and decided what to do about them.

One way of ensuring daily success is to modify some part of your behavior in that direction. If you want to smile more, modify your behavior to mold your attitude and habit; practice smiling twenty times a day before a mirror and ten times without one. Before long your subconscious (working on your life goal) and your facial muscles are working in consonance as behavioral modification reinforces the life goal imprinted on your subconscious.

Behavioral modification is a shortcut that pays handsome dividends. It is like telling yourself you are "good" each morning rather than trying to pronounce "supercalifragilistic-expialidocious," which means "good" in *Mary Poppins*. Take the easy way to lay cobblestones, one at a time with a success each day. Secretary of State Dean Acheson was right about the future when he said, "Perhaps the best thing about the future is that it only comes one day at a time." The same is true of daily successes produced by behavioral modification.

Volunteering is one way of ensuring daily success. Surveys report that about 30% of people over age sixty contribute their time to volunteer efforts. Where? At any of a hundred places and activities that include libraries, museums, hospitals, nursing homes, Big Brother and Big Sister organizations, churches, and schools (assistants and mentors). Helping small business people and minority businesses, serving on boards and commissions—the list is almost endless.

Volunteer work makes successful days by building self-esteem, an important ingredient of life in the sunset years. Just as you have a hard time loving others without loving yourself, so it is hard to help yourself without helping others. Steady volunteerism is part of a survival plan for retirement, and it brings the added gift of cobblestones and wandering sidewalks as you pursue old and new interests.

At any age volunteering makes a contribution to the human fraternity. Once a rabbi asked his students how they could tell when the night had ended and the day was on its way back. "Could it be," one student asked, "when you see an animal in the distance and can tell whether it is a sheep or a dog?" "No," the rabbi answered. "Could it be when you can look at a tree in the distance and can tell if it is a fig tree or a peach tree?" asked another. "No," answered the rabbi. "Well then, when is it?" the pupils demanded. "It is when you look on the face of any woman or man and see that she or he is your sister and brother? Because if you cannot do this, no matter what time it is, it is still night." Volunteering empowers people to recognize others as brothers and sisters.

In retirement, travel is a sign of freedom that can also contribute significantly to daily success. Any person can make paths of his own apart from travel, but traveling is a way to stake out your territory, if only for a day.

Books tell more than we want to know about where to travel and how to get there. None of them explain why state highway construction crews erect signs that say, "Detour ahead. This construction is for your convenience." Watch your teeth and shock absorbers during the detour!

Travelers often debate the relative merits of destinations. One time a person championed the beauties of a certain place in an extended speech. After he finished another man offered a five-word response: "There is no there *there*." It is good that we do not believe everything we hear about destinations. In 1861 Lieutenant Joseph Ives of the Corps of Topographical Engineers said about the Grand Canyon, "It is, of course, altogether valueless...Ourselves are the first, and doubtless will be the last, party of whites to visit this profitless locality. It seems intended by nature that the Colorado River shall be forever unvisited and undisturbed."[161]

Retirees planning to visit the country with travel trailers may know the popular Travel Bare legend, but if not they should learn it, especially the men. Newspapers have carried many versions of this legend, such as this one datelined Prince Albert, Saskatchewan, on August 3, 1962.

> *It was really quite simple, an American tourist explained to Royal Canadian Mounted Police who found him wandering along a highway near here clad in his undershorts. His story: His wife was driving the family car while he relaxed in the trailer. She stopped to let some bears cross the road and the husband stepped out to see what the trouble was. His wife drove on. The police drove seventy miles before overhauling his wife and reuniting the couple.*[162]

Many of these accounts float around the country, all revolving around the male's fear of being found nude in public.

Do you want to try something different in your travels? So did John A. Krohn. He was thirty-five years old in 1908 when he decided to walk the perimeter of the United States, pushing a wheelbarrow. Before returning to Maine he covered over 9,000 miles, mostly on railroad tracks. His expenses included eleven pairs of shoes, 112 pairs of socks, and five wheels and three tires for the wheelbarrow. His total bill was $1,356, about $3 a day for the 367-day trip.[163]

Because it broadens perspective at any age, travel can put your life goals into action as you pursue old and new interests. Seeing real cobblestones and wandering sidewalks can help you design your own.

New Tricks

Canine experts argue about whether they can teach old dogs new tricks, but psychologists answer with a resounding "Yes!" if the subject is people. A person who shuts down his learning mechanism anytime in life might as well crawl into a kennel since he has already retreated from being human.

An old sign in my father's office combined German and English words to read, "Ve get too soon olt and too late schmardt." It joked about how age often thwarts the search for knowledge and wisdom, but it did not say, "Ve get too old fer lerning." This powerful myth about aging is also held by many seniors. In the mid-seventies a Harris poll discovered that 27% of the public over age sixty-five felt they were too old to learn.[164]

People fail to distinguish between learning and memory because they misunderstand the mind. The mind is not a data warehouse or giant memory dump but an instrument of learning. We can learn as long as we have a mind, although some powers of memory diminish. I probably could not memorize the Old Testament kings as rapidly as thirty years ago, but in the intervening period my passion for learning has increased, not diminished.

Some people who like books and reading are baffled by book depositories (I am not talking about the one in Dallas). Libraries exist for the mind; they are not labyrinths to puzzle through. A course on using the library is a good investment for anyone, retired or not, since it can help us pursue old and new interests.

Books and libraries bring new learning and lead us down new paths. For instance, have you ever wondered how you would get rid of a dead cat if you lived in a large city and could not bury it? Consult the wisdom of the ages. The urban legend "Dead Cat in a Box" tells about a woman who puts her dead cat in a shoe box while on her way to bury the cat in the suburbs. She stops in a downtown department store, and while shopping she places the box on a counter. The box disappears, but a few minutes later the store detective finds a female shoplifter who has passed out in the powder room with an open shoe box on her lap.[165] Almost without effort you can learn how city people are supposed to bury cats and how to catch a shoplifter!

Community colleges and universities offer hundreds of courses for people of all ages, and senior citizens often enroll for half tuition or less. Well over a million seniors above age sixty-five return to educational institutions each year. Many schools have specialized senior programs for intellectual and cultural growth, and seniors are sometimes the course leaders. These experiences include credit and non-credit courses, lecture and travel series, workshops, and other activities. Combining cultural and language courses for a country such as Mexico puts real zip into travel plans. That could be an exciting life goal: traveling for a month in Mexico, appreciating its culture and history firsthand, and conversing in the native tongue.

Throughout life, learning experiences clarify personal goals and give a strong sense of accomplishment and self-worth. Educational programs offer social contacts and increase communication skills as people with common goals and interests gather around the pursuit of learning. Campuses and other learning sites add a refreshing dimension to life, and thousands of clubs and non-traditional programs spread the wealth widely. Museums, lecture programs, travel clubs, and other learning opportunities are available in most urban areas.

There are clubs for every imaginable interest, including Elvis, of course. Try these on for size: the International Wizard of Oz Club, Count Dracula Society, Titanic Historical Society, Society for Creative Anachronism (preserving the best of the Middle Ages), National Society for the Preservation of

Covered Bridges, Friends of Cast Iron Architecture, Sons and Daughters of the Soddies (preserving sod houses), Midwest Old Settlers and Threshers Association, American Sunbathing Association, Tattoo Club of America, Goose Island Bird and Girl Watching Society, International Frisbee Association, Cigar Smokers of America, International Lefthanders, Redhead League, Mothers-in-Law International, Cannon Hunter's Association of Seattle (they hunt cannons), Circus Fans' Association, National Button Society (1,600 members), American Homebrewer's Association, and the Jim Smith Society (if your name is Jim Smith). If that list is too short, try the Amphibious Auto Club of America (with annual swim meet) or American Association of Aardvark Aficionados. Are you still undecided? You belong in the Procrastinators Club of America.[166]

Cultivating "public" and "private" sides of life is an art that we can pursue throughout life. Some people are more effective and at ease in small groups and one-on-one conversations, while others excel in larger groups and public meetings. Marriages often attract opposites, so one spouse may be a private person and the other a public person.

Life goals help us pursue a new interest if we decide to strengthen our private or public side. A man who is ill at ease in idle chitchat can strengthen his personal and social skills in retirement. His spouse may expand the public side of her personality, strengthening and confirming her poise with groups of people. This give-and-take makes life exciting, whether in retirement or in middle-age. Walking on cobblestones and wandering sidewalks gives us the opportunity to strengthen our weaker personality traits.

With life goals fixed in your mind and emblazoned on your subconscious through visioning, you will find new sidewalks and cobblestones to wander. Life goals help retirees—and all of us—use old skills and abilities and cultivate new ones. Pursuing old and new interests helps us decide where to settle in retirement. Goals set the stage for daily success, which translates into monthly and yearly success as we modify behavior. Through our life goals we learn new tricks and use our minds as instrument of learning, not as mere depositories of information. This happens tomorrow since tomorrow is all that we have. It is more than enough for it is a new day, as the poet says:

Send tomorrow with its feel
of the softness of soil,
the grease of engines,
the splatter of paint,
the sound of music,
the joy of debate, and
the calmness of forgiveness.
Give us tomorrow and its new work,
new smell,
new touch,
new thoughts,
new hopes.
Lord, tomorrow
give us a new day.[167]

Sidewalk Cracks

Remember flying downhill on your skates or scooter? The faster you went the faster you passed over those sidewalk cracks. Everything was fine until you hit a big slit in the cement, or collided with a large crack opened by the winter freeze. Then came spill-time.

Negotiating regular or irregular cracks is child's play compared with the fissures that you pass over in life. Some bumps cause little hurt while others can throw you for a spill. Life goals enable you to endure life's little bumps and persevere through the big ones. They are ways of adapting to aging, health setbacks, second moves, and relations with your children and grandchildren. You are finding ways to jump the cracks when you impress these goals on your subconscious.

Aging and Health

Most of us have no desire to grow old—gracefully or any other way. That is why we keep our distance from aging by telling jokes. Did you hear about the man who was bragging about his new hearing aid? "It's the most expensive one I have ever bought, cost $3,000," he said. His friend turned to him and asked, "What kind is it?" The man looked at his wrist-watch and said, "Quarter past two."

Like it or not, we are as old as we feel, as old as we say, and as old as we are. All three are true. Imaging and positive self-talk can moderate the advances of age but can never turn back the clock since the crack of aging is here to stay. The best that we can do about it is not take it so seriously that we promote its cause. We should be like Sam, who visited his doctor for a pain in his right arm. "For Pete's sake, Sam," the doctor said, "what do you expect at 101?" "Dammit," Sam yelled back, "my left arm is also 101 and it does not hurt a bit!"

People keep saying, "At your age..." You can complete the sentence any way you want, but that does not make it true. Aging and achievement are not mutually exclusive. Here is some evidence. Bertrand Russell participated in international peace drives at ninety-four and George Bernard Shaw wrote the play *Farfetched Fables* at ninety-four. Eamon de Valera was president of Ireland at ninety-one and Adolph Zukor chairman of Paramount Pictures. At eighty-nine Arthur Rubenstein gave one of his greatest recitals at Carnegie Hall. Albert Schweitzer headed a hospital in Africa at the same age, and Konrad Adenauer was German chancellor at age eighty-eight.[168]

Health is part of aging and how we feel about aging, but probably no one is as boring as the constant health complainer. This kind of person deadens the air waves with ailments ranging from weekend constipation to supposed ringing in the eyes. When asked about health the older person should answer as if talking to the IRS: answer the immediate question and then shut up. Do not divulge your full medical history, including the tortures of bunion removal twenty-two years ago.

If one of your life goals is an image of good health, you will endure life's little health bumps and persevere through the big ones with aplomb. Marian MacDowell was a concert pianist who established a summer colony for artists after her composer-husband died. Late in life she constructed studios so artists of all kinds could work the full day without interruption. She offered this advice about afflictions and ills as she neared her 100th birthday.

Everyone in this busy world tends to have something in the way of discomfort, but I think most of us try to forget our physical ailments and go ahead with our work...I'm not going to write about my ailments. They're just the natural ones that any old woman who is nearly 100 is apt to have.[169]

One survivor of the airliner crash at LaGuardia Airport in 1992 had good reason to complain about health. Bleeding and soaking wet, he was struggling up the embankment from the water where the plane rested when a rescuer met him and asked, "Are you from the plane crash?" "No," the survivor said humorously. "I made a wrong left off the parkway."[170]

Good nutrition is integral to good health. Two of three deaths in the United States are linked with four nutritionally-related diseases, namely, cancer, diabetes, high-blood pressure, and heart disease.[171] Persons interested in a life goal of good health concentrate on three items: fat, salt, and fibre. They seek less of the first two and more of the third.

Many people consider sex a taboo subject for retirees since apparently seniors never engage in it. Probably the best advice I have read on sex came from an English romantic novelist. When all else fails, try her advice—or lacy underwear and a stiff drink. She wrote that

white sugar is the curse of civilization—it causes fatigue and sexual apathy between husband and wife. My recipe against sexual fatigue is to take honey in large quantities; two Gev-E-Tabs, ten vitamin E pills, four wheatgerm oil tablets, four vitamin A pills, four bonemeal tablets, six liver-plus tablets, two dessert-spoons of Bio-Strath Elixir, twice a day.[172]

Sex in the sunset years is like sex throughout life: it is less satisfying if the sun sets on love.

We are not making a joke of marital attachment, especially when it endures to the sunset years. Marriages that last through retirement bring days of joy and difficulty, depending partly on earlier times. Perhaps a man does well to accept Charles Dickens' advice in his story *Bleak House*, in which Mr. Bagnet is an ex-artilleryman and Mrs. Bagnet "a soldierly looking woman." In the course of conversation Mr. Bagnet tells his friend, George: "You know me. It's my old girl that advises. She has the head. But I never own to it before her. Discipline must be maintained. Wait till the greens is off her mind. Then, we'll consult. Whatever the old girl says, do—do it!"[173]

A retired man suffers a tremendous jolt if the "old girl" dies. For any retired couple, bidding farewell to a mate is one of life's most wrenching experiences. When death strikes we go through the five stages of grief so ably described by Dr. Elizabeth Kübler-Ross, but each phase seems to take an eternity as we move through denial, anger, bargaining, depression, and finally acceptance.

Most seniors take this as part of aging, although the grief is real. What is often more difficult to accept are the lifestyle changes or change in residence that follow. Dignity stands front and center in all these considerations.

As persons we want dignity at every stage in life, whether at age six or sixty. I remember entering grade school as a child just as World War II ended. Clothes were so scarce that I wore my sister's hand-me-down underwear. What made this unbearable was that the panties were made of some material that my classmates knew was not "normal" for boys. I lost all dignity as we lined up at the bathroom urinals, and I learned a powerful lesson about the need for dignity at all ages.

We do not like to think about nursing homes and other forms of assisted living, partly because of our fear of losing personal dignity. But increased life expectancy makes this a prime concern for all. The facts are that for a person aged sixty-five the chances of needing nursing home care are better than two out of five (43%). Furthermore, of this group 24% will spend at least two years in a nursing home, and 9% will spend at least five years. About 35% of all persons in nursing homes have been residents less than a year, 31% one to three years, 14% three to five years, and 18% five years or more. The average nursing home occupant has been in residence for almost three years, and today nursing home care costs about $35,000 annually.

One retirement life goal should address this issue of long-term care. People dutifully insure their cars although only one in seventy is involved in an accident each year. The same goes for houses, where one in eighty-eight catches fire annually. Despite the high percentage of people who will need convalescent or nursing care, few purchase the necessary protection. Some mistakenly rely on Medicare and Medicaid, which pay only about 50% of all nursing home costs in the United States and require divestiture of certain assets.

Children and Grandchildren

"Dear God, help me be the type of person my dog thinks I am." Public speaker Cavett Robert overheard that statement from a fourteen-year-old girl during a prayer breakfast in Australia.[174] Many a grandparent has probably prayed this prayer with a grandchild in mind.

An old Russian proverb says that grandparents get along better with grandchildren than with their children, and it is probably true. Parents often have such high expectations that no child grows up exactly like he or she should. Grandchildren are another story! Natural camaraderie develops between skip-generations, partly because each finds something lacking in-between. That is part of the generational ebb and flow we call the human tide.

Grandparents usually have an abiding interest in their

grandchildren. Books tell them how to be good grandparents, but few need them. Looking at a grandchild, grandparents may experience the feeling described by Robert Frost's short poem, "The Span of Life."[175]

The old dog barks backward without getting up.
I can remember when he was a pup.

Life goals about relations with children and grandchildren should be an integral part of retirement planning. This is too big a patch of ground to leave untilled. Little bumps and big cracks need jumping on retirement sidewalks, and some of them arise in family relationships.

Consciously cultivating grandchildren takes time and energy because it is an investment in the next generation. On the other hand, sometimes one's own children finally can be who they are when seniors move away in retirement. Clear-cut life goals allow you to negotiate the best path for you, your children, and grandchildren.

Grandparents should master the art of story-telling. Though often ignored, this genre makes a big impact on grandchildren. They want to know about you, and you must tell the story winsomely and sometimes in exaggerated style so they hear what you say and catch what you mean. Some adults grow older without acquiring this skill, so theirs is the challenge of learning to use the art for grandchildren and others. Part of staying alive and exciting is to avoid the boredom of having no stories to tell. Learning to tell stories well generates other stories to be told.

Some seniors limit their repertoire of stories to uninspiring chronicles of what they did on the job. These are not stories so much as company reports in oral form, or overblown statements of personal skill and success. They sometimes sound like a man who worked in the Research Department of the British Foreign Office. His service dates were the war years from 1903 to 1950, but he boasted at his retirement ceremony, "Year after year, the worriers and fretters would come to me with awful predictions of the outbreak of war. I denied it each time. And I was only wrong twice."[176] Telling good stories deflates boredom and passes tales of human experience from generation to generation.

Part of story-telling is recording your life memories on video, tape, or paper. This is a time for exaggeration! Remember how much colder the winters were back then? The stand-off with the bear in the woods? Your children and grandchildren will bless you for your memories and life-story, and you will enjoy personal rejuvenation and the excitement of sharing life's experiences.

Aging, health, another move, and relating to children and grandchildren are sidewalk cracks to be negotiated in the senior years, like much of life. When we create and envision vital life goals in these areas, we find ways to endure life's little bumps and persevere through the big ones.

Do Not Enter

The sign on the sidewalk says, "Do Not Enter." What lies beyond is new construction, and we must wait for now. Life goals serve the function of planning beyond life and arranging affairs so we pass that boundary in peace.

Have you ever recalled an incident in your life and suddenly understood how it now makes sense, in view of later developments? Is that wisdom? Is it a wise person who understands that the end gives perspective to all that precedes it?

You are entitled to your opinion. Mine is that our sense of mortality is the most critical factor in how we understand life. Seeing life backwards from death is seeing life as it really is and can be. Once you understand that death is the worst possible thing that can happen to you in this material world, you can lay solid plans. Marty Haugen's folk song "Canticle to the Son" says it well:

Praise to our death, that makes our life real,

The knowledge of loss that helps us to feel;
The gift of Yourself, Your presence revealed
To lead us home.

Psychiatrist M. Scott Peck says it differently: "The only real security in life lies in relishing life's insecurity."[177] Note his term "relishing."

There is nothing morbid about sensing mortality for the process liberates us by concentrating the mind and focusing our energy. Kids learn about it while jumping rope and singing,

Mother, mother, I am ill.
Call for the doctor over the hill.
Doctor, doctor, will I die?
Yes, my dear, and so will I.

You probably know all the household tricks for avoiding death. Never, ever rock an empty rocking chair. Never put a broom on a bed. Keep open umbrellas outside. Never wash a flag. Don't turn a chair on one leg. Keep your cat off the piano keys. Don't wash clothes on New Year's Day. Do all your sweeping before sundown. Sleeping with your head at the foot of the bed is fatal. Avoid these and all the other dangers of life and you will live forever—unless of course you fail to identify one.

Is it too simple to say that we are unprepared until we have learned enough about the meaning of life to be ready to die? That is one of the functions of life goals. They help us discover the meaning of our lives, including planning beyond life. Life goals are life's teaching path, and part of what we have to learn is the meaning of the "Do Not Enter" sign at life's end.

A contemporary novel tells the story of a young priest who was stricken with a terminal illness. The doctor told the priest's bishop (but not the priest) that he had two or three years to live. The bishop then assigned the young man to the most difficult parish in the diocese, serving native Indians in

British Columbia. Petty concerns fell away as the priest confronted life on its fundamental level. His work flourished, including motivating Indian youth to see new vistas, but his health was failing. Finally the bishop visited and discussed why this tiny parish had become so important. The bishop said that for him "it has been easier here, where only the fundamentals count, to learn what every man must learn in this world." "What is that," the young priest asked? "Enough of the meaning of life to be ready to die," the bishop replied.[178]

At every stage of life people should use life goals to plan beyond life. It is not a death wish to have a legal will and living will, power of attorney and durable medical power of attorney, estate plans, and life insurance. The encompassing life goal is the desire to provide security and a sense of ease for those left behind when you pass "Do Not Enter."

If you gamble or play the lottery (the odds of winning in Arizona are 5,000,000 to 1), remember that life expectancy tables lay out your odds black on white. For instance, the 1958 Consumers Standard Ordinary Mortality Table, used by many life insurance companies to calculate mortality, tells the tale for people from age thirty-five to forty.

Age	Number of Living	Deaths Each Year	Rate Per 1,000
35	100,000	257	2.57
36	99,743	271	2.73
37	99,472	288	2.90
38	88,184	310	3.13
39	98,874	335	3.39
40	98,538	363	3.68

It is easy to see why life insurance costs more as you get older. The odds are stacked against you. Cowboys used to say, "A dead man's shroud has no pockets," so good planning assigns assets where you want them to go since your pockets will be empty when your number is up.

Nonetheless, do not depart until you are carried across the "Do Not Enter" line. Will Rogers said it right: "Dear God, don't let me die until I'm dead." Life goals plan beyond life without taking you there. They help you understand that while you are still here your approval of self is a hundred times more important than the approval of others. Even Charles Schulz, famous for thousands of "Peanuts" cartoons, suffered loss of face from not being recognized. "In 1965, the class I graduated with was planning its twenty-fifth reunion," he wrote. "I was on the list of people they didn't know what had happened to."[179] Fame and fortune cannot prepare you for the exit like the meaning of life can.

We are at the chapter's end, and luckily the next page provides an exit. Our decision is to push back sidewalk-rollers with life goals that seize the future. Whatever our age, the future is all that remains, so we plan for it by exercising all our faculties and practicing the values that are precious to us. We build cobblestone and wandering sidewalks with goals that pursue old and new interests. Changing, growing, and learning, we use goals to exercise old skills and abilities and develop new ones. Hobbies, daily successes, and choosing where to live are important throughout life, as is learning. Life goals help us negotiate the little bumps and endure the big ones, including aging, and the "Do Not Enter" sign intensifies our commitment to plan beyond life. Seeing that sign with clarity contributes to life's meaning.

What we seek is a well-punctuated life. It will include question marks that point to life's mysteries and quotation marks to show our indebtedness to others. Life's exclamation points confirm our enthusiasm for living, and we underline the values we hold dear. Our apostrophes prove Whose we are. Finally, the period at life's end tells us to live life one day at a time, not in a lump.[180]

VIII
For Better...For Worse

Through the years marriage partners have pledged their faithfulness with that ominous-sounding phrase, "for better or for worse." I remember muttering it in a different context some years ago when my young daughter and I were visiting an amusement park. The words tumbled out of my mouth just as we climbed into a roller coaster.

For years I had successfully avoided speed demons like this coaster, and for good reason. I knew that my premonitions were right when I felt the monster's shakes and sounds and experienced so many rapid changes that I lost count. A thunderous roar followed dead silence; one second I was sitting peacefully with hands limp on a bar and the next I was floating upside down. At times I could not scream or move, then I shook like the pilot of an Olympic bobsled. My feelings careened between mountaintop thrill and bottomless fear, and rational and irrational thoughts pulsed through me like electricity.

As we dismounted a sobering thought struck me: there are hundreds of these iron monsters all around the United States, each one a heaven and hell on wheels! Annually about 300 million people ride these twisted piles of steel and wood and experience sensations of bobsledding, bronco busting, and sky diving.[181] Each roller coaster ride buys you a ticket to change, for better or for worse.

The long view makes it easier to see the changes in life. For instance, consider how much America has changed since the turn of the 1800's. At that time the United States had no public libraries, every gentleman powdered his hair, and the country's only hat factory made cocked hats. Virginia held a fifth of the country's population, and whipping posts decorated downtown Boston and New York. To take up the collection church ushers used poles with bags fastened to the end—and bells to awaken sleepers.

Though we do not always have the long view to see it, life changes much, with many ups and downs. Some lives resemble roller coasters rides while others glide across the continent like Pullman cars. All of our lives have peaks and valleys of varying height and depth.

This chapter tells how people of all ages set realistic life goals as they hit life's peaks and sit in its valleys—or travel in-between. Goals are for all life circumstances, but here we concentrate on the "ups" and "downs" since potentially they can give us clarity of vision. In these pages we discuss joy and suffering to see whether our goals reflect a balanced triad of feeling, thinking, and acting. Then we turn to the self's role in controlling the triad, and the relationship between goals and success in life.

Do not desert us if now you are traversing one of life's valleys. In the chapter's second half we follow a similar approach for those frightful times when life's roller coaster brings a sinking experience. Life goals are for better *and* for worse.

Hilltops

Have you noticed that the Book of Ecclesiastes seems to have been written for the other person? Probably you have heard a familiar quotation in a speech or at a funeral. "There is a time to be born and...die, a time to sow and...reap, a time to weep and...laugh, a time to mourn and...dance." These are fine words—usually for the other person. Actually, life includes all of us in the pages of its great book. We are born and die. Sowing and reaping, weeping and laughing, and mourning and dancing are part of life. We enjoy hilltops and tolerate life below sea level in our valleys.

Hilltops are life's natural highs, not drug or alcohol-induced but life-produced. They exhilarate us because there we breathe reinvigorating air. So what items are found in your list of life's hilltops? Your confirmation or bar/bath mitzvah? First love? High school and college graduation? Marriage? Children? Your first steady job? Satisfaction in a new job? Recognition for your charitable activities? Honors from trade or professional colleagues? Advanced degrees? Material success? Deep religious experiences? Satisfying relationships with your spouse? The happiness of good friends? Burning the mortgage? Family reunions and family love? Your first grandchild? Retirement?

Whatever your highs have been or now are, they all share one characteristic. They took in most or all of your personhood, including your capacity to feel, think, and act. You are the way you *feel*, *think* and *act*, though at times you mix these ingredients in different proportions. If a supposed hilltop experience or event does not acknowledge the presence of one of these three, chances are good that you will not list it in your Book of Hilltop Remembrances.

During life we continually review that Book to see how well its entries measure up to the way we now feel, think, and act. Occasionally after broadening our range of emotions we delete an earlier hilltop that no longer is significant. Sometimes we add new hilltops to the list; perhaps we have come to think differently, and a hilltop we once ignored makes more sense.

Blessing strikes twice if you are now camping on one of life's hilltops. Your hilltop is about how you feel, think, and act, and from that hill you can evaluate how well your life goals reflect that great triad.

Joy and Suffering

The ancient Egyptians believed that the god Osiris would ask two questions to determine a person's life journey after death. "Did you bring joy? Did you find joy?" These questions lie out of earshot for some people, and H. L. Menken liked to poke fun at their cynicism by saying that if they smelled flowers they immediately began looking around for a coffin.[182]

Like the words hush, chimes, lullaby, and murmuring, joy is an onomatopoeic word that sounds like what it is. Even the Germans agree in their guttural tongue. Joy is "Freude" (froydeh), and saying the word turns your lips into a smile and makes your facial muscles happy. Pronouncing the English word "joy" makes happy faces too.

Joy falls on people in varying amounts. Some of it we earn, but most joy comes as a gracious and unmerited gift. Sometimes joy pops into our thinking, sometimes into feeling, and sometimes into our actions, but when it strikes all three at once we are enjoying one of life's hilltops, without doubt.

Maybe you are now camping on one of life's joy hilltops. If so, it is good for you to ask what is happy and joyful about your marriage, job, material success, or whatever the hilltop is. You can learn to ask good questions about the joy-balance of your goals by reviewing the hilltop joy you are experiencing. Is your marriage joyful chiefly because you *feel* good about it? Excellent! Then ask these additional questions: How does your marriage show joy in the way you *think* about it and its future? How do your *actions* show joy in your hilltop marriage?

The more you review your hilltops' joys, the more you will

insist that your life goals manifest all three parts of joy (thinking, acting, feeling). In the process you are learning two important lessons: first, how to broaden hilltop experiences and extend your plateau of happiness as far as possible; and second, how to incorporate joy when you compose and revise your life goals.

Playing is one source of joy, and we can learn much from children since they know how to play, and they know the happiness of playing. Amusing themselves with body and soul, they have little respect for halfhearted fun. Hide and seek is a dead-earnest game that brings the joy of unexpected discovery and the happiness of deception without injury (whether the Ninja Turtles game does this is another question).

For their part, adults pursue life-enriching play with varying success. For some people games ended in childhood, and all that remains of play is competition on the job or softball field. Others find the joy of play in mind-games like chess or crossword puzzles that exercise thinking. Walking barefoot in the mud brings out playful emotions and reminds us of simpler times. Probably the most difficult form of play for adults is to incorporate action. Among hundreds of options in this area are practical jokes, acting out humor, exchanging wild and crazy letters and cards, and playful intimacy in intercourse. The following questions are important for examining the role of play in our lives. How does my play include thinking, feeling, and acting? Which of the three is my strongest suit, and why? What personal resources should I marshall to open myself to other kinds of play? How do my goals reflect the need for the joy of play?

Many people find joy in material success. There is little question that we need material goods to survive, for even anchorite monks craved food and shelter in the desert. But once we meet the basic needs for self-preservation, a wide array of material goods can become sources of pleasure. Marketing experts ply us with the joy that comes from electronic equipment, fat-free ice cream, and beer served by beautiful women.

Some people keep the joys of material goods in proper perspective. For them, material possessions are like a fleeting sunset that spreads happiness and then vanishes for twenty-four hours. Other people reach the mistaken conclusion that everything they have or want is a prerequisite for happiness, and materialistic joy becomes a life support system, like the air they breathe. Materialistic pleasure must fill nearly every waking hour.

If you are occupying a hill of material prosperity, what does the terrain look like? For years people have told us to simplify, but we keep proving the old saying right: the more we have, the more we want. Sometimes wanting more deprives us of the joys we already have. We can evaluate other openings for happiness by examining the specific joys that a possession brings us. For instance, I would not trade my computer's word processing capability for the fleeting joy of a sunset, so I ask, how does the computer bring me joy? To what extent does it engage and expand my thinking, feeling, and acting? If my answer is a great deal in all three areas, it holds potential for joy because of what it does emotionally, rationally, and in my behavior.

Ask yourself these kinds of questions as you evaluate the relationship between material possessions and joy. To what extent are these possessions sources of joy in the way you feel, think, and act? Do they feed one of these levels more than another? Which possession makes little thinking sense or would do little to expand the joy of your thinking? (Given my financial status, I will tell you one: a Rolls Royce!) All too often we expect material goods to fill unsatisfied joys in our lives.

I have met many successful people over the years, and some of them—but not all—also won the capitalist war, as their fruits of victory showed. They enjoyed the toys of grown men and women; their house cleaners were busy and their garages full of cars; municipal bonds dragged in tax-free interest; and they were whiz-bangs at their jobs and outperformed competitors.

Some of these victors loaded all of their joy-chips into feeling, others into thinking, and still others into action that was loosely anchored in feeling and thinking. Perhaps they ended up with a hilltop mansion by channeling all their goals into material goods, but then one morning a small voice cried out for release, for interaction with people without competition, for intimacy with another. Or a spouse wanted out of marriage because the materialistic voyage on Love Boat failed to deliver on promises of happiness.

Your Midas touch may bring problems if everything you touch—except money—turns into a muffler. If now you are enjoying the hilltop of a major material success, take the time to consider the life of Timothy Dexter. Born in 1747, he was a man who wanted to be called Lord of Newburyport (Massachusetts). A financial wizard by accident and intention, he took his share of booty in bonds and currency issued by the Continental Congress. For him and others the loot came from selling British ships and cargo that had been captured during the Revolutionary war. In his shop Dexter also exchanged goods for the same paper, stacking boxes of it behind beds. People said that he was crazy since the scrip would be worth nothing, and the end of the war proved them right. But his bet paid off handsomely when Thomas Jefferson and Alexander Hamilton vowed to stop inflation with a new banking system, and the nearly worthless paper was valid again. Suddenly Dexter was so wealthy that he bought a large mansion and sought the title of "Lord." He also succeeded in other speculations, including buying up all of the cats brought to his wharf and shipping them to a plantation island covered with thousands of mice and rats. There he sold the cats for $2.50-$5.00 apiece.

But Dexter's social success never matched his material success. He was eccentric, an alcoholic, a wife-beater, and an egomaniac who held a fake funeral to see how people would react to his death. Since his wife shed nary a tear he sent her away for her heartlessness.[183]

Furnishing a playroom with all of life's toys while remaining an emotional cripple or social failure is no formula for success. This kind of person can expand joy by revamping his life to include more than material possessions. A mother who trades her child's love for a Mercedes Benz needs to review the multiple sources and meanings of joy. Another person might enjoy material success through pyramid credit, arguing that prosperity is that splendid time when you can always get enough credit to live beyond your dreams. But credit-mongers should examine joy's rational side before bombs fall, loans pop, and joy's wine turns into vinegar.

Since most of us occupy hilltops of varying prosperity, we should consider the relation of altruism and joy in light of material success. Bringing joy to others is probably the purest and noblest form of joy. The opposite of egotism is altruism, the unselfish concern for the well-being of others. No set of life goals is complete without targeting some form of this joy. How can altruism help you reach a deeper sense of joy? If you use all available time and energy for shoveling dirt up your materialist hill, where will you find the emotive joy of a shared laugh that helps another? Where will your mind find the joy of designing help for persons who have fewer material blessings? Are you willing to act on another's behalf without expecting something in return?

I discovered in life that I turned more altruistic as my material success multiplied. Of course, one reason for charitable giving is a sense of responsibility to the broader society; people expect it. More than that, I found that imparting joy to others brings real joy. Although it cost me thinking time, emotional outlay, and action garbed in physical and monetary clothes, it returned much more in joy.

Suffering is the opposite of joy. If joy exercises unused facial muscles and makes the spirit bubble, suffering wrinkles the face and makes the spirit cry. Each has its place in life's ebb and flow, even during our highs.

Suffering is part of life for without it there is no growth. Tell me, which child was born without a mother suffering? Have you ever expanded your sphere of life without gritting your teeth, bearing what at the time may seem unbearable, and dipping a toe into icy waters? A folk hymn says it well:

Never saw a sunrise that didn't follow night,
Hardly saw it shining till a shadow blocked its light.
Never took a journey and not leave some place behind,
Not feel some anguish before some peace of mind.

Without clouds the rain can't wash the land,
Without rain the grass won't hide the sand,
Without grass the flower's bloom won't grow;
Without pain the joy in life won't show.

The university of life includes suffering in the core curriculum. We learn to avoid the hot stove the second time. We know the wisdom of not trying something complicated without preparation, not bluffing our way through a forty-five minute speech, and not lying since it hurts to get caught. Suffering is a great teacher that constantly reviews life's ABC's with us; it walks old paths we want to forget and leads us down new forks we prefer to avoid. Someone said that we can tell if we are on the right path if it is upgrade; as long as we keep moving upgrade we know that suffering is keeping us on track.

Whatever hilltop we are experiencing, to examine suffering we must again invoke the triad of feeling, thinking, and acting. Life has plenty of personal suffering that is obvious on the surface, but probing more deeply shows that hidden suffering teaches much even to those on hilltops.

Some people owe their life-highs to shelling out feeling, thought, or action one by one rather than in combination, and that often brings suffering. For example, I have met bubbly people who never seem to let thinking interfere with life. They admit as much and say that they do not like to think, or that thinking is not fun. Perhaps they are overemphasizing emotion because thinking hurts too much; they may have a bad case of suffering-overload.

On the other hand, you have probably met people who

walk around looking like thought incarnate. If they are placed on a hot stove they ask if perhaps someone turned on a griddle. Extensive suffering may have shrunk their capacity for emotion and robbed them of the gift of emotional joy.

Others avoid thinking or feeling through over-activity. These busy bees get much done, but life lacks coherence and seldom brings them emotional satisfaction. For example, some materially successful people suffer from a constant need to be doing something. They are not at home with themselves and are not guests in their own hotel. Finding joy only in one third of our triad cheats us of the joy that comes from the other two, and often causes suffering.

In a real sense you created the hilltop that you now occupy. It could be material success, a happy marriage, a satisfying job, credibility with colleagues, a happy retirement, or whatever it is. But watch out what you build, and carefully evaluate the joys your creation brings. If you miscreate and encounter suffering you can blame only yourself. In his book *The Wounded Healer*, Henri Nouwen recounts a masterful tale from ancient India that describes our capacity to create what can devour us. He wrote:

> *Four royal brothers decided each to master a special ability. Time went by, and the brothers met to reveal what they had learned. "I have mastered a science," said the first, "by which I can take but a bone of some creature and create the flesh that goes with it." "I," said the second, "know how to grow that creature's skin and hair if there is flesh on its bones." The third said, "I am able to create its limbs if I have the flesh, the skin and the hair." "And I," concluded the fourth, "know how to give life to that creature if its form is complete."*
>
> *Thereupon the brothers went into the jungle to find a bone so they could demonstrate their specialties. As fate would have it, the bone they found was a lion's. One added flesh to the bone, the second grew hide and hair, the third completed it with matching limbs and*

the fourth gave the lion life. Shaking its mane, the ferocious beast arose and jumped on his creators. He killed them all and vanished contentedly into the jungle."[184]

Self-History and Self-Control

Hilltops teach much about life, for better or worse. From them we learn about ourselves and the challenges of handling self-anger, exercising self-control, and turning loose of useless pasts. Through it all the truth about ourselves must prevail.

Will Rogers once said, "A lot of what everybody knows ain't necessarily so." For example, while we suppose that Mrs. O'Leary's cow started the Great Chicago Fire in 1871, the fact is that a reporter created the cow to enliven a newspaper story. Similarly, many "truisms" about self are untrue. One of them is that we are not angry with ourselves after reaching a successful milestone or hilltop vista. That ain't necessarily so. Sometimes we become angry that it took so long to attain the goal of material success, marital intimacy, or social approbation. Self-anger rears its ugly head in many circumstances, some of them involving our highs.

Self-anger and self-control are life's Mutt and Jeff, two sides of the same coin. If we control self in the three triad areas of feeling, thinking, and acting, we have less reason to be angry with ourselves for not measuring up on some count. Seldom does self-discipline in healthy doses coexist with self-anger. People who are most angry with themselves most often lack self-discipline; they complain about themselves but take no steps to change direction.

Self-control insulates and shields the self as a target for anger. Self-discipline patches weak spots so anger cannot burn through; it applauds your strengths while constraining pride. Disciplining self is not applying a rod to your emotions, thoughts, and actions, but plugging personality holes, opening personhood to new opportunities, and moving from strength to strength in considered fashion. Self-control imposes your will on feeling, thinking, and acting so that self-anger has fewer sitting ducks to shoot. It is dangerous not to recognize that we can be sitting ducks. A Civil War general named John Sedgwick should have learned that lesson. When he raised his head above a parapet in the Battle of the Wilderness, reportedly his last words were, "Nonsense, they couldn't hit an elephant from this dis—"

Self-control also turns loose of the past when that is necessary. Many people experience self-anger about incidents or events that nothing in the world can change. Clinging to these life memories is like booking passage after we know what happened on the Titanic's maiden voyage. Maybe a thought recurs because at one time we should have expressed it but did not. Perhaps we cannot release a strong negative feeling about old Aunt Ann, who is dead and gone, or we continually review past actions through the dark lens of remorse. Whatever that past, turning loose of it is a necessary part of self-control.

Our highs give us a perspective for exercising self-control in new ways. They present extra resources of emotional, rational, and action-joy (one or all three) to root out the anger we want to dispel. Using these resources, our self-control can extinguish those useless flash-points from the past.

Any person can release parts of the past that anger and consume him, but people of faith have the added comfort that a caring God rescues them from their past. Religious faith allows believers to stuff an unwieldy past into sealed boxes for God to guard. This is our nuclear dump for past failings. In Roman Catholicism, Lutheranism, and other groups, private confession and absolution can exorcise the tormenting devils of a remembered past. Another resource is counseling, although one wit called psychoanalysis confession without forgiveness. Close friends and spouses can seal a penitent's self-release with reassurance and continuing companionship.

You see by now that self-control, thwarting self-anger, and turning loose of one's past are important components of a life-goal system that works. Our earlier discussion in this chapter showed the need to account for joy and suffering. Managing depression is another element in living on hilltops, and also a factor in self-history.

Depression afflicts both the high and mighty and the low and weak. As part of life, depression can invade life's hilltops and its valleys. Here we are talking not about clinical depression but the daily "blues" that strike without warning, when even gourmet coffee tastes flat. Depression socks our life when the mind outruns us in recognizing the need for growth and change. It is like the sky's pain when the dark of night gives way to the morning's rays. Depression is life's caterpillar-butterfly combination, when the caterpillar must slough off the old to take on the new. Why does it hurt? Because our mind knows that something old must make way for something new, and this kind of change seldom happens without pain.

Some theologians hint that depression foreshadows the last change, life's final sloughing-off. People who recognize depression's affinity with death may have an easier or more difficult time with depression, depending on many variables. But if death changes temporal life into something different, much like birth pushes the fetus into living air, we should fear depression and death about as much as birth.

The tested triad of feeling, thought, and action provides a good framework for reviewing depression, which often spreads from one realm to another. If your depression usually starts with emotions, it is good to ask whether you have given your emotions enough room for joy, play, breadth, and self-control. If depression is a recurring problem in several areas of the triad, your goals should confront it head-on, and you may also need professional help. The key is discipline applied to self, or self-control.

Finally, part of living on life's hilltops is self-analysis of one's talents, gifts, skills, and abilities. We should identify which gift(s) brought us to a summit, which ability is weak from lack of exercise, and which skill is loafing at half-speed. An old codger gave me some healthy advice when I received my doctoral degree. "You now have your Ph.D. Stick around, son, and life will teach you the rest of the ABC's," he said. Life's alphabet soup comes in large doses of institutionalized learning and in daily digging where we discover something new. Part of that education is understanding how our skills served us in major experiences.

Try this experiment sometime. Take a piece of paper and draw two columns headed "formal education" and "informal education." In the proper column list major life experiences and incidents that taught you, improved your skills, and brought new abilities to the fore. Add the central ability or gift that was involved in each major experience. Then ask the following questions about your entries. Where is my joy in this ability? My suffering? Self-control? Self-anger? How did the skill help bring me to this hilltop? How did it stop me from reaching a new high?

What we are seeking is a workable philosophy for life. What a price a publisher could charge for one that is tailored to your life! Even then you might be unhappy, like the woman whose friend asked, "Why study philosophy? It doesn't make you any happier." "No," the first replied, "but it helps me be unhappy more intelligently."

With goals you use your life's ABC's to write a life philosophy for yourself. Others can point, lead, cajole, and encourage, but for better or for worse your life is your show. If it includes a solid sense of self, your life philosophy has a better chance of teaching you how to enjoy highs and suffer lows with grace. You will not get past the first page in writing your life philosophy if you ignore the trusty triad of feeling, thinking, and acting.

Life Goals and Successes

I operate with a rather simple formula that says you can have successes without life goals, but not life goals without success. The reason is simple. Life successes alone (hilltops) may not adequately deal with deficiencies of joy or surpluses of suffering. Hilltop successes do not ensure a healthy dose of self-control, turning loose of the past, or evaluating personal resources, but life goals can bring you to all three.

Attaining a success is different from reaching a life goal. Grady Nutt says that life moves from "roots to shoots,"[185] and it is a mistake to call a temporary shoot a permanent root. Sometimes we attain a success almost haphazardly, like catching the flu. Other successes come over time from many small steps. Clearly, root goals cause life successes that meet our vision of joy, our need for self-control, and our capacity to release the past.

Here is a way to measure the difference between successes and achieving life goals. Stripping away a person's success does not deprive him of the drive for life, but removing even an unconscious life goal rips at the fabric of life. Stealing goals takes away life's breath while planting life goals in the heart instills vision and new vigor.

The Holocaust of Hitler and his henchmen teaches a powerful lesson about the difference between life successes and life goals. Psychiatrist Viktor Frankl was imprisoned in the Auschwitz death camp but outlived the experience. In his book *Man's Search for Meaning*, he tells how dreams lit the way in the darkness of the camp's brutality. In one set of barracks men looked for a way to preserve their human dignity, decency, and self-pride. Their solution was to live as if they were in the continued presence of a beautiful woman, an esteemed lady who loved them and cared for them. While they knew this to be a fantasy, it was preferable to reality because it gave them a way to endure. Subtle changes in appearance and relationship followed as the men took on the fantasy; they cleaned up their language, appeared as neat as possible under the circumstances, and shaved daily with pieces of broken glass. The men responded with imagination and pride amid daily devastation, inhumanity, and selection for death, and their human spirit won out.[186]

If you have children, consider the relation of success and life goals in the light of your parental responsibility. You cheat your children if you offer only success as a model. In your gut you may know that you will never win them all, that some hilltops remain out of reach, but how can you impart this wisdom if success is your only model? On the other hand, solid life goals offer a plethora of questions and issues for a child's consideration and growth. At any stage in life your slate of goals embodies your life philosophy, but no matter what their number, successes alone can never be the sum and substance of that philosophy.

Your life goals will bring success, so this is a good time to evaluate and revise your list of goals. This is a continuing task, month in and month out. As you review your goals, the questions in the accompanying table can help you decide how well they incorporate "for better or for worse."

LIFE GOAL EVALUATION
Which life goal embodies most effectively the joy you seek in life? Why? Which invites you to the joy of altruistic sharing?
How do your life goals account for life's inevitable suffering?
To what extent does each life goal incorporate feeling, thinking, and acting, the three parts of our triad?
Which life goal relies on self-control and self-discipline in specific ways?
Which life goal reflects a conscious decision to turn loose of a part of your past?
If you are inclined toward depression in feeling, thinking, or action, which life goal confronts that tendency head-on, and how?

For most people, one or more life goals naturally focuses on attaining a material target. This goal shows that you have a healthy instinct for self-preservation and are reaching beyond immediate physical needs (food, clothing, shelter) for other gains. Evidently you do not need a lesson in playing "King of the Mountain" in the material realm. You probably agreed when Senator William Proxmire presented a Golden Fleece Award to the U.S. Army for spending \$20,000 for 30,000 colored pamphlets describing the schoolyard game.

On the other hand, overloading life goals with materialistic ambition sets people up for internal collapse. Such a narrow focus on joy does not fully exercise your talents and abilities. Having only materialistic goals limits your personhood in areas where it needs to breathe, exercise, and play. Restricting goals to material success shows that the goal-setter lacks self-control and will not turn loose of imagined wants to broaden life's vision.

There is another point that shows the need for linking life successes and life goals. Part of wisdom is learning how to descend from a hilltop of success or a life-goal achievement. No hill or mountain extends forever, not even Mt. Everest, and no life-high lasts forever. Life continues serving up unexpected events like the end of an athlete's career, a business failure or capricious economy, the onslaught of illness, and the death of a spouse or child. It takes wisdom to know how to scramble down from the top. Jesus' disciples wanted him to remain on the Mount of Transfiguration, not descend to the plain; staying put in those glorious surroundings seemed wise but was foolish.

Experienced mountaineers know that coming down is often more difficult and dangerous than climbing. As a young man Barry Rugo decided to scale Mt. Everest, although it had snatched his brother's life in 1980. The 29,028 ft. summit of the "Goddess Mother of the Earth" towered above them as team members began their climb in the spring of 1991, and it was pitch dark as the party launched its final ascent to reach the summit about 10:00 A.M. the next day, May 15. The top of the mountain was a narrow platform only five by twenty feet. As the team began descending, two members a hundred feet ahead of Rugo yelled back to ask if all was going well. "I'll see you at the camp. Go ahead down," he replied. While pausing to rest at 28,700 ft. he heard the hiss of his oxygen unit go dead, and at that elevation clouds blocked his view of the team while swirling snow erased their footprints. Despite a well-conditioned body, Rugo was exhausted and managed only twenty steps without a rest. Lacking supplementary oxygen, his brain was susceptible to fatigue, although later he said that he "wasn't having any problems with the mental part of it." Then suddenly he stumbled over two corpses perfectly preserved by the cold, and that unnerved him. Despite these problems, he staved off uncontrollable panic and moved toward the nearby base camp, which he found without further difficulty.[187] Knowing how to descend from the mountaintop was a matter of survival.

Finally, visioned goals are sometimes incremental steps toward a larger life goal made up of several interim successes. Take, for example, a high school student with a life goal of becoming a physician. That goal is important for visioning, but so are the steps needed to get there, such as graduating from high school and college. The student should vision these more proximate life goals along with the long-term goal.

Just imagine the incremental life-goals on your list if you wanted to inaugurate human flight from scratch. The trek took nearly a thousand years. Reportedly in 1000 A.D. a Benedictine monk with artificial wings broke his legs while jumping from a tower. In the 15th century Leonardo de Vinci's drawings included models of parachutes and helicopters (toy helicopters were popular as early as the 14th century). In 1670 a Jesuit priest designed an airship with four vacuum cylinders. Its purpose was to wreck ships and set houses ablaze with fireballs from the sky, but luckily as a man of peace the priest abandoned the idea. A century later (1783) Frenchmen floated aloft in hot air balloons. In 1886 an American suggested harnessing ten eagles with reins to take man aloft.

In 1891 Otto Lilienthal teetered through the air after hurtling from a "flying hill" near Berlin. Standing between two fixed wing poles and then jumping off the hill while suspended from a glider, he glided about twenty yards at a height of sixteen feet. In five years he had nearly 3,000 flights under his belt, using storks as his mentors and steering the machine with his body. He offered copies of his glider for sale for 500 marks, but in 1896 the apparatus he was on crashed from a height of fifty feet. Lilienthal broke his neck and died the next day, but he had given the world its first heavier-than-air flying machine by showing how to achieve lift with curved, fixed wings. His last reported words were, "You have to make sacrifices."[188]

Many people thought the Wright brothers were dreaming when they unloaded a strange contraption on a sand dune at Kitty Hawk. The Wright boys were dreamers all right that December in 1903, but they achieved their aim when the contraption briefly took to the air. The long-range goal of powered human flight became a reality after many incremental steps, and that is also how we reach our highest hilltops.

Valleybottoms

Though our language finds no problem with the word "hilltop," it fails to provide us with the word "valleybottom." That is one of the strange things about valleys, or about living in valleys. We seldom use synonyms of "valley" to talk about life's low spots. Do people refer to life's "dales," "glens" or "vales?" Seldom or never. In Arizona a valley is a "small canyon," but no one complains about life's "small canyons."

We use the term "valley" for life's low points since it can mean almost anything we want it to mean. The Phoenix Valley covers several hundred square miles, just as some of life's valleys may drag on for years. A steep and sudden business reversal can be a valley, like a narrow gorge into which you tumble from a mountainside. These are life's lows, when things are not going well in some area. Possibly we feel secure in our material success but are low in self-esteem; this is a valley. Or our religious life brims with excitement while relations with our extended family slog through an endless, bitter valley.

Sometimes, when a part of life is not going well, we get "kneak in the wees" and our "tangues get tongled." This is a valleybottom, and we are going to call it that. It may include economic reversal, a wayward child, illness, marital difficulties, problems in relationships, extended grief, moving to a new city, and a host of other afflictions.

We probably should not resort to a crass description of a domestic accident to describe a valleybottom, but the following story makes an unforgettable point. Management analyst Jerry B. Harvey took delight in his grandfather's ability to tell tales. The old man's favorite was what happened to a well-endowed neighbor lady, Mrs. Lenora Thrusher, when

> *during an unaccountable lapse of concentration, she leaned over the motor-driven wringer of her new electric washing machine and got one (or more) parts of her anatomy temporarily entangled in its workings. I can still remember my grandfather's description of her, perched on the rooftop of her house, clinging to the chimney, shouting to Beecher, her husband, "Get rid of the damn thing before it maims us all."*

Harvey concludes, "Today, when I hear someone use the trite expression, 'I got caught in the wringer,' I know all too well—perhaps better than the speaker—the origin of the comment and the earthly reality of its meaning."[189]

Pleasure and Pain

Visitors to Death Valley report that the Valley's sublime beauty includes colorful rock formations, exquisite plants of small size, and other surprises. Death Valley is not a pit, nor does it lack distinguishing characteristics. Our valleybottoms are much the same. If we inspect them closely we will see their variegated nature, the complex forces that create and sustain them, and the potential for change that they offer.

Many people find it easier to compile a Book of Valleybottom Remembrances than one for hilltops, and that is not surprising. Life's lows drag us down and we remember them; it may be scary to take a plunge on a roller coaster, and bungee-jumping may be worse. So now is the time to list your life's valleybottoms. And what is today's low point for you?

Using the trusty triad of feeling, thinking, and acting, determine whether your valleys show a pattern. Are you more inclined to suffer emotional bottoms than thought bottoms? What inaction, over-action, or over-reaction has brought you the most bottoms? Valleybottoms teach us something about pleasure by showing how life suffers from its absence. Life-lows show that one part of our trusty triad is not a happy camper. To discover why, we should carefully examine the terrain of valleybottoms.

Using humor to release emotion is one joy that we can keep alive in a valley, sometimes through sheer willpower. When the checking account is sucking air and bills are flying, we should remember what a man told his wife as the mailman delivered a bill marked "**FINAL**." He said, "Thank goodness they're giving up on this bill, it's their final notice."

The joy of altruistic giving shines with diamond-like brilliance when we are in a low. In these circumstances, giving freely can open us to gifts that we may desperately need from others. A kind word or simple thank-you from someone, or their psychological support, may be pivotal in how you arise from a low spot. Most people find it easier to give than to receive; in a valleybottom your generous gifts may open you to healing gifts from others.

In a valley it is important to focus on those parts of life still above sea level. Like a drop of dye in water, a little joy goes a long way. Find those emotional outlets that still impart pleasure and play them at full volume. Look for intellectual pleasures that are old favorites and hear their drumbeat again. Invigorate yourself with activities that bring happiness and help your body sing a hallelujah chorus to life.

Some pain or suffering is like a skin rash that is here today and gone tomorrow while other forms strike deeper and last longer. For them, topical treatment is ineffective. Our power to endure and transform suffering controls, in part, its intensity and duration. For example, some people feel a good deal of suffering from flak they receive on the job while others can dismiss it like the weather. Sonny Jurgensen of the Washington Redskins used to say that every week of the football season a quarterback is either in a penthouse or an outhouse. Flak rolled off him like water off a duck.

Whatever its form, suffering is an opportunity for growth. It may cause you to expand your repertoire of emotions, consider thinking in ways you had not envisioned, and act with commitment when inaction seemed best. The Chinese combine the characters for the words "risk" and "opportunity" to make the character for "crisis." Suffering is risk with opportunity, a hurt that can be healed, a life-turn that can go from worse to better.

I know people who at their own hands suffer unmercifully from worry. They agonize so much that one or another thing might happen that their feelings suffer, they warp their way of thinking, and they pull back from acting because of possible consequences. This is like fearing alligators while living in the desert! But—they insist—sometimes these things really happen. Right, I reply, and one time tumbleweeds invaded Morbridge, South Dakota, filled the streets, blocked access to the hospital, and buried thirty homes to the roof![190] They should run for office as County Tumbleweed Defender!

People in valleybottoms often endure unnecessary suffering by relying excessively on one side of our triad and ignore the balancing and enriching power of the other two sides. Some thinking-types suffer too long in a valley while their emotions are starved for air. An overly-emotional person would do well to lighten up on the gravity of the situation by measuring the worst possible result. Either of these persons will find relief by pursuing activities that turn off the spigots of preoccupation. Valleybottoms usually include suffering, but no law of the universe says a valley must run forever.

There is light at the end of the tunnel, and reminding ourselves of that fact is one way to see while it is dark. One Good Friday the pastor of Mount Carmel Baptist Church in West Philadelphia preached a well-known sermon entitled "It's Friday, But Sunday's Coming." For ninety minutes he preached that line repeatedly: It's Friday, but Sunday's coming. He began in a soft voice, saying "It was Friday; it was Friday and Jesus was dead on the tree. But that was Friday, and

Sunday's coming." A deacon shouted, "Preach, Brother, preach," and the preacher felt a boost. Louder still he said, "It was Friday and Mary was crying her eyes out. The disciples were running in every direction, like sheep without a shepherd, but that was Friday, and Sunday's coming." His volume increased as the minutes passed. By the end of the sermon he was exhausted and the people were swaying with excitement. Finally he shouted at the top of his lungs, "It's Friday!" With one voice the congregation answered, "Sunday's coming!"[191]

We need to hear that Sunday comes to valleybottoms. A maxim that serves me well is, "This too will pass." Though it sounds solemn and stoic, the phrase turns our eyes to a future when the suffering is over. It may give us courage to wait and do what we can to hasten that day.

Sometimes raw courage can help a person keep on keeping on. During a live TV circus show a trainer stood in a small cage with Bengal tigers surrounding him. He began his usual routine, using a whip and chair for control, when suddenly the lights went out. The tigers could see him in pitch darkness but he could not see them, and he could rely only on the whip and chair. Thirty seconds seemed like an eternity until suddenly the lights reappeared with all the tigers in their places. The trainer finished his act and then answered questions about the experience. He said that he kept cracking his whip and talking in a normal voice since the tigers were unaware that he could not see them.[192] Raw courage prevailed.

Self-Understanding and Self-Restraint

All that we said about self-control, self-restraint, and applying the will to our trusty triad applies here too. In valleybottoms, Alexander Graham Bell's words about closed doors ring true. He said, "When one door closes, another opens; but we often look so long and so regretfully upon the closed door that we do not see the one which has opened for us."

Valleybottoms offer two natural vistas. We can look across the valley floor and worry about its expanse, or up the mountainsides that surround us. Exercising self-control in a valley means taking time to understand our suffering; we review the dynamics that brought us to this life-low, and turn loose of parts of life that prefer the pits.

Valleybottoms are crucibles for learning—if we have the discipline to discover what road brought us there and the wisdom to avoid it the next time. It is unfortunate for a person to learn little or nothing from a major setback in the material realm. Did the plunge result from ambition gone wild? From over-stressing a Type A personality? From purposely pulling back from success when the brass ring was in reach? What plans and preparations should have been in place to counteract the timing, market action, or economic collapse over which you had no control? Imagine the trials and errors that are required for major medical discoveries like organ transplants and DNA, and the learning at each step of the way. We need to investigate our trough, turn from self-anger, and reinforce the personhood that gives us our future.

Defeat can make champions. Some analysts claim that defeat in military battles teaches more than victory, although "victory has a hundred fathers and defeat is an orphan." The Alamo spawned both the legend of Davy Crockett and the state of Texas. Most of us like clowns and comics and laugh at losers so long as we are not in their circle. One writer suggests that April 1 should be called "National Losers Day" and that losers should have a monument that reads, "They also serve who only stand and lose."[193]

The next time you get angry with yourself and question the value of self-restraint, think about the pitiful record of this American. He failed in business as a young man and then lost his bid for the state legislature. Again he failed at business, but the voters finally elected him to the legislature. His sweetheart died, and he suffered a nervous breakdown. Three defeats followed: for Speaker of the House, elector, and the national Congress. He finally won a congressional seat but lost his second bid. Opponents beat him in a run for the Senate, for the Vice Presidency, and again for the Senate. Finally in the greatest race of his life he became President of the United States. What if Abraham Lincoln had retired early from politics with the comment, "Aw shucks, forget it?"

Part of self-control is remembering that tomorrow is important, that valleybottoms have hills to look up to. There is a story about Margarite Higgins, journalist and Pulitzer prize winner, when she was with the Marines during the Korean War. Fifteen thousand men had held off a hundred thousand communist troops for several bitter cold days, and they were dead tired. One large Marine leaned against a truck with a dirty and unshaven face, using a trench knife to fork beans from a can, when a reporter asked him, "If I could grant you one wish, what would it be?" Perhaps he wanted to be at home with his family, or on a trip. The man glanced up and said, "Just give me tomorrow."[194] Tomorrow is always important.

Part of valleybottom-review is a disciplined release of our past in favor of tomorrow. Religious faith can offer many resources since it brings the capacity to change, grow, mature, and move on, especially when we face a crisis. Faith gets the harmony flowing between life on the inside and outside, and the leap of faith helps people make changes for full harmony. As we reach a deeper understanding of valleybottom tensions, we see potential there too. With crisis and tension around us, we mature and move on—or crawl back into our cocoons.

Reviewing skills and abilities comes harder in a trough, but it is required to gain wisdom for life's trek. We must open ourselves to new possibilities if what we see of ourselves cannot meet the present challenge. Perhaps our behavior no longer provides meaning for life, or maybe values and ideas of our past have lost their grip. Whatever the cause, we gather strength to make a transition and move on. That means correcting shortfalls, changing self based on who we are, and modifying guideposts for behavior.

Many of us like to draw on other people's resources instead of using our own. For example, citizens of Palm Beach knew Bertha Adams only as a beggar. The old woman begged door to door and regularly got food and clothing from the

Salvation Army, but when she died her mattress held over a million dollars worth of stocks and certificates. She never used these resources for herself or others. Why not?

When it comes to imposing self-control in valleybottoms, consider drawing strength and guidance from the disciplined power of your body. Do you know that your eyes can distinguish nearly 8,000,000 color differences and your ears 300,000 tones? Your heart pumps five quarts a minute, almost 2,000 gallons a day, and you could lift twenty-five tons if all 600 muscles pulled one way. One cubic inch of bone can withstand a two-ton force. With over a thousand square feet, your lungs' surface is more than twenty times the skin's. The epidermis has no monopoly on skin cells for they also cover parts of your stomach, eyes, and lungs. But do not ignore liabilities. For every pound of fat you need 200 miles of extra capillaries, and your hands and feet contain over half of the body's 206 bones, all of them breakable.[195]

Life Goals and Successes

Visioning life goals brings the successes you seek. Visioning is an act of self-restraint and self-discipline, especially when you are suffering a valleybottom's insults. What you need most seems like the hardest thing to do, but do it! Seeing your goals in Technicolor is good medicine when clouds and storms cover the sky. Visioning goals helps you see alternatives and motivates you to use resources to regain the life you want, so visioning brings success.

Imaging your future is important when your feet are caught in quicksand. Imaging is a giant power for directing your future; it is your future's dynamo. Without it your subconscious has few alternatives except to project images from a past that you should release. Painting action-pictures on the canvas of the subconscious brings results because visioning is powerful. It works.

It is important to redirect skills and abilities as life circumstances change. Reportedly all our body cells change completely in about seven years, but some people take longer than that to redirect skills and abilities into new channels when old ways lose their utility. Constantly evaluating capabilities, redirecting strengths as required, and cultivating and improving skills and abilities are necessities, not options.

For instance, say that you are suffering in a valleybottom of marital discord, and with the help of a marriage counselor you and your spouse uncover a major problem. Your spouse expects more expressions of love than you normally offer. She has entered a "touchy-feely" phase, and she needs more frequent communications of love and physical affection.

You do a quick check of your basic skills and abilities and how they appear in your emotions, thinking, and actions, and you find that generally you are weakest in the emotional area. You decide to make a correction by redirecting interpersonal skills (especially with your spouse) to reflect more accurately your feelings of attachment and love. You review several books on expressing emotion and a video series on affection and conclude that you should change your life goals to reflect this redirection. Then you add a statement like this to your life goal list: "I feel warm and fuzzy all over as I hold Mary's hand on the seashore and tell her eye-to-eye, 'Mary, you mean the world to me, and I want to say it while holding your hand!'" This life goal can directly affect your marriage if you visualize it several times a day.

During the Revolutionary War, one preacher showed how to redirect resources. In the last big battle on Jersey soil, a thousand Americans clashed with 5,000 enemy troops under the command of a Hessian general. The Reverend James Caldwell was returning from the funeral of his wife, who had been killed at the hands of an enemy soldier. Entering the thick of battle, he found the Americans in bad straits since they could not fire their rifles. The paper wadding used in their guns was gone. Caldwell quickly broke the lock of the historic Springfield Church, then returned with a load of famous Watts hymn books. Soon his voice rang out over the noise, "Give 'em Watts, boys, give 'em Watts!" As the pages turned into rifle wadding the Americans rallied, and the Hessians never again seriously threatened Washington's troops.[196] That was redirecting resources!

Some persons feel helpless as they sit in a valleybottom, but they are lucky if they are parents since their parenting responsibility may move them off dead center. Kids know instinctively when their parents are in trouble, and in these circumstances more is caught than taught about how to handle a life-trough. If you assert self-responsibility, admit errors, practice self-control, redirect resources, and vision your goals, you are giving your children good instruction about handling life's hardballs. Let's hope they catch what you throw. So, if necessary, use your modeling role to make this a valleybottom for better, not for worse.

Check counterfeiters have given a bad name to forgery, and so have the world's great forgers. In 1971 novelist Clifford Irving perpetrated one of the century's most publicized hoaxes when he convinced a New York publisher that he had a commission from Howard Hughes to write the wealthy recluse's autobiography. Irving wrote a 1,200 page book "by Hughes," and forged nearly two dozen handwritten letters and contracts from Hughes to support his claim. In a rare breach of secrecy, Swiss banks helped expose the hoax by revealing that Irving's wife had an account there.

Irving laid no claim on being the consummate forger of all time. He reserved that honor for someone else, saying that "by definition, the identity of the greatest forger of all time, whether man or woman, is unknown to us. For he (or she) must have been—or must be—far too clever and skillful to ever have been suspected or exposed. *Caveat emptor* [Buyer beware]."[197]

Each of us carries part of the consummate forger inside of us, and we perpetrate the biggest case of forgery against ourselves. Not distinguishing between life's hilltops and valleybottoms is forgery on self, and it is self-deception not to discern the joys and sufferings in both. It is a self-hoax to ignore the triad of feeling, thinking, and acting as we evaluate joy and suffering. Seething with self-anger, playing cat and mouse with self-control, and holding fast to a past that needs release are frauds against self. It is duplicity to think that attaining success is the same as achieving life goals. Only a master counterfeiter would turn away from the power of visioned goals and rely on a child's world-view to overcome adult problems.

Forgers of the world, unite! Drop the shackles of self-delusion and use life goals to make all your hilltops and valleybottoms for better, not for worse.

Notes

CHAPTER I

[1] Dialogue Sermon Preached at Washington Cathedral, Washington, D.C., May 1, 1983, by Chaplain, Major General, John A. Collins, Chief of Chaplains, USAF, and Chaplain, Brigadier General, Stuart E. Barstad, Deputy Chief of Chaplains, USAF.

[2] See Jane Goodsell, *Not a Good Word About Anybody* (New York: Ballantine Books, 1988).

[3] Peter McWilliams, *The Personal Computer Book* (Los Angeles: Prelude Press, 1990), p. 44.

CHAPTER II

[4] Richard Thomas, a New York state wildlife expert working with the Department of Environmental Conservation, published the results of his cogitation on this intriguing question in the department's bi-weekly newsletter, *Fin, Fur and Feather Facts.*

[5] Quoted in a *Washington Post* interview (1977), as cited by Charles Colson in *Loving God* (Grand Rapids: Zondervan Publishing House, 1983), p. 11.

[6] Ray Geiger, ed., *American Farm & Home Almanac, 1976* (Lewiston, Maine: Almanac Publishing Co., 1975), p. 50.

[7] David Wallechinsky, Irving Wallace and Amy Wallace, *The Book of Lists* (New York: Bantam Books, 1978), p. 157.

[8] Roger Fish and William Ury, *Getting to Yes; Negotiating Agreement Without Giving In* (New York: Penguin Books, 1983), p. 154.

[9] Frederic A. Brussat in *Here Comes the Future*, ed. Frank W. Klos (Minneapolis: Augsburg Press, 1981), p. 22.

[10] Jeffrey J. Mayer, *If You Haven't Got the Time to Do It Right, When Will You Find the Time to Do It Over?* (New York: Simon and Schuster, 1990), pp. 11-46.

[11] In his book Mayer emphasizes that people who thrive on crises kid themselves into thinking they are doing the most important thing. Use your most productive time to do your most important work. Trivial chores lead to other trivial chores, so watch the sequence. Schedule blocks of time for yourself to finish your most important work. Fill slack time with less important work. Politely fend off people who try to invade the time you set aside for an important task. Consider closing your office door and using other means to get time needed for important projects. Avoid procrastinating by doing absolutely nothing until you start the project, think through the whole project, or start with one small step and schedule the rest. Using deadlines is important; consider moving them up to give you momentum with a project. Ruthlessly eliminate work that is not essential and avoid the "just say yes" syndrome.

Delegate responsibly as a team member, don't waste time at meetings that are unimportant, and give all agendas a bite. Use breakfast and luncheon meetings for serious business. Do not wait for someone to return a call; tell the party answering that you will call back so you control your schedule, and put all your calls in a block. Rely on your notes; they are more reliable than memory. Sift and sort your in and out boxes at a specified time each day, not throughout the day.

[12] Philip Rosenberg, "James and John Stuart Mill," *New York Times Book Review*, April 6, 1975.

[13] Among other works, see Neil Postman, *Amusing Ourselves to Death: Public Discourse in the Age of Show Business* (New York: Penguin Books, 1985), and William Fore, *Television and Religion* (Minneapolis: Augsburg Press, 1987).

[14] Brochure from *Atocha* Commemorative, Boca Raton, Florida, undated [1986-87?].

[15] Grady Nutt, *So Good, So Far...* (Nashville: Impact Books, 1979), pp. 30-31.

[16] In Klos, ed., *Here Comes the Future*, p. 29.

[17] Colson, *Loving God*, pp. 27-34.

[18] Frank W. Klos and Robert N. Bacher, *Here Comes the Future, Leader Guide* (Minneapolis: Augsburg Press, 1981), p. 52.

[19] Wayne Coffey, *303 of the World's Worst Predictions* (New York: Tribeca Communications, Inc., 1983), pp. 12, 21, 59, 83.

[20] Nutt, *So Good, So Far...*, p. 150.

[21] *Hercules Herald*, Pope AFB, NC, November 25, 1983.

[22] Communication Research Associates, *A Workbook for Interpersonal Communication*, 2nd edition (Dubuque, Iowa: Kendall/Hunt Publishing Company, 1978), p. 196, quoting from *Mad Magazine*, December 1970.

CHAPTER III

[23] Reported in the *Sourdough Sentinel*, Elmendorf AFB, AK, March 4, 1988.

[24] Wayne E. Oates, *Nurturing Silence in a Noisy Heart* (Garden City, NY: Doubleday & Company, Inc., 1979), pp. 22-24.
[25] *The Old Farmer's Almanac, 1991* (Dublin, NH: Yankee Publishing, Inc., 1991), pp. 93-94.
[26] M. Scott Peck, *The Road Less Traveled* (New York: Simon and Schuster, 1978), p. 53.
[27] Robert Drake, "I Don't Know What He's Doing Now," *Christian Century*, July 6-13, 1988, p. 641.
[28] Philip Ziegler, *The Black Death* (New York: Harper and Row, Publishers, 1971).
[29] "The Twelve Months," by George Ellis, died 1815.
[30] Charles M. Schulz, *You Don't **Look** 35, Charlie Brown!* (New York: Holt, Rinehart and Winston, 1985), no pagination.
[31] See Abraham J. Twerski, *Like Yourself and Others Will Too* (Englewood Cliffs, NJ: Prentice Hall, 1978).
[32] Edwin C. Bliss, *Getting Things Done* (New York: Charles Scribner's Sons, 1976), pp. 69-70.
[33] In Frank W. Klos, ed., *Here Comes the Future* (Minneapolis: Augsburg Publishing House, 1981), p. 69.
[34] See Patricia Neal, *As I Am: An Autobiography* (New York: Simon & Schuster, 1988).
[35] Peter McWilliams, *The Personal Computer Book* (Los Angeles: Prelude Press, 1990), pp. 368-71.
[36] Simon Schama, *The Embarrassment of Riches: An Interpretation of Dutch Culture in the Golden Age* (New York: Alfred A. Knopf, Inc., 1987).
[37] Clarissa M. Silitch, ed., *Mad and Magnificent Yankees* (Dublin, NH: Yankee, Inc., 1973), p. 110.
[38] Drake, "I Don't Know What He's Doing Now," p. 642.
[39] Robert Frost, *A Further Range*, Book Six (New York: Henry Holt and Company, 1936), p. 69.
[40] See Michael Spino, *Running Home, The New Guide to Total Family Fitness* (New York: Berkley Publishing Corporation, 1977), and other books on this subject.
[41] Norman Cousins, *Anatomy of an Illness as Perceived by*

the Patient (New York: Norton, 1979).

[42] Schulz, *You Don't Look 35, Charlie Brown!*, no pagination.

[43] *Health Action*, Aid Association for Lutherans, Vol. 4, No. 7 (July/August 1988), pp. 4-5.

[44] Klos, ed., *Here Comes the Future*, p. 21.

[45] Dr. Jean Houston makes this comment in Klos, ed., *Here Comes the Future*, p. 72.

[46] Peck, *The Road Less Traveled*, p. 16.

[47] Klos, ed., *Here Comes the Future*, p. 70.

CHAPTER IV

[48] Daniel J. Boorstin, *Hidden History; Exploring Our Secret Past*, selected and edited by Daniel J. Boorstin and Ruth F. Boorstin (New York: Vintage Books, 1989), pp. 288-96.

[49] Boorstin, *Hidden History*, pp. xvii-xxiv.

[50] Boorstin, *Hidden History,* p. xvii.

[51] Jerry B. Harvey, *The Abilene Paradox and Other Meditations on Management* (Lexington, Massachusetts: D. C. Heath and Company, 1988), pp. 9-10.

[52] Boorstin, *Hidden History,* p. 243.

[53] Warren Bennis, "Organizations and the Future," in *Here Comes the Future*, ed. Frank W. Klos (Minneapolis: Augsburg Publishing House, 1981), p. 81.

[54] G. Lloyd Rediger, *Coping with Clergy Burnout* (Valley Forge, Pennsylvania: Judson Press, 1982), pp. 11-12, 15-16.

[55] Roger Fisher and William Ury, *Getting to Yes; Negotiating Agreement Without Giving In* (New York: Penguin Books, 1983), p. 25.

[56] Harvey, *Abilene Paradox*, p. 20.

[57] Harvey, *Abilene Paradox*, pp. 20-25.

[58] Harvey, *Abilene Paradox*, pp. 38-45.

[59] Boorstin, *Hidden History*, p. 224.

[60] Boorstin, *Hidden History*, p. 27.

[61] M. Scott Peck, *The Road Less Traveled* (New York: Simon and Schuster, 1978), pp. 30-31.

[62] *The Old Farmer's Almanac, 1990* (Dublin, NH: Yankee Publishing Incorporated, 1989), p. 192.
[63] Martha R. McPartland, "A Strange and Wonderful Inheritance," in *Mad and Magnificent Yankees*, ed. Clarissa M. Silitch (Dublin, NH: Yankee, Inc., 1973), pp. 24-29.
[64] David Wallechinsky, Irving Wallace and Amy Wallace, *The Book of Lists* (New York: Bantam Books, 1978), pp. 295-96.
[65] Ibid., pp. 480-81.
[66] *The Teacher Brothers Modern-Day Almanac, 1982* (Philadelphia: Running Press, 1981), p. 77.
[67] John Wareham, *Secrets of a Corporate Headhunter* (New York: Berkley Publishing Group, 1980), p. 35.
[68] *Old Farmer's Almanac, 1990*, pp. 221-22.
[69] Harvey, *Abilene Paradox*, p. 50.
[70] Richard Nelson Bolles, *What Color is Your Parachute, A Practical Manual for Job-Hunters and Career Changers*, 1986 Edition (Berkeley, CA: Ten Speed Press, 1986), pp. 11, 14, 16, 42-43, 69. This is a quality study that all job-hunters and career-changers should consult in the most recent edition.
[71] Levinson is quoted by J. Bill Ratliff in *When You Are Facing Change* (Louisville, KY: Westminster/John Knox Press, 1989), p. 35.
[72] Ratliff, *When You are Facing Change*, pp. 39-40.
[73] Ratliff, *When You Are Facing Change*, pp. 41-104 and passim. Ratliff presents a masterful description of the three stages and tells how to use available resources in each.
[74] Wayne E. Oates, *Nurturing Silence in a Noisy Heart* (Garden City, NY: Doubleday & Company, Inc., 1979), p. 3. This book is a gem on nurturing silence.
[75] Wallechinsky et al., *The Book of Lists*, p. 12.
[76] Bolles, *What Color is Your Parachute*, p. 65.
[77] Wallechinsky et al., *The Book of Lists*, p. 456.
[78] *The Business Journal* (Phoenix, Arizona), May 1, 1992. The article used the *Business Week* Executive Pay Surveys and the Bureau of Labor Statistics as sources.
[79] *Wall Street Journal*, April 22, 1992.

[80] Ibid.
[81] Wallechinsky et al., *Book of Lists*, pp. 470-73.
[82] Harvey, *Abilene Paradox*, pp. 61-63 and passim.
[83] *Old Farmer's Almanac*, 1990, p. 197, from Howard Rheingold's book, *They Have a Word for It* (1988).

CHAPTER V

[84] The seven words are the, of, and, a, to, in, is, you, that, it, he, and for. See David Wallechinsky, Irving Wallace and Amy Wallace, *The Book of Lists* (New York: Bantam Books, 1978), p. 160, drawing on *American Heritage Word Frequency Book* (1971).
[85] *Arizona Republic*, March 18, 1992.
[86] Richard T. Hise, *Effective Salesmanship* (Hinsdale, IL: The Dryden Press, 1980), pp. 40-43.
[87] Mack H. McCormack, "What Makes a Great Salesman," *Wall Street Journal*, June 20, 1988.
[88] See Carole Jackson, *Color for Men* (New York: Ballantine Books, 1984). Similar programs are available for women.
[89] *Washington Post*, December 31, 1989.
[90] Wallechinsky et al., *Book of Lists*, p. 135.
[91] Wayne E. Oates, *Nurturing Silence in a Noisy Heart* (Garden City, NY: Doubleday & Company, Inc., 1979), p. 66.
[92] William R. White, *Stories for the Journey* (Minneapolis: Augsburg Publishing House, 1988), p. 30.
[93] Harlan Cleveland, "The Role of Leadership in Facing the Future," in *Here Comes the Future*, ed. Frank W. Klos (Minneapolis: Augsburg Publishing House, 1981), pp. 120-27.
[94] Roger Fisher and William Ury, *Getting to Yes, Negotiating Agreement Without Giving In* (New York: Penguin Books, 1983), pp. 11-98.
[95] George A. Miller, *The Psychology of Communication* (Baltimore: Penguin Books, 1969), pp. 132-33.
[96] *The Teacher Brothers' Modern-Day Almanac, 1980* (Philadelphia: Running Press, 1979), p. 47.

[97] Ibid., p. 45.
[98] Peter McWilliams, *The Personal Computer Book* (Los Angeles: Prelude Press, 1990), p. 231.
[99] Wallechinsky et al., *The Book of Lists,* p. 39.
[100] Fisher and Ury, *Getting to Yes*, p. 34.
[101] Herbert A. Leggett, *Arizona Soliloquies*, Vol. III (Phoenix: n.p., 1961), p. 20.
[102] Art Ulene, *Feeling Fine* (New York: Ballantine Books, 1977), pp. 192-93.
[103] Collis Harman, "Belief Systems and the Transformation of Human Values," in Klos, ed., *Here Comes the Future*, p. 61.
[104] *Old Farmer's Almanac, 1990* (Dublin, NH: Yankee Publishing Incorporated, 1989), pp. 118-121.
[105] *Washington Post*, December 31, 1989.

CHAPTER VI

[106] Walter Wangerin, Jr., *As For Me and My House, Crafting Your Marriage to Last* (Nashville: Thomas Nelson Publishers, 1987), p. 23. Wangerin adds that for Christians two other critical ingredients of marriage are faith in God and forgiveness.
[107] "Census Bureau Says Average American Household is 2.63 People," UPI press release, Washington, D.C., April 22, 1992.
[108] Recently a Stanford University professor of biological sciences, Jonathan Roughgarden, showed through computer simulation that sexually reproducing species have the edge over asexual types. Though it would appear that an asexual species would have the advantage, with each individual capable of producing offspring instead of only half of them, his computer simulation of 5,000 generations showed that the sexual population maintained its numbers more successfully than the asexual one. Roughgarden said that "recurring catastrophes mean the (asexual) population is always caught off balance." The sexual population shuffled genes at reproduction and achieved a more equal distribution of genes for each

generation. In essence, sex buffers the population from changes in the environment. The computer study confirmed what many have known for a long time: sex is good. See *Stanford Observer*, March-April 1992.

[109] *Arizona Parenting*, March 1992; Chaplain, Lieutenant Colonel, Denis B. Baum, USAFR, "The Family as Caring Community," in *People Who Care*, USAF Chaplain Service Resource Board, 1990, pp. 43-44.

[110] *Newsweek*, March 23, 1992.

[111] *Arizona Republic*, May 19, 1992.

[112] See Dolores Curran, *Traits of a Healthy Family* (Minneapolis: Winston Press, 1983), pp. 4-7 and passim.

[113] Ibid., pp. 4-7, 10.

[114] For a more complete description of privatism and individualism, see Robert Bellah et al., *Habits of the Heart: Individualism and Commitment in American Life* (New York: Harper and Row, 1986).

[115] *Newsweek*, April 6, 1992.

[116] Ross Campbell, M.D., *How to Really Love Your Teenager* (Wheaton, ILL: SP Publications, Inc., 1988), p. 23.

[117] See Elmer Bendiner, *The Fall of Fortresses* (New York: G. P. Putnam's Sons, 1980).

[118] "Speaking 'Parentese'," *Stanford Observer*, March-April 1992.

[119] M. Scott Peck, *The Road Less Traveled* (New York: Simon and Schuster, 1978), pp. 123-26.

[120] Campbell, *How to Really Love Your Teenager*, p. 35.

[121] "Anger Tied to Multitude of Troubles," *Arizona Republic*, May 20, 1992.

[122] See Robert U. Akeret, *Photoanalysis: How to Interpret Hidden Psychological Meaning of Personal and Public Photographs* (New York: Pocket Books, 1975).

[123] *Military Chaplains' Review*, Spring 1987.

[124] Peck, *The Road Less Traveled*, p. 153.

[125] Ibid., pp. 160-61, 168.

[126] *Arizona Parenting*, March 1992.

[127] Wayne W. Dyer discusses dependent and independent

families in *Your Erroneous Zones* (New York: Avon Books, 1976), pp. 198-217. Recently a number of books have appeared on co-dependency in marriage and other relationships.

[128] Campbell, *How to Really Love Your Teenager*, pp. 10-11, 14, 24, 27, 45ff.

[129] Ibid., pp. 25, 45-51.

[130] Quoted by Martin Marty in "The Begats," *Christian Century*, April 12, 1989, p. 399. Sullivan's book was published in New York by Paulist Press in 1988.

[131] Baum, "The Family as Caring Community," p. 45.

[132] Ibid. Baum expresses credit to Morton Kelsey for his book, *Caring: How Can We Love One Another?* (New York: Paulist Press, 1981).

[133] Chaplain, Major General, John A. Collins, Chief of Chaplains, USAF, and Chaplain, Brigadier General, Stuart E. Barstad, Deputy Chief of Chaplains, USAF, Dialogue Sermon, Washington Cathedral, Washington, D.C., May 1, 1983.

[134] John Wareham, *Secrets of a Corporate Headhunter* (New York: Berkley Publishing Group, 1983), p. 65.

[135] Jan Harold Brunvand, *The Vanishing Hitchhiker; American Urban Legends and Their Meanings* (New York: W. W. Norton, 1981), pp. 22-23, 125- 29.

[136] Campbell, *How to Really Love Your Teenager,* pp. 52-54.

[137] Charles M. Schulz, *You Don't* ***Look*** *35, Charlie Brown!* (New York: Holt, Rinehart and Winston, 1985), no pagination.

[138] Data on the religious awakening is found in the *Princeton Religion Research Center Emerging Trends*, Vol. 10, No. 8 (October 1988), p. 5.

[139] See, among others, Gregory Stock, *The Kids' Book of Questions* (New York: Workman Publishing, 1988), for a series of interesting questions that may prompt children to enter the maze of ethics and religion.

CHAPTER VII

[140] *Arizona Republic,* February 26, 1989.

[141] Wilbur Cross and Carol Florio, *You Are Never Too Old to Learn* (New York: McGraw-Hill Book Company, 1978), p. 205.

[142] Deborah Chase, "Aging in America," *Correspondent*, Spring 1992, p. 10.

[143] Ibid.

[144] Wayne Coffey, *303 of the World's Worst Predictions* (New York: Tribeca Communications, Inc., 1983), p. 51.

[145] Frank W. Klos and Robert N. Bacher, *Here Comes the Future, Leader Guide* (Minneapolis: Augsburg Press, 1981), pp. 48-49.

[146] Chase, "Aging in America," p. 13; *How to Swing into Retirement without Stumbling* (Appleton, Wisconsin: Aid Association for Lutherans, 1991), p. 3.

[147] Jan Harold Brunvand, *The Vanishing Hitchhiker; American Urban Legends and Their Meanings* (New York: W. W. Norton & Company, 1981), p. 20.

[148] Vic Oliver, quoted in *The Teacher Brothers, Modern-Day Almanac, 1983* (Philadelphia: Running Press, 1982), p. 59.

[149] Robert Frost, *A Further Range*, Book Six (New York: Henry Holt and Company, 1936), p. 69.

[150] J. Robert Evans, *Personal Productivity Through Creative Living* (Dubuque: Kendall/Hunt Publishing Company, 1981), pp. 58-59, based on Milton Rokeach, *The Nature of Human Values* (New York: The Free Press, 1973). I modified some entries slightly.

[151] *The Christian Century*, September 23, 1987, p. 807.

[152] Mary Birling, "Life in the 90s," *Correspondent*, Spring 1992, p. 7.

[153] Evans, *Personal Productivity*, p. 9.

[154] Ibid., p. 14,

[155] Charles W. Colson, *Loving God* (Grand Rapids: Zondervan Books, 1987), pp. 133, 211-14.

[156] Chase, "Aging in America," p. 12.

[157] Cross and Florio, *You Are Never Too Old to Learn*, pp. 7-8.

[158] William S. Ellis, "A Mountain of Determination," *Mad and Magnificent Yankees*, ed. Clarissa M. Silitch (Dublin,

NH: Yankee, Inc., 1973), p. 55.

[159] Leo Buscaglia, *Bus 9 to Paradise* (New York: Fawcett Columbine, 1986), p. 99.

[160] Pope John XXIII, *Journal of a Soul*, translated by Dorothy White (New York: McGraw-Hill Book Company, 1965), pp. 325-26.

[161] Coffey, *303 of the World's Worst Predictions*, p. 29.

[162] Brunvand, *The Vanishing Hitchhiker*, p. 132.

[163] William Edward Mason, "A Big Wheel Around America," *Mad and Magnificent Yankees*, pp. 95-98.

[164] Cross and Florio, *You are Never Too Old to Learn*, p. 24.

[165] Brunvand, *The Vanishing Hitchhiker*, pp. 104-105.

[166] *Teacher Brothers, Modern-Day Almanac, 1983, p. 41; Teacher Brothers, Modern-Day Almanac, 1980* (Philadelphia: Running Press, 1979), p. 72.

[167] Frank W. Klos, ed., *Here Comes the Future* (Minneapolis: Fortress Press, 1981), p. 91. The prayer is by Herbert Brokering.

[168] David Wallechinsky, Irving Wallace and Amy Wallace, *The Book of Lists* (New York: Bantam Books, 1978), p. 3.

[169] Carl Carmer, "Maker of Memories," *Mad and Magnificent Yankees*, p. 36.

[170] *Arizona Republic*, March 24, 1992.

[171] Deborah Lampe, "Six Steps You can Take Today for a Healthier Tomorrow," *Correspondent*, Spring 1992, p. 16.

[172] Coffey, *303 of the World's Worst Predictions*, p. 85.

[173] Vivian H. Galbraith, "Afterthoughts," in *The Historian's Workshop*, ed. L. P. Curtis, Jr. (New York: Alfred A. Knopf, Inc., 1970), pp. 20-21.

[174] *Arizona Business Gazette*, March 13, 1992.

[175] Frost, *A Further Range*, p. 69.

[176] Klos, ed., *Here Comes the Future*, p. 127.

[177] M. Scott Peck, *The Road Less Traveled* (New York: Simon and Schuster, 1978), p. 136.

[178] Margaret Craven, *I Heard the Owl Call My Name* (Garden City, NY: Doubleday and Co., 1973), pp. 149-50.

[179] Charles M. Schulz, *You Don't **Look** 35, Charlie Brown!* (New York: Holt, Rinehart and Winston, 1985), no pagination.

[180] Credit for the idea of the punctuated life goes to R. Maurice Boyde, *A Lover's Quarrel with the World* (Philadelphia: Westminster Press, 1985).

CHAPTER VIII

[181] Some roller coasters make riders feel 3 1/2 times their weight, then flip upside down for sudden zero gravity. Federal statistics show 25 deaths since 1973, about one fatality per 200 million rides. See *Wall Street Journal*, May 28, 1992.
[182] Leo Buscaglia, *Bus 9 to Paradise* (New York: Fawcett Columbine, 1986), pp. 23, 25-26.
[183] Ian Nicholas, "Lord of Newburyport, Earl of Chester, and Merchant Extraordinary," in *Mad and Magnificent Yankees*, ed. Clarissa M. Silitch (Dublin, NH: Yankee, Inc., 1973), pp. 10-19.
[184] Henri J. M. Nouwen, *The Wounded Healer; Ministry in Contemporary Society* (Garden City, NY: Doubleday & Co., 1972), pp. 5-6.
[185] Grady Nutt, *So Good, So Far...* (Nashville: Impact Books, 1979), p. 29.
[186] Viktor E. Frankl, *Man's Search for Meaning; An Introduction to Logotherapy* (New York: Simon & Schuster, Inc., 1984).
[187] Peter Routman, "Cold Sweat," *University of Chicago Magazine*, February 1992, pp. 21-22.
[188] Dieter Vogt, "A Man With a Vision," *Northwest Airlines Magazine*, August 1991, pp. 38-41.
[189] Jerry B. Harvey, *The Abilene Paradox and Other Meditations on Management* (Lexington, Massachusetts: D. C. Heath and Company, 1988), pp. 7-8.
[190] *Washington Post*, December 31, 1989.
[191] Chaplain, Major General, Stuart E. Barstad, Chief of Chaplains, USAF, Easter Sunrise Service, Patrick AFB, FL, April 3, 1988.
[192] Chaplain, Brigadier General, Stuart E. Barstad, Deputy Chief of Chaplains, USAF, "Living in the Real World,"

National Prayer Breakfast Observance, Keesler AFB, MS, February 7, 1985.

[193] Michael J. O'Neill, "Let's Hear It for Losers," *Newsweek*, November 2, 1987.

[194] Chaplain, Brigadier General, Stuart E. Barstad, Deputy Chief of Chaplains, USAF, Veterans Day Address, Birmingham, AL, November 11, 1983.

[195] *The Teacher Brothers, Modern Day Almanac, 1982* (Philadelphia: Running Press, 1981), p. 53.

[196] *American Farm and Home Almanac*, Vol. 11 (Lewiston, Maine: Almanac Publishing Co. and Simon & Schuster, Inc., 1975), p. 40.

[197] David Wallechinsky, Irving Wallace and Amy Wallace, *The Book of Lists* (New York: Bantam Books, 1978), p. 48.

Index

A

B

C

D

E

F

G

H

I

N

O

P

R

S